Property Coverages

Property Coverages

Edited by
Arthur L. Flitner, CPCU, ARM, AIC, AU

2nd Edition • 1st Printing

The Institutes
720 Providence Road, Suite 100
Malvern, Pennsylvania 19355-3433

2nd Edition • 1st Printing • October 2014

Library of Congress Control Number: 2014948305

ISBN 978-0-89463-785-8

Foreword

The Institutes are the trusted leader in delivering proven knowledge solutions that drive powerful business results for the risk management and property-casualty insurance industry. For more than 100 years, The Institutes have been meeting the industry's changing professional development needs with customer-driven products and services.

In conjunction with industry experts and members of the academic community, our Knowledge Resources Department develops our course and program content, including Institutes study materials. Practical and technical knowledge gained from Institutes courses enhances qualifications, improves performance, and contributes to professional growth—all of which drive results.

The Institutes' proven knowledge helps individuals and organizations achieve powerful results with a variety of flexible, customer-focused options:

Recognized Credentials—The Institutes offer an unmatched range of widely recognized and industry-respected specialty credentials. The Institutes' Chartered Property Casualty Underwriter (CPCU®) professional designation is designed to provide a broad understanding of the property-casualty insurance industry. Depending on professional needs, CPCU students may select either a commercial insurance focus or a personal risk management and insurance focus and may choose from a variety of electives.

In addition, The Institutes offer certificate or designation programs in a variety of disciplines, including these:

- Claims
- Commercial underwriting
- Fidelity and surety bonding
- General insurance
- Insurance accounting and finance
- Insurance information technology
- Insurance production and agency management
- Insurance regulation and compliance
- Management
- Marine insurance
- Personal insurance
- Premium auditing
- Quality insurance services
- Reinsurance
- Risk management
- Surplus lines

Ethics—Ethical behavior is crucial to preserving not only the trust on which insurance transactions are based, but also the public's trust in our industry as a whole. All Institutes designations now have an ethics requirement, which is delivered online and free of charge. The ethics requirement content is designed specifically for insurance practitioners and uses insurance-based case studies to outline an ethical framework. More information is available in the Programs section of our website, www.TheInstitutes.org.

Flexible Online Learning—The Institutes have an unmatched variety of technical insurance content covering topics from accounting to underwriting, which we now deliver through hundreds of online courses. These cost-effective self-study courses are a convenient way to fill gaps in technical knowledge in a matter of hours without ever leaving the office.

Continuing Education—A majority of The Institutes' courses are filed for CE credit in most states. We also deliver quality, affordable, online CE courses quickly and conveniently through CEU. Visit www.CEU.com to learn more. CEU is powered by The Institutes.

College Credits—Most Institutes courses carry college credit recommendations from the American Council on Education. A variety of courses also qualify for credits toward certain associate, bachelor's, and master's degrees at several prestigious colleges and universities. More information is available in the Student Services section of our website, www.TheInstitutes.org.

Custom Applications—The Institutes collaborate with corporate customers to use our trusted course content and flexible delivery options in developing customized solutions that help them achieve their unique organizational goals.

Insightful Analysis—Our Insurance Research Council (IRC) division conducts public policy research on important contemporary issues in property-casualty insurance and risk management. Visit www.insurance-research.org to learn more or purchase its most recent studies.

The Institutes look forward to serving the risk management and property-casualty insurance industry for another 100 years. We welcome comments from our students and course leaders; your feedback helps us continue to improve the quality of our study materials.

Peter L. Miller, CPCU
President and CEO
The Institutes

Preface

Property Coverages is one of the textbooks for the property track in The Institutes' Associate in Claims (AIC) designation program.

The purpose of *Property Coverages* is to provide the learner with a basic understanding of property coverages involved in the handling of property claims.

The text examines coverages for homeowners property, other personal lines property, commercial property, business income, commercial crime, equipment breakdown, inland marine, ocean marine, businessowners property, farm property, and other specialty property coverages.

The text's content is adapted from two other Institutes texts, *Personal Insurance* and *Commercial Insurance*.

The Institutes are thankful to the individuals who contributed to the development of previous forms of the content, including manuscript reviewers and advisory committee members.

For more information about The Institutes' programs, please call our Customer Service Department at (800) 644-2101, email us at customerservice@TheInstitutes.org, or visit our website at www.TheInstitutes.org.

Arthur L. Flitner

Contributors

The Institutes acknowledge with deep appreciation the contributions made to the content of this text by the following persons:

Richard Berthelsen, JD, CPCU, AIC, ARM, AU, ARe, MBA

Pamela J. Brooks, MBA, CPCU, AAM, AIM, AIS

Doug Froggatt

Donna J. Popow, JD, CPCU, AIC

Contents

Segment A

Assignment 1
Property Loss Exposures and Homeowners Coverage

Assignment 2
Other Personal Lines Property Coverage

Assignment 3
Commercial Property Insurance, Part I

Assignment 4
Commercial Property Insurance, Part II

Direct Your Learning

1

Property Loss Exposures and Homeowners Coverage

Educational Objectives

After learning the content of this assignment, you should be able to:

- Describe the property loss exposures that individuals and families might face in terms of each of the following:
  - The assets exposed to loss
  - The causes of loss
  - The financial consequences of loss
- Describe how individuals and families can use the Insurance Services Office, Inc., (ISO) 2011 Homeowners insurance program to address their personal risk management needs.
- Describe what is insured by each of these coverages contained in the 2011 Homeowners 3—Special Form (HO-3) policy:
  - Coverage A—Dwelling
  - Coverage B—Other Structures
  - Coverage C—Personal Property
  - Coverage D—Loss of Use
  - Additional Coverages
- Describe what is covered and what is excluded by these provisions in the 2011 Homeowners 3—Special Form (HO-3) policy:
  - Perils Insured Against for Coverages A and B
  - Perils Insured Against for Coverage C
  - Section I—Exclusions
- Summarize each of the 2011 Homeowners 3—Special Form (HO-3) policy provisions in Section I—Conditions.

Outline

Educational Objectives, continued

- Given a scenario describing a homeowners property claim, determine whether the 2011 HO-3 policy Section I—Property Coverages would cover the claim and, if so, the amount the insurer would pay for the claim.
- Compare the coverage provided by each of the following 2011 homeowners forms to the coverage provided by the 2011 Homeowners 3—Special Form (HO-3):
  - HO-2 Broad Form
  - HO-4 Contents Broad Form
  - HO-5 Comprehensive Form
  - HO-6 Unit-Owners Form
  - HO-8 Modified Coverage Form
- Summarize the coverages provided by various 2011 ISO Homeowners policy endorsements.

Property Loss Exposures and Homeowners Coverage

1

PROPERTY LOSS EXPOSURES

Virtually all individuals and families have property. Property used, stored, enjoyed, or displayed is property that may be exposed to loss. Such property may include a family's house, an individual's television, or a child's framed photograph. Losses to property can result in serious financial consequences to those who suffer the losses.

All property is subject to **property loss exposures**. Property may be destroyed, damaged, stolen, or lost, or may otherwise suffer a decrease in value because of a particular cause of loss (or peril).

Property loss exposure

A condition that presents the possibility that a person or an organization will sustain a loss resulting from damage (including destruction, taking, or loss of use) to property in which that person or organization has a financial interest.

Individuals and families face countless situations in their daily lives that present the possibility of a property loss that has financial consequences. For example, an individual's belongings could be destroyed by a flood, or a family's home and its contents could be destroyed by a tornado. These situations, and many more, are loss exposures that individuals and families might face.

Property loss exposures can be examined in terms of three loss exposure elements:

- Assets exposed to loss
- Causes of loss
- Financial consequences of loss

Assets Exposed to Loss

Assets exposed to loss are any items of property that have value. A common method of classifying property uses two broad categories—**real property** and **personal property**. Much like the term "real estate," real property includes land, buildings, attached structures, plants growing on the land, and anything embedded in the land, such as minerals. All other property, such as a bicycle or a sofa or a computer, is classified as personal property. Individuals and families can be faced with loss exposures by owning or having a legal interest in one or both of these types of property. See the exhibit "Examples of Assets (Property) Exposed to Loss."

Real property (realty)

Tangible property consisting of land, all structures permanently attached to the land, and whatever is growing on the land.

Personal property

All tangible or intangible property that is not real property.

Examples of Assets (Property) Exposed to Loss

Real Property	Land, buildings, other structures attached to the land (swimming pool, storage shed, flagpole), whatever is growing on the land (trees, crops), and anything embedded in the land (foundations, underground pipes)
Personal Property	Dwelling contents, high-value articles (jewelry, silverware), rare or unique property (antiques, art work), business personal property, motor vehicles, trailers, watercraft, and aircraft

[DA00140]

Real Property

Individuals and families face property loss exposures that can arise from several types of owned real property. All real property is tangible property having a physical form that can be seen or touched.

For example, a single-family home purchased by an individual could pose a significant real property loss exposure. The land also indicates an additional real property loss exposure, as may any foundations or underground pipes. Any sheds attached to the land, or anything growing on it, such as trees, also could present real property loss exposures.

Personal Property

Listing all the specific kinds of personal property that individuals and families can own that are exposed to loss would be virtually impossible, when one considers the scope of the personal property definition. A general sampling of some personal property loss exposures includes those experienced by homeowners, renters, or condominium owners, who likely own furniture, televisions, and other electronic entertainment equipment. Additional household personal property can include computers, appliances, dishes, carpets, sports equipment, clothing, tools, books, jewelry, cameras, and digital recording devices. A homeowner could park a car in the driveway (the car is personal property) or have a boat at a vacation home (the boat is personal property). Additionally, personal property can include intangible property such as patents or copyrights (which are also often referred to as intellectual property). See the exhibit "Insuring and Pricing Personal Property Loss Exposures—Personal Property Categories."

Causes of Loss

Many causes of loss (or perils) can damage or destroy both real and personal property. In terms of real property, causes of loss faced by individuals and families include fire damage to a dwelling or storage shed, lightning damage to a tree, earthquake damage to a swimming pool, and wind damage to roof shingles. Personal property causes of loss can include theft of a car or damage

Insuring and Pricing Personal Property Loss Exposures—Personal Property Categories

For the purpose of identifying, insuring, and pricing personal property loss exposures, personal property can be divided into these categories:

Dwelling contents—the broadest category of personal property. A dwelling's contents may include furniture, appliances, draperies, electronics, kitchenware, groceries, clothing, sports equipment, tools, toys, and many other items common to the use of a dwelling as a home. Such items are generally insured as a group rather than individually.

High-value personal property—items of personal property worth considerable sums of money. Examples include jewelry, silverware, furs, and firearms. These items may be partially covered under the category of dwelling contents. However, they usually require a more specific type of insurance, because many property insurance policies limit the maximum amount of coverage available under specific loss conditions (for example, jewelry coverage is more limited for a theft loss under a homeowners policy than for a fire loss), for this category of personal property.

Rare or unusual property—items whose value comes from their unique characteristics. These items may often be one of a kind or one of a very few in existence in terms of like kind and quality and are not easily replaced. Examples of this type of property are antiques, works of art, coin or stamp collections, and other collectibles. Such items should be specifically listed for insurance purposes because most insurance policies limit the amount that an insurer will pay for this type of personal property.

Business personal property—personal property, such as office furniture and computer equipment, used for business purposes. Because most personal insurance policies limit or exclude coverage for business personal property, additional insurance coverage may be necessary.

Motor vehicles, trailers, watercraft, and aircraft—mobile property typically excluded (or covered only up to a certain limit) in policies covering dwellings and their contents. Because these items present unique loss exposures, they should be separately insured using the appropriate coverage form.

To keep the cost of personal insurance reasonable, personal insurance policies are designed to cover the loss exposures faced by the average person or family. If personal policies included unlimited coverage for all types of personal property, premiums needed to provide such coverage would be higher than most people could afford or would be willing to pay. For example, the cost to insure individual, expensive jewelry items against theft is not automatically included in homeowners policy premiums. Insurance professionals can help individuals and families understand the relationship between cost and coverage by explaining that, in order to keep insurance premiums reasonable for the average consumer, it is fair for those persons who own valuable or unusual items to pay an additional premium to insure them.

[DA00139]

to a car in an accident, disappearance of luggage and its contents while the owner is on vacation, and loss of a diamond that falls from its setting in a ring. Even damage to a motorboat that collides with a dock is a personal property loss. Any loss that results from the countless possible causes of loss that can affect an individual's or a family's property has consequences in terms of asset value.

Financial Consequences of Loss

When property is damaged or destroyed, individuals and families sustain certain financial consequences. Financial consequences of loss can include one or more of these outcomes:

- Reduction in value of property—The difference between the value of the property before the loss (preloss value) and after the loss (post-loss value). For instance, if an individual severely damages the front bumper of an auto by colliding with a tree, the auto would be worth less after the accident than it was worth before the accident.
- Increased expenses—Expenses in addition to normal living expenses that are necessary because of the loss. For example, increased living expenses could include the expenses an individual incurs following a dwelling fire, such as the cost of renting a hotel room, while the dwelling is temporarily uninhabitable.
- Lost income—Loss of income that results if property is damaged. For example, if a hurricane damages a home rented to others, the owner might not be able to collect rent on the property until the house is repaired or replaced.

ISO HOMEOWNERS COVERAGE

The Insurance Services Office, Inc. (ISO) Homeowners insurance program's policy forms are designed to meet the personal risk management needs of individuals and families.

The parties eligible for coverage under the ISO 2011 Homeowners (HO) insurance program fall into three general categories:

- Individuals and families who own a private home in which they reside—This is typically a single-family dwelling, but sometimes an eligible two to four-family dwelling. A mobile home is not eligible for unendorsed coverage. Dwelling and mobile home insurance policies are available for insuring residences that are not eligible for homeowners policies.
- People who rent or lease the premises in which they reside—The residence might be an apartment, a house (either a single-family house or other type), a mobile home, a trailer home, a house trailer, or a condominium unit.
- Individuals and families who own private condominium units used for residential purposes—Most insurers provide homeowners policies to people who own and live in condominium units. However, some insurers also provide such coverage when the insureds own but do not live in the

condominium as long as the condominium unit is used as a residence by one family or by one or two tenants.

To address these parties' needs, the ISO Homeowners program offers six policy forms:

- Homeowners 2—Broad Form (HO-2)
- Homeowners 3—Special Form (HO-3)
- Homeowners 4—Contents Broad Form (HO-4)
- Homeowners 5—Comprehensive Form (HO-5)
- Homeowners 6—Unit-Owners Form (HO-6)
- Homeowners 8—Modified Coverage Form (HO-8)

Individuals and families should select a form based on their risk management needs and whether they meet the form's eligibility requirements. See the exhibit "How the ISO Homeowners Program Policy Forms Address Personal Risk Management Needs."

How the ISO Homeowners Program Policy Forms Address Personal Risk Management Needs

ISO Policy Form	Example of Personal Risk Management Need Addressed
HO-2— Broad Form	Meets most needs of owner-occupants for dwelling, other structures, and personal property coverage at a lower premium than the HO-3 or HO-5 coverages.
HO-3— Special Form	Meets the needs of owner-occupants of dwellings who want coverage on their dwellings and other structures that is broader than the HO-2 offers.
HO-4— Contents Broad Form	Meets the needs of tenants and other apartment or dwelling occupants who do not require coverage on the dwelling.
HO-5— Comprehensive Form	Meets the needs of owner-occupants of dwellings who want the broadest coverage available among ISO's forms for their dwellings, other structures, and personal property.
HO-6— Unit-Owners Form	Meets the needs of owners of condominium units and cooperative apartment shares.
HO-8— Modified Coverage Form	Meets the needs of owner-occupants of dwellings who may not meet insurer standards required for other policy forms.

[DA00300]

The HO-2—Broad Form (HO 00 02), simply known as the HO-2, provides named perils coverage for dwellings, other structures, and personal property. The HO-2 is designed to meet the risk management needs of owner-occupants of dwellings.

Forms HO-2, HO-3, HO-5, and HO-8 can be issued only to the owner-occupant of a one-, two-, three-, or four-family dwelling. Rules prohibit issuance to owners who do not occupy the dwelling. Further, the forms may not be issued to cover dwellings on farm premises. Persons purchasing a dwelling under a long-term installment contract, without legal title to the property, are eligible in the same manner as titled owners and occupants under a life estate arrangement. Also, a dwelling under construction is eligible if the named insured is the intended owner-occupant.

The HO-3—Special Form (HO 00 03), called the HO-3, provides special form coverage on dwellings and other structures (rather than the named perils coverage provided by the HO-2). Special form coverage, also known as open perils coverage, protects property against direct physical loss that is not otherwise excluded by the coverage form. Note that the HO-3 provides named perils coverage for personal property, as does the HO-2. The HO-3 is designed to meet the risk management needs of owner-occupants of dwellings who want broader coverage on their dwellings and other structures.

The HO-4—Contents Broad Form (HO 00 04), or HO-4, provides coverage for a tenant's personal property on a named perils basis. The HO-4 does not provide coverage for dwellings or other structures. This policy form is designed to meet the risk management needs of tenants and other occupants of apartments or dwellings. For example, a young woman who has recently graduated from college, started a new job, and moved into an apartment should obtain an HO-4 if she is no longer an official resident of her parents' insured household and would like her own personal property and liability insurance protection. Form HO-4 can be issued to a tenant who maintains a residence in any kind of structure. Persons who maintain a residence in a building that they own but that is not a one- or two-family dwelling are also eligible.

A homeowners policy (other than HO-4) may also be issued in the name of a trust and trustee(s) when legal title to a one-, two-, three-, or four-family dwelling or condominium unit is held solely by the trust and when the trustee, beneficiary, or grantor regularly resides there. If a portion of the premises is used for other-than-private-residential occupancy, eligibility rules permit (1) not more than two roomers or boarders per family unit and (2) an incidental business occupancy, such as an office, private school, or studio. Occasional rental of the premises to others is also allowed.

The HO-5—Comprehensive Form (HO 00 05), known as the HO-5, provides open perils coverage on dwellings, other structures, and personal property. The HO-5 is designed to meet the risk management needs of owner-occupants of dwellings who would like the broadest coverage available among ISO's forms for their property. A homeowner who desires the broadest available coverage for his home and contents, and is willing to pay the increased premium for it, should select the HO-5.

The HO-6—Unit-Owners Form (HO 00 06), or HO-6, provides coverage for personal property on a named perils basis, with limited dwelling coverage (unit improvements and betterments). The HO-6 is designed to meet the risk management needs of the owners of condominium units and cooperative apartment shares. The HO-6 is similar to the HO-4, but it includes special provisions for loss exposures inherent in condominium and cooperative unit ownership. For example, a couple that purchases a vacation unit in a seaside condominium community should obtain additional homeowners coverage under an HO-6.

Only owners of condominium units and cooperative apartment shareowners are eligible for the HO-6, although the insured is not required to be an occupant of the unit. If a two-, three-, or four-family dwelling is co-owned by the families who reside there, one of the owner-occupant forms may be issued in the name of one of the owner-occupants, with the others named on an Additional Insured Endorsement (HO 04 41) to cover each party's interest in the building. The other parties may be issued an HO-4 for their personal property. This combination of coverages gives all co-owners complete homeowners coverage.

The HO-8—Modified Coverage Form (HO 00 08), called the HO-8, provides coverage for a dwelling, other structures, and personal property on a limited, named perils basis. A special valuation clause specifies that damage will be covered on a **functional replacement cost** basis. The HO-8 is designed to meet the risk management needs of owners-occupants of dwellings that may not meet insurer underwriting standards required for other policy forms (such as when the replacement cost of a dwelling significantly exceeds the dwelling's market value). For example, a couple may own a historic home in a city where local property values, including the value of the historic home, are far below replacement cost. This couple may opt for homeowners coverage under an HO-8.

Functional replacement cost
The cost of replacing damaged property with similar property that performs the same function but might not be identical to the damaged property.

Apply Your Knowledge

A homeowner wishes the broadest possible coverage for his home and contents. Which of the six ISO Homeowners program forms would be most appropriate for his coverage needs?

Feedback: The HO-5—Comprehensive Form (HO 00 05), known as the HO-5, provides open perils coverage on dwellings, other structures, and personal property and is designed to meet the risk management needs of owner-occupants of dwellings who would like the broadest coverage available among ISO's forms for their property.

HO-3 SECTION I—PROPERTY COVERAGES

The Insurance Services Office, Inc. (ISO) 2011 Homeowners 3—Special Form (HO-3) provides coverage for a house and its contents. It is designed to cover the property loss exposures that most individuals and families face.

Section I—Property Coverages of the HO-3 policy provides four basic property coverages and twelve Additional Coverages:

- Coverage A—Dwelling
- Coverage B—Other Structures
- Coverage C—Personal Property
- Coverage D—Loss of Use

Coverage A—Dwelling

Coverage A applies to the dwelling on the residence premises listed on the Declarations page. "Residence premises" includes not only a one-family dwelling, but also a two-, three-, or four-family dwelling where the named insured resides in at least one of the units. It also applies to structures (such as a garage or a deck) attached to the dwelling and to materials and supplies located on or next to the covered dwelling and used to construct or repair the dwelling. Coverage does not apply to the land at the residence premises.

Coverage B—Other Structures

Coverage B—Other Structures applies to structures on the residence premises that are not attached to the dwelling and are separated from it by "clear space." A fence, utility line, or similar connection linking another structure with the dwelling does not make it an attached structure.

An additional amount equal to 10 percent of the Coverage A limit is available for other structures. This 10 percent limit applies collectively to all "other structures" at the residence premises.

Coverage B has three important exclusions:

- A structure rented to anyone who is not a resident of the dwelling. However, a structure that is rented to others for use as a private garage is covered.
- A structure from which any business is conducted.
- A structure used to store business property. However, a structure containing business property is covered if the business property is solely owned by an insured or a tenant of the dwelling, provided that the business property does not include gaseous or liquid fuel, other than fuel in a permanently installed fuel tank of a vehicle or craft parked or stored in the structure.

Coverage C—Personal Property

Coverage C—Personal Property applies to items the insured owns or uses, anywhere in the world. It can also cover loss of or damage to personal property of others while that property is on the residence premises, if the named insured requests such coverage after a loss. Coverage C can also cover loss of or damage to personal property of a guest or residence employee while it is in any residence occupied by an insured.

The standard limit for Coverage C is 50 percent of the Coverage A limit, and it applies in addition to that limit. The Coverage C limit can be increased simply by changing the amount appearing on the Declarations page and charging an additional premium.

Only 10 percent of the Coverage C limit or $1,000 (whichever is greater) is available for property usually located at a residence other than the one listed on the Declarations page. This same limitation applies to property kept by an insured in a self-storage warehouse.

The 10 percent or $1,000 limitation does not apply to personal property removed from the residence premises because the house is being repaired, renovated, or rebuilt and is not fit to live in or to store property in. An insured who is moving from one principal residence to another will have the full limit of Coverage C available at both locations for thirty days.

Special Limits of Liability

Some categories of personal property are subject to sublimits, called special limits of liability, within the Coverage C limit. Items within these categories pose a higher-than-average risk of loss (for example, jewelry) or are types of property not contemplated in homeowners insurance premiums (for example, business property). The special limits for three personal property categories (jewelry and furs; firearms and related items; and silverware, goldware, platinumware, and pewterware) apply only when loss is caused by theft. The special limits for eight other categories of personal property apply when loss is caused by any covered peril. See the exhibit "Special Sublimits Within Coverage C."

Special Sublimits Within Coverage C

Personal Property	Special Limit of Liability
Liability Sublimits Applicable to All Covered Perils	
Money and precious metals, including stored value cards, such as gift cards	$200
Securities, documents, records, and stamps, including cost to research and replace information that has been lost	$1,500
Watercraft, including trailers, equipment, and motors	$1,500
Trailers (other than used with watercraft)	$1,500
Portable electronic equipment	$1,500
Antennas, tapes, wires, records, disks, or other media	$250
Property Used Primarily for Business Purposes	
On the residence premises	$2,500
Away from the residence premises	$1,500
Sublimits Applicable to Theft (No Sublimit for Other Perils)	
Jewelry, furs, precious stones, and semiprecious stones	$1,500
Firearms and related items	$2,500
Silverware, goldware, platinumware, and pewterware	$2,500

[DA07598]

Property Not Covered

The HO-3 policy specifically excludes all coverage for some categories of personal property. In most cases, these items are usually insured through policies other than a homeowners policy:

- Articles separately described and specifically insured in this or other insurance. (For example, jewelry separately described on an endorsement or in a separate policy is Property Not Covered.)
- Animals, birds, or fish.
- Motor vehicles, parts, and electronic equipment that operates solely from the vehicle's electrical system. (Coverage is provided for vehicles not required to be registered, such as riding mowers and wheelchairs.)
- Aircraft and hovercraft.
- Property of roomers and boarders unrelated to the insured.
- Property in an apartment rented to others. (Coverage for such property is provided as an Additional Coverage.)
- Property rented or held for rental to others off the residence premises.
- Business data, including drawings, stored either on paper or electronically.

- Credit cards or electronic fund transfer cards. (Coverage for such property is provided as an Additional Coverage.)
- Water or steam. (For example, there is no coverage for replacing water in a damaged swimming pool.)

Coverage D—Loss of Use

Coverage D applies to the insured's exposure to financial loss, apart from the property damage itself, if the residence premises are damaged so badly that they are not fit to live in. Coverage D applies only if the damage is the result of a loss that is covered under Section I—Property Coverages of the policy. The Coverage D limit is 30 percent of the Coverage A limit, and it applies in addition to the Coverage A limit. The limit can be increased by changing the amount on the Declarations page and paying an additional premium.

Three coverages are grouped under Coverage D:

- Additional living expense—If the insured must live elsewhere until the dwelling has been repaired, this pays for any necessary increase in living expenses required to maintain the household's normal standard of living.
- Fair rental value—If part of the residence is rented to others, the insurer will reimburse the insured the lost rental value (less expenses that do not continue) until repairs are made.
- Loss of use due to civil authority—Even if an insured's property is undamaged, civil authorities may prohibit access to the home because of damage to neighboring property. In this case, the expenses of living elsewhere and lost rental income are covered for a maximum of two weeks.

Additional Coverages

The Additional Coverages insure against various types of losses that would not otherwise be covered under Section I of the policy. In addition to the basic descriptions of coverage provided in the bulleted list, the exhibit states whether each Additional Coverage creates an additional amount of insurance (as opposed to being payable within the applicable policy limit), whether each is subject to the policy deductible, and whether each must be triggered by another covered loss:

- Debris Removal—Covers reasonable expenses for removing debris of covered property that has been damaged by an insured peril or by ash, dust, or particles from a volcanic eruption that has caused direct loss to a covered building or property in the building. It also covers, subject to special conditions, the cost to remove fallen trees, not to exceed $500 for any one tree or $1,000 in any one loss.
- Reasonable Repairs—Covers reasonable costs incurred to protect covered property or repair other property damaged by an insured peril.

- Trees, Shrubs, and Other Plants—Covers loss caused by fire or lightning, explosion, riot or civil commotion, aircraft, vehicles not owned or operated by a resident, vandalism or malicious acts, or theft up to an additional 5 percent of the dwelling limit with a maximum of $500 for any one item. Property grown for business purposes is excluded.
- Fire Department Service Charges—Pays up to $500 for fire department charges incurred to save or protect insured property from a covered loss if the responding unit is from beyond the property's regular fire protection district.
- Property Removed—Covers property removed from premises endangered by an insured peril. While removed, the property is covered for direct loss by any cause (not limited to perils insured against) for up to thirty days.
- Credit Card, Electronic Fund Transfer Card or Access Device, Forgery, and Counterfeit Money—Pays up to $500 for legal obligation due to unauthorized use or theft of a credit card or an electronic fund transfer card or access device. It also covers loss due to forgery of a negotiable instrument or acceptance in good faith of counterfeit paper currency. There is no coverage for a card used by a resident of the household or by someone to whom the card was entrusted, and the insured must have complied with all terms of the issuing company. Losses arising from business use or dishonesty of the insured are excluded.
- Loss Assessment—Pays up to $1,000 for assessments charged by a corporation or an association of property owners for loss to collectively owned property caused by an insured peril.
- Collapse—Covers abrupt collapse of a building or part of a building resulting from an insured peril, hidden decay, insect or vermin damage, weight of contents or inhabitants, weight of rain, or defective material or construction. There is no coverage if the building was showing visible signs of deterioration before the collapse.
- Glass or Safety Glazing Material—Covers breakage of building glass, including breakage caused by earth movement. Direct physical loss to covered property caused solely by the broken glass is covered, but not resulting damage caused because the glass is broken (for example, rain damage). There is no coverage if the dwelling has been vacant for more than sixty days.
- Landlord's Furnishings—Pays up to $2,500 of the policy limit to cover damage caused by an insured peril other than theft to appliances, carpeting, and other household furnishings in apartments rented to others.
- Ordinance or Law—Pays up to 10 percent of the Coverage A limit to cover increased costs incurred due to the enforcement of any ordinance or law regulating the construction, demolition, remodeling, renovation, or repair of the insured building. There is no coverage for any costs relating to pollutants.
- Grave Markers—Covers grave markers, including mausoleums, for damage by an insured peril, up to $5,000.

Additional Coverages

Additional Coverages	Does this coverage create an additional limit?	Does the deductible apply?	Is this coverage dependent on another covered loss?
1. Debris Removal	Yes, if primary limits are exhausted, an additional 5 percent of the limit of liability is available.	Yes*	Yes, damage to covered property by a covered peril or volcanic eruption must occur.
2. Reasonable Repairs	No.	Yes*	Yes, damage to covered property by a covered peril must occur.
3. Trees, Shrubs, and Other Plants	Yes, up to $500 is provided for each item up to a total of 5 percent of the Coverage A limit.	Yes*	No.
4. Fire Department Service Charge	Yes, payment up to $500 is an additional limit.	No	No, there must be a threat of a covered peril, but there is no requirement that the peril actually occur.
5. Property Removed	No.	Yes*	No, the removed property is covered against direct loss from any cause.
6. Credit Card, Electronic Fund Transfer Card or Access Device, Forgery, and Counterfeit Money	Yes, an additional total of $500 is available for any series of acts committed by any one person. Defense coverage is also provided.	No	No.
7. Loss Assessment	Yes, for an additional $1,000.	Yes**	No, not to property of the insured. But there must be a loss from a covered peril to association property.
8. Collapse	No.	Yes *	No, other property need not be damaged, but the collapse must result from a covered peril.
9. Glass or Safety Glazing Material	No.	Yes*	No, other property need not be damaged, but the glass breakage must result from a covered peril.
10. Landlord's Furnishings	No.	Yes*	No.
11. Ordinance or Law	Yes, an additional limit of 10 percent of Coverage A is available.	Yes*	Yes, to the dwelling or an "other structure."
12. Grave Markers	No.	Yes*	No.

*Not a separate deductible. Only one deductible is subtracted from the total loss of a covered event.

** Only one deductible applies per unit to the total amount of any one loss, regardless of the number of assessments.

[DA00379]

HO-3 SECTION I—PERILS INSURED AGAINST AND EXCLUSIONS

The Insurance Services Office, Inc. (ISO) Homeowners 3—Special Form (HO-3) protects policyholders against loss from a variety of perils to their homes, other structures, and personal property.

Special form coverage

Property insurance coverage covering all causes of loss not specifically excluded.

Named perils coverage

An insurance policy in which the covered causes of loss are listed or "named" in the policy.

The HO-3 contains these divisions in Section I—Perils Insured Against:

- Coverage A—Dwelling and Coverage B—Other Structures are provided on a **special form coverage** basis, commonly referred to as open perils coverage.
- Coverage C—Personal Property is provided on a **named perils coverage** basis.

No covered perils are listed in Section I—Property Coverages for Coverage D—Loss of Use or for the policy's Additional Coverages, because Coverage D and three of the Additional Coverages apply only when other covered losses occur. The remaining Additional Coverages individually describe when coverage applies. Certain exclusions from coverage apply in Section I—Exclusions.

Perils Insured Against for Coverages A and B

Insured perils for Coverage A—Dwelling and Coverage B—Other Structures are grouped together because both provide open perils coverage for real property with similar exposures to loss. Open perils coverage begins with this broad grant of coverage: "We insure against direct physical loss to property described in Coverages A and B."

This statement is followed by a list of excluded perils. Any peril not listed in these exclusions is covered. The excluded perils are these:

- Any peril excluded in Section I—Exclusions, discussed subsequently. Examples of excluded perils are flood, earthquake, and war.
- Collapse—However, collapse that results from some other cause is provided for under Section I—Property Coverages.
- Freezing of a plumbing, heating, air conditioning, or sprinkler system or a household appliance—If the insured fails to take reasonable precautions to prevent pipes and hoses from freezing and bursting, coverage is excluded for any resulting damage.
- Freezing, thawing, pressure, or weight of water or ice—Damage to external property (such as fences, pavement, patios, swimming pools, foundations, piers, and docks) caused by freezing, thawing, and water or ice pressure is excluded.
- Theft of construction materials—Theft in or to a dwelling under construction or of construction materials and supplies is excluded until the dwelling is finished and occupied.
- Vandalism and malicious mischief to vacant dwellings—Coverage for vandalism, including ensuing losses such as fire damage, is excluded for dwellings that have been vacant for more than sixty consecutive days.
- Mold, fungus, or wet rot—Coverage for loss resulting from these causes is excluded unless the mold, fungus, or wet rot is hidden and results from an accidental leak of water or steam from a plumbing, heating, sprinkler,

or air conditioning system; from a household appliance; or from a storm drain or water, steam, or sewer pipes off the residence premises. Sump pumps and roof drains are not considered part of the plumbing, heating, sprinkler, or air conditioning system or household appliance.

- Natural deterioration—Losses caused by wear and tear, marring, deterioration, mechanical breakdown, latent defect, inherent vice, smog, rust, other corrosion, and dry rot are excluded.
- Smoke from agricultural smudging or industrial operations—Damage that results from smoke caused by agricultural smudging or industrial operations is excluded. Agricultural smudging intentionally creates a dense smoke to protect plants from frost.
- Pollutants—The policy excludes coverage for damage to property caused by pollutants. An exception is made if the pollutants are released or escape as the result of any of the perils insured under Coverage C.
- Settling of the dwelling—Losses caused by settling, shrinking, bulging, or expansion of foundations, footings, patios, pavements, bulkheads, and the building structure are excluded.
- Animals—The HO-3 excludes damage caused by animals that an insured owns or keeps or by birds, rodents, or insects.

Unless the loss is otherwise excluded, the HO-3 covers water damage resulting from an accidental discharge or overflow of water or steam from a plumbing, heating, air conditioning, or sprinkler system; from a household appliance; or from a storm drain or water, steam, or sewer pipe off the residence premises. Coverage is provided for damage caused by the water, including the cost of tearing out and replacing any part of the building to make repairs. However, the loss to a damaged system or appliance is not covered.

Ensuing losses not specifically excluded by the HO-3 are covered. For example, settling of foundations is excluded, but if a settling foundation causes a water pipe to break, the ensuing water damage would be covered.

Perils Insured Against for Coverage C

Coverage C covers the contents of a home and other personal property. In contrast with the open perils coverage for Coverages A and B, Coverage C applies on a named perils basis, meaning that coverage applies only if covered property is damaged as a result of a cause of loss named in the policy. While open perils and named perils cover many of the same causes of loss, open perils coverage sometimes includes causes of loss that are not among the named perils.

For example, melting snow can back up beneath roof shingles because of the accumulation of frozen water (called an "ice dam") in the roof gutters. The water then enters the building, causing water damage to the building and personal property within. Ice dam is not a named peril under Coverage C, but it is a covered peril for purposes of Coverages A and B because it is not excluded. Therefore, any resulting water damage to the building is covered by Coverage A or B, but water damage to personal property in the building is not covered by Coverage C.

These are named perils that apply to Coverage C:

- Fire or lightning.
- Windstorm or hail—However, damage caused by rain, snow, sleet, sand, or dust is covered only if wind (including hurricane and tornado) or hail first damages the building, causing an opening in a roof or wall through which the cause of damage enters. Watercraft and their equipment are covered only while inside a fully enclosed building.
- Explosion.
- Riot or civil commotion—State laws commonly define a "riot" as a violent disturbance involving three or more (in some states, two or more) people. Civil commotion is a more serious and prolonged disturbance or violent uprising.
- Aircraft.
- Vehicles—For example, damage to personal property in the back seat of a car involved in an auto accident would be covered.
- Smoke—Sudden and accidental smoke damage to personal property, including damage by soot, fumes, or vapors from a boiler or furnace, is covered. Loss caused by smoke from agricultural smudging or industrial operations is excluded.
- Vandalism or malicious mischief.
- Theft—Theft is generally understood to mean any unlawful taking of property. The theft peril states that it "includes attempted theft and loss of property from a known place when it is likely that the property has been stolen." Thus, for example, the peril includes damage to covered property that results from an attempted but unsuccessful theft, such as when thieves break through a door but flee before stealing anything because a burglar alarm sounds.
- Falling objects—Coverage is provided if a falling object breaks through the dwelling's roof or wall and damages the contents.
- Weight of ice, snow, or sleet—Coverage applies only for damage to property contained in a building.
- Accidental discharge or overflow of water or steam—The water or steam must be accidentally released by a plumbing, heating, air conditioning, or fire-protective sprinkler system or by a household appliance.
- Sudden and accidental tearing apart, cracking, burning, or bulging—Coverage applies if a hot water heating system, an air conditioning system, an automatic fire-protective sprinkler system, or an appliance for heating water suddenly and accidentally tears apart, cracks, burns, or bulges, resulting in a loss.

- Freezing—Damage resulting from the freezing of a plumbing, heating, air conditioning, or fire-protective sprinkler system or of a household appliance is covered provided that the insured has taken reasonable precautions to maintain the heat or has shut off and drained the system or appliance.
- Sudden and accidental damage from artificially generated electrical current—Loss to tubes, transistors, or electronic components or circuitry of appliances, computers, or home entertainment equipment is not covered.
- Volcanic eruption—This peril does not include loss caused by earthquake or tremors. Damage caused by airborne shock waves and ash, for example, is covered. An earthquake caused as a consequence of a volcanic eruption, however, is not covered.

Several noteworthy limitations apply to the theft peril. See the exhibit "Limitations Applicable to Theft Peril."

Limitations Applicable to Theft Peril

- Theft committed by an insured is excluded.
- Theft from a building under construction and theft of construction materials are excluded.
- Theft from a part of the insured premises rented to someone other than an insured is excluded.
- Theft of personal property from another residence the insured owns, rents, or occupies is excluded unless the insured is temporarily living there.
- Theft of property of an insured who is a student residing away from home (such as in a dormitory) is excluded unless the student has been there during the ninety days before the loss.
- Theft is excluded for watercraft, including furnishings and equipment, away from the residence premises.
- Theft of trailers, semi-trailers, and campers is excluded.

[DA07720]

Section I—Exclusions

The HO-3 Section I exclusions apply to Coverages A, B, and C:

- Ordinance or law—This exclusion eliminates coverage for losses resulting from any ordinance or law that reduces the value of the property; requires testing for or cleaning up of pollutants; or requires demolition, construction, or debris removal. However, the HO-3 Additional Coverages section provides limited ordinance or law coverage for buildings or structures damaged as a result of an insured peril. The Additional Coverage applies to losses resulting from any ordinance or law that requires construction, demolition, remodeling, renovation, or repair beyond the typical repairs needed to restore the structures after a loss.

- Earth movement—Earthquakes and other types of earth movement, such as landslides, mudslides, mudflows, subsidence, and sinkholes, are excluded perils. This exclusion applies regardless of the cause of the earth movement, whether natural or otherwise. Damage caused by an ensuing fire or explosion is covered.
- Water—Coverage for losses caused by flood, surface water, waves, water, or waterborne material such as sewage that backs up through sewers and drains is excluded regardless of the cause of the water-related loss. Losses resulting from the "escape, overflow, or discharge" of "water or waterborne material from a dam, levee, seawall, or any other boundary or containment system" are also excluded. Ensuing losses from fire, explosion, or theft resulting from water damage are covered.
- Power failure—Damage resulting from a loss of electrical power or utility service because of a problem away from the insured residence premises is not covered. However, if power is interrupted by an insured peril that occurs on the premises, resulting losses are covered.
- Neglect—An insured is expected to use all reasonable means to protect property during and after a loss. The HO-3 provides no coverage for losses that result from the insured's failure to do so. Under an Additional Coverage, the insurer agrees to pay the cost of reasonable repairs to protect damaged property.
- War—Losses that result from war, including the discharge of nuclear weapons (on purpose or by accident), are excluded. This exclusion includes undeclared war, civil war, insurrection, rebellion, revolution, or military war-like action. Destruction, seizure, or use of insured property for military purposes is also excluded.
- Nuclear hazard—Losses that occur because of a nuclear hazard are excluded. A nuclear hazard is defined in Section I—Conditions as any "nuclear reaction, radiation, or radioactive contamination."
- Intentional loss—The HO-3 excludes any loss arising out of an act any insured commits or conspires to commit with the intent to cause a loss.
- Governmental action—Property described in Coverages A, B, and C is not covered against destruction, confiscation, or seizure by order of any governmental or public authority. This exclusion does not preclude coverage for governmental action taken to prevent the spread of fire.

Section I—Exclusions contains three additional exclusions that apply only to Coverage A—Dwelling and Coverage B—Other Structures:

- Weather is an excluded peril only if it contributes to any of the previously excluded perils. For example, torrential rain that causes a mudslide would not be a covered peril, because earth movement (mudslide) is excluded. However, if the weight of rainwater that has collected on a roof causes the roof to collapse, coverage is provided under the Collapse form of Additional Coverage.

- Acts or decisions—including the failure to act or decide—of any person, group, organization, or government body are excluded.
- Damage that results from faulty planning, zoning, surveying, design specifications, workmanship, construction, renovation, materials, and maintenance is excluded. However, if faulty construction of a chimney in the insured's house results in a fire, the damage caused by the fire would be covered.

HO-3 SECTION I—CONDITIONS

Eighteen major conditions apply to the Section I coverages in the Insurance Services Office, Inc. (ISO) Homeowners 3—Special Form (HO-3). Both the insured and the insurer must meet these conditions.

Section I—Conditions of the ISO HO-3 policy describes the conditions that must be met by both the insured and the insurer and provides a majority of the information required for the insured and insurer to comply with the mutual "promise" made in the insuring agreement.

Insurable Interest and Limit of Liability

The Insurable Interest and Limit of Liability condition limits the maximum payment for any single loss to the applicable limits shown on the Declarations page, regardless of the number of insureds who have an insurable interest in the property. This condition further limits loss payment to any insured to the extent of that insured's insurable interest in the property at the time of the loss.

Deductible

The Deductible condition specifies that the policy deductible applies on a per-loss basis and that only the highest deductible applies when two or more apply to a loss. Before the 2011 revision, this condition had appeared after the Definitions section, but now follows the Insurable Interest and Limit of Liability condition in the Conditions section. This placement reinforces the policy's intent that the deductible only applies to Section I losses.

Additionally, the minimum deductible for the ISO Homeowners program is $500. This is an increase from the previous minimum deductible amount under Section I, which was $250.

Your Duties After Loss

The Your Duties After Loss condition lists the insured's duties after a property loss. Because the cooperation of an insured is essential to the investigation, settlement, or defense of any claim, this condition clarifies that the insurer can deny coverage when an insured fails to fulfill the contractual duties listed.

In any given claim settlement, the insurer's claims representative might not require the performance of all of the listed items. However, this clause entitles the representative to require performance of any of the duties that may be helpful in the claim settlement process. These are the listed duties:

- Give prompt notice
- Notify the police
- Notify the credit card, electronic fund transfer card company, or access device company
- Protect the property from further damage
- Cooperate with the insurer
- Prepare an inventory
- Verify the loss
- Sign a sworn proof of loss

Loss Settlement

The Loss Settlement condition establishes the process for determining the amount to be paid for a property loss. There are two settlement methods, with the first method established for Coverage C—Personal Property and other miscellaneous items, and the other established for Coverage A—Dwelling and Coverage B—Other Structures.

The deductible amount shown on the Declarations page is subtracted once from the total of all losses payable under Section I and caused by a single loss event. (Two additional coverages do not have the deductible applied to them—one dealing with fire department service charges and the other with credit cards and other types of money cards.)

Losses to personal property listed under Coverage C—Personal Property, as well as awnings, carpeting, appliances, antennas, outdoor equipment, structures that are not buildings, and grave markers or mausoleums, are settled at the lesser of two amounts:

- Actual cash value (ACV) at the time of the loss
- The amount required to repair or replace the items

The loss settlement for buildings depends on how the limit of insurance compares to the replacement cost value of the damaged buildings at the time of the loss. These are the methods for determining the loss settlement for a building:

- If the limit of insurance is 80 percent or more of the replacement cost, the insurer will pay for the replacement cost of the damage up to the limit of coverage.
- If the limit of insurance is less than 80 percent of the replacement cost, the insurer will pay the greater of two amounts. The first amount is the ACV of the damage. The second is the proportion of the cost to repair or replace the damage that the limit of insurance bears to 80 percent of the replacement cost. This second method is sometimes easier to understand as a formula.

$$\text{Loss payment} = \frac{\text{Limit of insurance}}{80\% \times \text{Replacement cost}} \times \text{Replacement cost of the loss}$$

Except for small losses, which are generally considered to be under $2,500, the insurer will not pay more than the ACV until repairs are completed. An insured who has not decided whether a structure should be rebuilt can seek loss settlement on an ACV basis. Should the insured then decide to complete the repairs, he or she has up to 180 days after the loss to notify the insurer of intent to complete the repairs and make settlement on a replacement cost basis rather than on the ACV basis. See the exhibit "Loss Settlement Examples."

The insured is not required to rebuild a damaged or destroyed building on the same location. However, if the building is rebuilt on different premises, the insurer will pay no more than it would have if the building were repaired or replaced at the original premises. Regardless of the method used to determine the loss settlement amount, the limit of coverage shown on the Declarations page is the maximum amount that will be paid for any loss.

The Additional Limits of Liability for Coverages A, B, C, and D endorsement increases the Coverage A—Dwelling limit to equal the current replacement cost of the dwelling if that amount exceeds the limit appearing on the Declarations page. The limits of liability for Coverage B—Other Structures, Coverage C—Personal Property, and Coverage D—Loss of Use will be increased by the same percentage applied to Coverage A.

Loss to a Pair or Set

Often, items that are in pairs or sets are more valuable together than they are individually. Because of the increased value of pairs or sets, the Loss to a Pair or Set condition establishes the amount an insurer will pay if an item that is part of a pair or set is damaged or lost.

For example, Cindy has a custom-made brass lantern on each side of her driveway. The matching lanterns were recently fabricated at a cost of $2,000. As a pair, the lanterns have an ACV of $2,000. One lantern, by itself—not

Loss Settlement Examples

These are examples of how the loss settlement for a dwelling would be determined. (These simple examples ignore any deductible that might apply.)

Example 1—Dwelling limit equals or exceeds 80 percent of the replacement cost: An insured has a home with a $200,000 replacement cost and an HO-3 with a Coverage A limit of $180,000. Lightning strikes the central air conditioning unit and destroys it beyond repair. The unit has a replacement cost of $5,000 and is five years old. The dwelling is insured for more than 80 percent of replacement cost ($180,000 is 90 percent of $200,000).

The insured would receive $5,000 to replace the unit.

Example 2—Dwelling limit is less than 80 percent of the replacement cost: If this same insured has an HO-3 with a Coverage A limit of $100,000 (50 percent of the replacement cost), the insured's coverage would be below the 80 percent replacement cost requirement, and the second loss settlement method would be used. The insured would then receive the greater of the following:

- The ACV of the air conditioner. The ACV would be the $5,000 replacement cost minus depreciation. If a central air conditioner has a useful life of ten years and is now five years old, this air conditioner would depreciate by 50 percent. The ACV would equal $2,500.
- The limit is calculated:

$$\$100{,}000 \div (80\% \times \$200{,}000) \times \$5{,}000 = \$3{,}125$$

The insured would receive the greater amount of $3,125.

[DA00299]

part of a pair—would have an ACV of $300 or could be exactly reproduced for $1,500. If one of Cindy's lanterns is stolen, the insurer has two options:

- Replace the missing lantern for $1,500 and restore the pair to its original value
- Pay Cindy the difference between the ACV of the lanterns as a pair and the ACV of the remaining single lantern ($1,700)

Replacing the missing lantern for $1,500 is the logical choice for the insurer in this case. However, if the missing lantern could not be replaced, the insurer might have no choice other than to pay $1,700 to compensate Cindy for the value lost. Whichever solution is chosen, the deductible will be subtracted from the final amount of the loss.

Appraisal

If the insured and the insurer cannot agree on the amount of a loss, the Appraisal condition outlines a method for resolving the disagreement. This method, commonly called the appraisal process, follows this procedure:

- The insurer and the insured each choose an appraiser to prepare an estimate of the value of the loss. Each party pays for its own appraiser.
- If the estimates differ, the two appraisers submit their differences to an umpire. The umpire is an impartial individual (often another appraiser or a judge) who resolves the differences. An agreement by any two of the three will set the amount of loss. The insurer and the insured share the cost of the umpire.

Other Insurance and Service Agreement

If two or more insurance policies cover the same loss, the Other Insurance and Service Agreement condition states that the loss will be shared proportionally by all policies.

This example demonstrates how the share is apportioned between two policies:

John has an HO-3 with an $80,000 Coverage A—Dwelling limit. Maryanne, John's wife, did not realize that John had purchased a homeowners policy. She also purchased a homeowners policy with a $120,000 Coverage A—Dwelling limit.

A fire destroys the couple's home, which has a $100,000 replacement cost at the time of the loss. After the fire, John and Maryanne discover that two policies exist to cover their home, with a total of $200,000 in coverage available ($80,000 from John's policy plus $120,000 from Maryanne's policy).

The two policies will share the loss proportionally:

- The insurer that issued John's policy will pay 40 percent of the loss ($80,000 ÷ $200,000 = 0.40), or $40,000.
- The insurer that issued Maryanne's policy will pay 60 percent of the loss ($120,000 ÷ $200,000 = 0.60), or $60,000.

An insured home or item of personal property might also be covered by a service plan, property restoration plan, home warranty, or service warranty agreement. The homeowners policy makes it clear in the Other Insurance and Service Agreement condition that homeowners insurance coverage applies as excess over any amounts payable under any such agreement.

Our Option

Insurers usually settle claims by paying the value of the loss, and the insured is responsible for repairing or replacing the property. However, the Our Option condition reserves the right for the insurer to repair or replace damaged property with similar property, should it choose to do so. Sometimes insurers exercise this right because they can purchase repairs or obtain replacement items at a deep discount. Repairing or replacing property is the insurer's option. The insured cannot require the insurer to repair or replace damaged property.

Loss Payment

As provided for in the Loss Payment condition, the insurer will adjust all losses with the insured or the insured's spouse (unless another person is named in the policy or is legally entitled to receive payment). A loss is payable sixty days after the insurer receives a proof of loss and either an agreement has been reached by the insurer and the insured or a court judgment or an appraisal award has been entered. (Time periods may vary according to state requirements.)

Abandonment of Property

The Abandonment of Property condition provides that if the insured abandons the property after it is damaged or destroyed, the insurer need not take responsibility for it. For example, after collecting insurance proceeds for a loss, an insured might prefer to walk away from a burned-out home in a neighborhood where property values have declined and turn the property over to the insurer, rather than remain liable for the damaged building. However, the insurer is not obligated to accept the property.

Mortgage Clause

The Mortgage Clause condition establishes these rights of the mortgagee listed on the Declarations page:

- If a loss occurs to property covered by Coverage A—Dwelling or Coverage B—Other Structures, the loss is payable jointly to the mortgagee and the insured. Typically, the mortgagee relies on this right to ensure that the insured uses the money to repair the property. The mortgagee is satisfied as long as the property is repaired and the insured continues to make mortgage payments.
- A mortgagee has rights that are independent of the insured's rights. If the insurer denies the insured's loss (if, for example, arson by the insured is discovered), the mortgagee retains the right to collect from the insurer its insurable interest in the property.
- An insurer must mail notice of cancellation or nonrenewal of a policy to the mortgagee (in addition to notice sent to the insured) at least ten days before the cancellation or nonrenewal.

No Benefit to Bailee

The No Benefit to Bailee condition states that a bailee who holds the property of an insured is responsible for the care of that property. For example, a dry cleaner who negligently damages an insured's clothing cannot avoid responsibility for the damage because the insured has coverage under the homeowners policy.

Loss Payable Clause

In the Loss Payable Clause condition, the insurer agrees to include the named loss payee when a claim is paid involving that personal property. For example, the Loss Payable Clause condition applies to a homeowner who uses leased or rented furniture. The homeowner might be asked to name the furniture leasing company as an additional insured for this property. This information would appear in the policy declarations. Ordinarily, this means that a claim draft would be payable to both the named insured and the loss payee. The loss payee is also entitled to notification if the policy is canceled or nonrenewed. See the exhibit "Other Section I Conditions."

Other Section I Conditions

Suit Against Us—Bars an insured from bringing legal action against the insurer unless the insured has complied with all policy provisions. Any legal action must be started within two years of the loss.

Recovered Property—Provides that if the insurer pays a claim for the loss of property, and the property is later recovered, the insured has the option of taking the property and returning the claim payment or keeping the claim payment and allowing the insurer to take over the property.

Volcanic Eruption Period—All volcanic eruptions that occur within a seventy-two-hour period are considered to be one volcanic eruption. If multiple eruptions should occur within that period, only one coverage limit and one deductible would apply.

Policy Period—Specifies that coverage applies only to losses that occur during the policy period.

Concealment Fraud—States any insured who conceals or misrepresents any material information, engages in fraudulent conduct, or makes false statements relating to the insurance is not covered under the policy. This condition applies whether the conduct occurred before or after a loss.

Nuclear Hazard Clause—Defines the nuclear hazard, for which coverage is excluded in the Section I—Exclusions. Excluded nuclear hazards encompass any radiation, contamination, explosion, or smoke resulting from a nuclear reaction. A direct loss by fire resulting from the nuclear hazard is covered.

[DA07730]

2011 HO-3 SECTION I—PROPERTY COVERAGE CASE STUDY

Knowing how to apply the Insurance Services Office, Inc. (ISO) Homeowners 3—Special Form (HO-3) policy to the facts of a case is an important skill. This case study will help you make the transition from knowing policy language to applying policy language to personal property losses to determine whether coverage applies. As you progress through this case study, you can check your understanding of the coverage provided by answering the Knowledge to Action questions.

Case Facts

Marvin and Lashonda own a single-family home, which is insured under an unendorsed HO-3 policy with a $300,000 dwelling limit. A carport is attached to the rear of the home, where Marvin stores a small fishing boat and trailer. On February 2, 20X1, as the couple is cooking dinner, visitors unexpectedly arrive. Marvin and Lashonda forget to remove a pot from the stove, the pot overheats, and a fire ensues. The fire department is called, and the couple and their guests safely escape. The fire, smoke, and water damage destroy the kitchen and several adjoining rooms and damage the carport area, which is adjacent to the kitchen. The boat and trailer are destroyed by the heat and fire. Kitchen furnishings and appliances are destroyed. The couple must temporarily live in a nearby hotel for one month until their home is safe to occupy. Marvin and Lashonda report the loss to their insurer promptly. They are in compliance with all policy conditions, including Coverage A replacement cost provisions. See the exhibit "Summary of Marvin and Lashonda's Damages."

Summary of Marvin and Lashonda's Damages

$50,000	Value of structural damage to home because of the fire
$3,000	Value of Marvin's fishing boat and trailer (total loss)
$8,000	Value of structural damage to the carport
$3,500	Cost to live in a hotel while damage to home is repaired
$25,000	Value of damage to furnishings and appliances, including those items valued at a total loss

[DA07743]

Given the facts presented in the case, will the claim for fire and related damage be covered under the HO-3? If so, what amount will the insurer pay for the claim? When answering the questions in this case-based activity, consider only the information provided as part of this case.

Necessary Reference Materials

To determine whether the HO-3 policy provides coverage for the losses Marvin and Lashonda incurred as a result of the fire and the ensuing damage, you need copies of the HO-3 policy form and the Declarations page.

Overview of Steps

When examining the policy forms to determine whether coverage applies to the loss(es), you can apply the four steps of the DICE method. ("DICE" is an acronym for categories of policy provisions: declarations, insuring agreement, conditions, and exclusions.) Doing this involves analyzing these provisions and determining whether any information found at each step precludes coverage at the time the losses occurred. You should also examine other categories of policy provisions, such as the insured's duties, general provisions, endorsements (if applicable), and terms defined in the policy in relation to the declarations, insuring agreement, conditions, and exclusions.

Next, you should determine the amounts payable for the losses under the applicable policy or policies. Doing this involves analyzing the limits of insurance and any deductibles that apply. It also involves determining whether more than one policy provides coverage for the same loss.

Determination of Coverage

To determine whether HO-3 coverage applies for Marvin and Lashonda's submitted fire claim, you can move sequentially through the four steps of the DICE method of policy analysis.

DICE Analysis Step 1: Declarations

The first DICE step is to review the Declarations page of Marvin and Lashonda's policy to determine whether it covers the loss. See the exhibit "Excerpt From Marvin and Lashonda's Declarations Page."

Excerpt From Marvin and Lashonda's Declarations Page

Homeowners Policy Declarations

POLICYHOLDER: (Named Insured)	Marvin and Lashonda Smith 216 Brookside Drive Anytown, USA 40000	**POLICY NUMBER:**	296 H 578661
POLICY PERIOD:	**Inception:** March 30, 20XX **Expiration:** March 30, 20X1	**Policy period begins 12:01 A.M. standard time at the residence premises.**	

[DA07744]

Knowledge to Action

Action Task: Review the Declarations page in Marvin and Lashonda's policy.

According to your analysis of the excerpt of Marvin and Lashonda's Declarations page, is coverage applicable for the property and individuals in question during the coverage period?

Feedback: The Declarations page confirms Marvin and Lashonda as insureds for the premises damaged. The loss occurred during the policy period.

DICE Analysis Step 2: Insuring Agreement

The second DICE step is to review Marvin and Lashonda's insuring agreement to determine whether it is applicable to the described loss.

Knowledge to Action

Action Task: Review the relevant portions of the insuring agreement in the HO-3 policy.

According to your analysis of the excerpt of the insuring agreement, did this loss trigger coverage under the HO-3 Insuring Agreement?

Feedback: Yes, coverage is triggered under the HO-3, in which the insurer agrees to pay for direct physical loss to property described in Coverages A and B (subject to certain exclusions) and for direct physical loss under Coverage C for certain named perils, including fire and subsequent smoke and water damage.

DICE Analysis Step 3: Conditions

The third DICE step is to review the policy conditions to determine whether they preclude coverage at the time of the loss. See the exhibit "HO-3 Policy Form (Unendorsed) With $500 Deductible."

Knowledge to Action

Action Task: Determine whether the HO-3 policy conditions preclude coverage for Marvin and Lashonda's loss.

According to your analysis of the excerpt of the HO-3 policy conditions, is coverage precluded for Marvin and Lashonda's loss?

Feedback: No, coverage is not precluded for Marvin and Lashonda's loss. They reported the claim promptly and are in compliance with all policy conditions. The $300,000 coverage under Coverage A meets the 80 percent Coverage A Replacement Cost provision.

HO-3 Policy Form (Unendorsed) With $500 Deductible

Marvin and Lashonda's Coverages

Marvin and Lashonda Smith
216 Brookside Drive
Anytown, USA

Policy Period: From 03/30/X0 to 03/30/X1 (12:01 a.m. Standard time at the location of the residence premises)

Cov. A—Dwelling	$300,000	Cov. B—Other Structures	$30,000	Cov. C—Personal Property	$150,000	Cov. D—Loss of Use	$90,000

[DA07745]

DICE Analysis Step 4: Exclusions

The fourth DICE step is to review the policy exclusions to determine whether they exclude or limit coverage of the loss. See the exhibit "Special Limits of Liability."

Knowledge to Action

Action Task: Review the "Special Limits of Liability" exhibit to determine whether one or more exclusions exclude or limit coverage of Marvin and Lashonda's loss.

According to your review of the "Special Limits of Liability" exhibit, do one or more exclusions exclude or limit coverage of Marvin and Lashonda's loss?

Feedback: Yes, one coverage limitation in Marvin and Lashonda's HO-3 applies to Coverage C—Personal Property. Under Coverage C, a $1,500 limit applies per loss to watercraft, including trailers and related equipment. This limitation would apply to Marvin's fishing boat and trailer.

Determination of Amounts Payable

Now that you have completed the DICE analysis, you can determine the amounts payable. Doing this involves analyzing the limit(s) of insurance available to pay for the loss and any deductibles that apply. It also involves determining whether more than one policy provides coverage for the same loss.

Special Limits of Liability

3. Special Limits Of Liability

The special limit for each category shown below is the total limit for each loss for all property in that category. These special limits do not increase the Coverage C limit of liability.

a. $200 on money, bank notes, bullion, gold other than goldware, silver other than silverware, platinum other than platinumware, coins, medals, scrip, stored value cards and smart cards.

b. $1,500 on securities, accounts, deeds, evidences of debt, letters of credit, notes other than bank notes, manuscripts, personal records, passports, tickets and stamps. This dollar limit applies to these categories regardless of the medium (such as paper or computer software) on which the material exists.

   This limit includes the cost to research, replace or restore the information from the lost or damaged material.

c. $1,500 on watercraft of all types, including their trailers, furnishings, equipment and outboard engines or motors.

d. $1,500 on trailers or semitrailers not used with watercraft of all types.

e. $1,500 for loss by theft of jewelry, watches, furs, precious and semiprecious stones.

f. $2,500 for loss by theft of firearms and related equipment.

g. $2,500 for loss by theft of silverware, silver-plated ware, goldware, gold-plated ware, platinumware, platinum-plated ware and pewterware. This includes flatware, hollowware, tea sets, trays and trophies made of or including silver, gold or pewter.

h. $2,500 on property, on the "residence premises", used primarily for "business" purposes.

i. $500 on property, away from the "residence premises", used primarily for "business" purposes. However, this limit does not apply to loss to electronic apparatus and other property described in Categories **j.** and **k.** below.

j. $1,500 on electronic apparatus and accessories, while in or upon a "motor vehicle", but only if the apparatus is equipped to be operated by power from the "motor vehicle's" electrical system while still capable of being operated by other power sources.

   Accessories include antennas, tapes, wires, records, discs or other media that can be used with any apparatus described in this Category **j.**

k. $1,500 on electronic apparatus and accessories used primarily for "business" while away from the "residence premises" and not in or upon a "motor vehicle". The apparatus must be equipped to be operated by power from the "motor vehicle's" electrical system while still capable of being operated by other power sources.

   Accessories include antennas, tapes, wires, records, discs or other media that can be used with any apparatus described in this Category **k.**

[DA00338]

Knowledge to Action

Under Coverage A, how much will Marvin and Lashonda receive for fire damage to their home?

Feedback: Under Coverage A, Marvin and Lashonda will receive $49,500 ($50,000 less the $500 deductible) for fire damage to the home (within the $300,000 Coverage A limit) at full replacement cost because the policy dwelling limit complies with policy replacement cost provisions (Note that for purposes of this case, the policy deductible is being applied here).

Under Coverage A, how much will Marvin and Lashonda receive for fire damage to their carport?

Feedback: Under Coverage A, Marvin and Lashonda will receive $8,000 for fire damage to their carport (considered part of the dwelling, not an "other structure"; within the $300,000 Coverage A limit).

Under Coverage C, before an adjustment is made for the depreciation and physical condition of the furnishings and appliances, how much would Marvin and Lashonda be entitled to receive for fire, smoke, and water damage to those items?

Feedback: Under Coverage C, Marvin and Lashonda would be entitled to receive $25,000 for fire, smoke, and water damage to furnishings and appliances (within the $150,000 coverage limit). However, the amount that they would actually receive would be reduced based on the actual cash value of the furnishings and appliances, which would reflect a diminished value based on the extent to which they've depreciated.

Under Coverage C, before an adjustment is made for the depreciation and physical condition of the boat and the trailer, how much would Marvin and Lashonda be entitled to receive for fire damage to each?

Feedback: Under Coverage C, Marvin and Lashonda will receive $1,500 for fire damage to the boat and trailer (leaving a $1,500 balance unpaid because of the special limit of liability; within $150,000 coverage limit). However, the amount that they would actually receive would be reduced based on the actual cash value of the boat and trailer, which would reflect a diminished value based on the extent to which they've depreciated.

Under Coverage D, how much will Marvin and Lashonda receive for the additional living expenses required for a one-month hotel stay while their home is made habitable?

Feedback: Under Coverage D, Marvin and Lashonda will receive $3,500 for their additional living expenses (within the $90,000 coverage limit).

COVERAGE VARIATIONS IN ISO HOMEOWNERS FORMS

The homeowners insurance program developed by Insurance Services Office, Inc. (ISO) includes five coverage forms in addition to the widely used HO-3 form. To meet customers' needs and preferences, an insurance professional must understand the differences between these forms.

The ISO homeowners insurance program includes six coverage forms:

- Homeowners 2—Broad Form, or HO-2
- Homeowners 3—Special Form, or HO-3
- Homeowners 4—Contents Broad Form, or HO-4
- Homeowners 5—Comprehensive Form, or HO-5
- Homeowners 6—Unit-Owners Form, or HO-6
- Homeowners 8—Modified Coverage Form, or HO-8

While HO-3 is the most widely used, the other forms address different coverage needs or preferences:

- Apartment dwellers and condominium unit owners do not need full insurance on the buildings in which they live.
- Some customers will accept more restricted coverage than the HO-3 provides in exchange for lower premiums.
- Some customers are willing to pay for broader coverage than the HO-3 provides.
- Some older homes that have depreciated substantially are not well-suited for the replacement cost coverage provided by the HO-3.

An ISO homeowners form exists to address each of these situations. The primary differences between the HO-3 form and the other homeowners forms are in each form's Section I—Property Coverages. The Agreement, Section II—Liability Coverages, and Section II—Conditions are identical in all ISO homeowners forms. See the exhibit "Homeowners Forms Comparison."

HO-2 Broad Form Compared With HO-3

Like the HO-3, the HO-2 is designed for the owner-occupant of a house. An HO-2 has a slightly lower premium than an HO-3, while covering the same property for the same limits. The lower premium results from the fact that the HO-2 covers the dwelling and other structures against fewer causes of loss.

The HO-3 provides open perils coverage (also known as special form coverage) for Coverage A—Dwelling and Coverage B—Other Structures and provides named perils coverage for Coverage C—Personal Property. In contrast, the HO-2 provides named perils coverage for Coverages A, B, and C. In

Homeowners Forms Comparison

Form	Used for Insuring	Coverage A—Dwelling	Coverage B—Other Structures	Coverage C—Personal Property	Section II—Liability Coverages
HO-2 Broad Form	Owner-occupied dwellings	Named perils	Named perils	Named perils	Same in all forms
HO-3 Special Form	Owner-occupied dwellings	Open perils	Open perils	Named perils	Same in all forms
HO-4 Contents Broad Form	Tenants in residential buildings	N/A	N/A	Named perils	Same in all forms
HO-5 Comprehensive Form	Owner-occupied dwellings	Open perils	Open perils	Open perils	Same in all forms
HO-6 Unit-Owners Form	Owners of condominium or cooperative units	Named perils	N/A Included in Coverage A	Named perils	Same in all forms
HO-8 Modified Coverage Form	Owner-occupied dwellings	Modified named perils	Modified named perils	Modified named perils	Same in all forms

[DA09181]

both forms, Coverage D—Loss of Use is triggered by any loss covered under Coverage A, B, or C that makes the building unusable.

In addition to insuring against more causes of loss than named perils coverage, open perils coverage has another advantage, which involves the burden of proof:

- With named perils coverage, such as the HO-2, the insured must prove the loss was caused by a covered cause of loss for coverage to apply. The burden of proof is on the insured.
- With open perils coverage, if a loss to covered property occurs, the initial assumption is that it is covered. To deny coverage, the insurer must prove the loss was caused by an excluded cause of loss. In this case, the burden of proof is on the insurer.

By shifting the burden of proof, open perils coverage can provide an important advantage to an insured who suffers a property loss as a result of an unknown cause.

The list of named perils in the HO-2 encompasses most common insurable perils faced by homeowners. It closely resembles the list of named perils applicable to Coverage C in the HO-3 with a few minor differences. These are two examples:

- The vehicles peril is found in both policies, but the HO-2 policy has an exclusion for loss to a fence, driveway, or walk caused by a vehicle owned or operated by a resident of the premises.
- For accidental discharge or overflow of water or steam, the HO-2 excludes coverage if the building is vacant for more than sixty consecutive days. The HO-3 does not mention vacancy under this peril.

HO-4 Contents Broad Form Compared With HO-3

The HO-4 is designed specifically for people who live in rented houses or apartments. The HO-4 is essentially the same as an HO-3 without Coverages A and B. The HO-4 differs from the HO-3 in other ways, including these:

- HO-4 Coverage C is written at a limit the insured selects as adequate to cover personal property. In the HO-3, HO-2, and HO-5, the Coverage C limit is typically 50 percent of the Coverage A limit.
- Coverage D in the HO-4 is provided automatically at 30 percent of the Coverage C limit, rather than as 30 percent of the Coverage A limit, as in the HO-2 and HO-3.
- The HO-4 provides an additional coverage for building additions and alterations, with a limit equal to 10 percent of the Coverage C limit.
- The HO-4 does not include an additional coverage for furnishings provided by a landlord, because the occupant-insured of the apartment does not have an insurable interest in such property.

- Both the HO-3 and the HO-4 provide an additional coverage for increased costs imposed by a building ordinance or law. The HO-3 limit is 10 percent of the Coverage A limit, while the HO-4 limit is 10 percent of the building additions and alterations limit.
- Trees, shrubs, and other plants are covered for 10 percent of the Coverage C limit in the HO-4 policy, while the HO-3 provides coverage for up to 5 percent of the Coverage A limit.

HO-5 Comprehensive Form Compared With HO-3

The HO-5 provides the broadest property coverage of any ISO homeowners form. The HO-5 is essentially an HO-3 modified to provide open perils coverage, not only for the dwelling and other structures, but also for Coverage C—Personal Property.

The HO-5 broadens personal property coverage in some areas simply by not excluding an exposure that has been excluded by the HO-3 policy:

- The HO-5 covers water damage, including flood damage, for personal property away from a location owned, rented, occupied, or controlled by an insured.
- The HO-5 covers personal property damaged by rain through an open window, door, or roof opening, even if the building itself is not damaged.

The HO-5 special limits of $1,500 for jewelry and furs, $2,500 for firearms, and $2,500 for silverware apply not only to items that are stolen, but also to items that are misplaced or lost. The HO-3 does not cover, for any amount, items that are misplaced or lost.

HO-6 Unit-Owners Form Compared With HO-3

The HO-6 is closely related to the HO-4. This form is tailored to cover the exposures faced by unit owners in a **condominium** or a **cooperative corporation**. The HO-6 provides coverage for unit owners' property and liability exposures. It differs from the HO-3 in these ways:

- The HO-6 defines residence premises as the unit where the insured resides. The HO-3 definition includes a one- to four-family dwelling where the insured resides.
- The HO-6 description of Coverage A—Dwelling under Section I—Property Coverages includes: (1) alterations, appliances, fixtures, and improvements that are part of the building contained within the insured unit; (2) items of real property that pertain exclusively to the insured unit; (3) property that is the unit owner's responsibility under a condominium or cooperative association's property owners' agreement; and (4) structures owned solely by the insured at the residence location (such as a storage shed or garage).

Condominium
A real estate development consisting of a group of units, in which the air space within the boundaries of each unit is owned by the unit owner, and all remaining real and personal property is owned jointly by all the unit owners.

Cooperative corporation
A form of real property ownership in which the real property is owned by a corporation whose shareholders are the tenants of the property.

- Coverage A—Dwelling in the HO-6 provides a basic limit of $5,000, which can be increased if needed.
- Coverage B—Other Structures coverage is eliminated from the HO-6 because Coverage A of the HO-6 includes other structures owned solely by the insured.
- Coverage C—Personal Property is subject to a limit the insured selects.
- Coverage D—Loss of Use is provided automatically at a limit that is 50 percent of the Coverage C limit, rather than 30 percent of the Coverage A limit.
- Section I—Perils Insured Against in the HO-6 provides named perils coverage for Coverages A and C, similar to the coverage provided in the HO-2.
- Loss Assessments coverage is identical in the HO-3 and the HO-6, although it is more applicable to a condominium or cooperative corporation than a private dwelling. Condominiums and cooperatives have many elements, such as driveways, outdoor lighting, and swimming pools, that belong to all unit owners collectively. Damage to any of these commonly owned elements could result in an assessment against each individual unit owner.
- Trees, shrubs, and other plants are covered for up to 10 percent of the Coverage C limit, in contrast to the HO-3 limit of 5 percent of the Coverage A limit. In the HO-6, this coverage applies to plants solely owned by the named insured on grounds at the insured unit (such as those in the yard of a townhouse-style condominium).
- The additional coverage for landlord's furnishings is not included in the HO-6 policy.
- In the HO-6 policy, coverage for debris removal does not cover the cost to remove trees that damage a covered structure or block a driveway or ramp. This cost would be the condominium corporation's responsibility.

HO-8 Modified Coverage Form Compared With HO-3

The HO-8 is designed for use when the replacement cost of an owner-occupied dwelling significantly exceeds its market value.

An example of a dwelling that might be covered under the HO-8 is an older house with obsolete construction or features that would be expensive to replace, such as hand-carved wooden moldings. Such a house could have a market value of $100,000, but the cost to rebuild might be $200,000. A homeowner may be unwilling to pay the high premium necessary to buy $200,000 of insurance on a house purchased for $100,000. In addition, the homeowner could receive more money by collecting the insurance proceeds than by selling the house, which creates an obvious moral hazard. As a result, many insurers are unwilling to write an HO-3 on such a house.

The HO-8 provision addresses this problem under Section I—Conditions. A provision in this section specifies that if the insured makes repairs after a loss, the insurer will not pay more than the cost of "common construction materials and methods" that are "functionally equivalent to and less costly than obsolete, antique, or custom construction."

The HO-8 policy covers only ten named perils, and it limits or eliminates other coverages found in the HO-3 policy. The additional coverages for collapse, landlord's furnishings, ordinance or law, and grave markers are not included in the HO-8 policy. The HO-8 policy provides limited coverage for property not on the insured premises. There are no special limits for jewelry, firearms, silverware, and similar items because the theft peril provides coverage only up to $1,000.

These are other limitations in an HO-8 policy:

- Smoke from a fireplace is an exclusion in the HO-8 that is not found in the HO-3.
- Glass or safety glazing material is limited to $100.
- Under debris removal coverage, the amount available is included in the policy limit with no additional insurance available if the policy limit is exhausted. The HO-3 provides for an additional 5 percent if policy limits are exhausted.
- Windstorm is the only peril covered for trees, shrubs, and plants and only up to a limit of $250 per item ($500 in the HO-3). The occurrence limit is the same as the limit in the HO-3 policy, which is 5 percent of the dwelling limit.
- There is no coverage for personal property owned by a guest or residence employee while the property is in any residence occupied by an insured.
- The theft peril provides off-premises coverage limited to property in banks, trust companies, self-storage facilities, and similar locations.

COMMONLY USED ENDORSEMENTS THAT MODIFY THE 2011 ISO HOMEOWNERS POLICIES

In many cases, a homeowners policy's coverage may be modified through endorsements to fit the insured's needs.

These common endorsements amend Insurance Services Office, Inc. (ISO) homeowners policies:

- Personal Property Replacement Cost Loss Settlement
- Scheduled Personal Property
- Inflation Guard

- Earthquake
- Assisted Living Care Coverage
- Credit Card, Electronic Fund Transfer Card or Access Device, Forgery and Counterfeit Money Coverage—Increased Limit
- Home Business Insurance Coverage
- Ordinance or Law—Increased Amount of Coverage
- Limited Water Back-Up and Sump Discharge or Overflow Coverage
- Supplemental Loss Assessment Coverage
- Additional Residence Rented to Others—1, 2, 3, or 4 Families
- Personal Injury Coverage

ISO homeowners policies meet homeowners' common insurance coverage needs for both property and liability losses. However, insureds can have individual needs that basic ISO policies do not cover. For example, some homeowners operate businesses out of their homes. Others have valuable personal property that requires special attention. Endorsements individualize policies to meet these needs.

Personal Property Replacement Cost Loss Settlement

On all homeowners forms, losses to items covered under Coverage C—Personal Property are settled on an actual cash value (ACV) basis. The Personal Property Replacement Cost Loss Settlement endorsement (HO 04 90) provides replacement cost coverage on personal property. Dwellings and other structures are usually covered for their replacement cost value on homeowners policies. This endorsement lists certain types of personal property, such as antiques and fine art, ineligible for replacement cost coverage.

For losses with a replacement value of more than $500, the insured must repair or replace the lost or damaged items before the insurer will pay the replacement cost. (ACV is paid until repair or replacement is made.) The insured can make an ACV claim at the time of loss and later make a claim for the additional replacement cost. To do so, the insured must notify the insurer within 180 days after the loss of his or her intent to repair or replace the damaged property.

The value of personal property based on replacement cost is usually higher than the value of personal property based on ACV. Accordingly, when this endorsement is used, many insurers require a Coverage C—Personal Property limit that is higher than the usual Coverage C limit of 50 percent of the Coverage A limit (used with actual cash value coverage).

Scheduled Personal Property

An unendorsed homeowners policy (except for the HO-5) covers personal property against only named perils. Additionally, all homeowners policies impose special sublimits on coverage for certain types of property, such as stamps and coins, regardless of the cause of loss, and they include special sublimits on coverage for theft of jewelry and other types of property.

The Scheduled Personal Property Endorsement (HO 04 61) provides **scheduled coverage** for specific items, such as jewelry, furs, musical instruments, silverware, fine arts, and rare coins.

Scheduled coverage

Insurance for property specifically listed (scheduled) on a policy, with a limit of liability for each item.

The Scheduled Personal Property Endorsement covers more causes of loss than the HO-3 and other homeowners forms. The special limits and Coverage C deductible do not apply to the endorsement.

Inflation Guard

The Inflation Guard endorsement (HO 04 46) is designed to help prevent underinsurance caused by economic inflation and rising replacement costs. Rather than increasing coverage by a fixed amount, the endorsement gradually and automatically increases limits for Coverages A, B, C, and D throughout the policy period by a percentage mutually agreed upon by the insured and insurer.

Earthquake

All unendorsed homeowners forms exclude damage resulting from any kind of earth movement—including earthquake and landslide. The Earthquake endorsement (HO 04 54) provides a means to buy coverage for this cause of loss. The mandatory deductible is usually 5 percent of the limit that applies to either Coverage A or Coverage C, whichever is greater, but not less than $500.

Assisted Living Care Coverage

Assisted Living Care Coverage (HO 04 59) provides Section I—Coverage C—Personal Property and Section II—Coverage E—Personal Liability Coverage to a relative of the insured who is a resident of a facility that provides assisted living services, such as meals, medical supervision, housekeeping, and social activities. This scheduled person must not be a resident of the insured's household. Special limits of liability apply to certain types of property, such as $250 for hearing aids and $500 for medical alert devices. Section II coverage excludes liability assumed by the facility before an occurrence and bodily injury to a staff member of the facility.

Credit Card, Electronic Fund Transfer Card or Access Device, Forgery and Counterfeit Money Coverage—Increased Limit

Section I of the homeowners policies provides coverage up to a limit of $500 for losses resulting from the unauthorized use of an insured's credit card, bank transfer card, check forgery, or acceptance of counterfeit money. The Credit Card, Fund Transfer Card or Access Device, Forgery and Counterfeit Money Coverage (HO 04 53) provides a higher limit of coverage to as much as $10,000.

Home Business Insurance Coverage (HOMEBIZ)

For insureds who operate an office or business from their homes, the Home Business Insurance Coverage, or HOMEBIZ, endorsement (HO 07 01) provides a comprehensive business package policy when attached to a homeowners form. The endorsement, which specifically excludes professional liability coverage, also lists many examples of professional activities that are excluded, ranging from legal, insurance, or accounting services to body piercing services.

There are minimum requirements for a home business to be covered under this endorsement, such as ownership by an insured, operation from the residence premises, and a maximum of three employees.

For eligible businesses, this endorsement provides valuable commercial coverages:

- Section I—Property Coverage provides full Coverage C—Personal Property limits for business property, accounts receivable, loss of business income, extra expense, and increased Coverage C limits for other property.
- Section II—Liability Coverages provides products-completed operations coverage up to an annual aggregate limit equal to the Coverage E—Personal Liability limit; provides all other business liability coverage (including personal and advertising injury).

Ordinance or Law—Increased Amount of Coverage

Any individual who owns a house could discover after a loss that repairs or upgrades must be made in order to comply with current ordinances or laws. The Ordinance or Law—Increased Amount of Coverage endorsement (HO 04 77) increases the coverage that is provided by an HO-3 policy of 10 percent of Coverage A by increments of 25 percent.

Limited Water Back-Up and Sump Discharge or Overflow Coverage

Unendorsed homeowners policies exclude property coverage for water or waterborne materials that originate from within the insured's dwelling and back up through sewers or drains, or that overflow from a sump, sump pump, or related equipment. The Limited Water Back-Up and Sump Discharge or Overflow Coverage endorsement (HO 04 95) adds this coverage back into the policy.

Supplemental Loss Assessment Coverage

Insureds living in communities with a neighborhood association are charged a monthly fee to cover the cost of the maintenance and upkeep of the common areas of the neighborhood. An association might assess homeowners for major expenses, such as the installation of a new roof on a club house or damages paid to a person injured on the association's property.

The unendorsed homeowners policy provides some limited coverage under the Additional Coverages of Section I—Property Coverages and Section II—Liability Coverages. The Loss Assessment Coverage endorsement (HO 04 35) supplements those additional coverages with an additional amount of insurance for the premises named in the endorsement. The insured can also list additional locations and schedule an amount of insurance for them (for example, if an insured owns a secondary residence with a neighborhood association).

Additional Residence Rented to Others—1, 2, 3, or 4 Families

The Additional Residence Rented to Others—1, 2, 3, or 4 Families endorsement (HO 24 70) is designed for insureds who own rental property not at the insured location. It extends Coverage E—Personal Liability and Coverage F—Medical Payments to Others to one- to four-family residences that are owned by the insured and rented to others. The location of any additional residence must be listed on the endorsement, and the number of families that occupy each must be specified.

Personal Injury Coverage

The Personal Injury Coverage endorsement (HO 24 82) expands the liability coverage of a homeowners policy by adding the definition of personal injury

Reality Check

Effect of Dog Bites on Liability Coverage in Homeowners Policies

Dog bites are a significant source of homeowners liability claims. ISO has introduced a canine liability exclusion endorsement that insurers can use to shield themselves from this type of claim. Insurers may ask insureds if they have a dog and, if so, what breed it is. However, several states have passed laws that prohibit insurers from discriminating against dog owners based only on breed. This endorsement could become a significant errors and omissions exposure for a producer who fails to notify an insured of its application to a policy. Therefore, an ISO rules filing requires the insured to acknowledge the endorsement in writing for it to be effective. The wording of this endorsement may cause another problem. The endorsement excludes coverage for bodily injury arising out of direct physical contact with the canine. Therefore, if a visitor tripped over a dog and was injured in the fall, coverage would be excluded.

[DA07796]

and then adding coverage for personal injury. Personal injuries are defined in this endorsement as injuries arising out of one or more of these offenses:

- False arrest, detention, or imprisonment
- Malicious prosecution
- Invasion of privacy, wrongful eviction, or wrongful entry
- Publication, in any manner, of material that slanders or libels another party or disparages the other party's goods, products, or services
- Publication, in any manner, of material that violates a person's right to privacy

Exclusions to this coverage relate to intentional acts, criminal acts, contractual liability, employment, business activities, bodily injury to an insured, civic or public duties performed for pay, and pollutants. See the exhibit "Summary of Endorsements."

Apply Your Knowledge

Mark and Heather's neighbor's house caught fire and sustained serious property damage. Concerned that the same type of loss could occur to them, they called their insurance agent the next day to discuss ways to strengthen the fire protection coverage of their homeowners policy. If their policy was unendorsed, what endorsements would the agent likely suggest?

Feedback: Without the Personal Property Replacement Cost Loss Settlement endorsement, their personal property that is damaged by a fire is replaced at its actual cash value. Replacement cost coverage would indemnify Mark and Heather for the current replacement cost of property with similar features.

Summary of Endorsements

Endorsement	Summary
Personal Property Replacement Cost Loss Settlement (HO 04 90)	Provides replacement cost (instead of actual cash value) coverage on personal property, awnings, carpeting, household appliances, and outdoor equipment.
Scheduled Personal Property (HO 04 61)	Provides coverage for insureds who own jewelry, furs, or other eligible property for which an unendorsed homeowners policy does not provide adequate protection.
Inflation Guard (HO 04 46)	Helps prevent underinsurance caused by economic inflation and rising replacement costs by gradually and automatically increasing limits throughout the policy period for Coverages A, B, C, and D.
Earthquake (HO 04 54)	Covers damage caused by earthquake and land shock waves caused by volcanic eruption.
Assisted Living Care Coverage (HO 04 59)	Provides personal property and liability coverage for a relative of an insured living in an assisted living facility.
Credit Card, Electronic Fund Transfer Card or Access Device, Forgery and Counterfeit Money Coverage—Increased Limit (HO 04 53)	Increases the $500 coverage provided by the unendorsed HO policy to as much as a $10,000 limit for losses resulting from the unauthorized use of an insured's credit card, bank transfer card, check forgery, or acceptance of counterfeit money; the insurance limit can be increased for this additional coverage
Home Business Insurance Coverage (HO 07 01)	Provides a comprehensive business package policy for home business when attached to a homeowners form and a wider range of coverages normally found only in a commercial insurance policy; excludes professional liability coverage and many professional activities.
Ordinance or Law—Increased Amount of Coverage (HO 04 77)	Covers repairs that must be made in compliance with current ordinances or laws.
Limited Water Back Up and Sump Discharge or Overflow Coverage (HO 04 95)	Covers direct losses from water or water-borne material that (1) backs up sewers or drains or (2) overflows or is discharged from a sump, sump pump, or related equipment.
Supplemental Loss Assessment Coverage (HO 04 35)	Supplements additional coverages for insureds in communities where monthly fees are charged to cover the maintenance and upkeep costs of the common areas; also allows the insured to list additional locations and schedule an amount of insurance for them.
Additional Residence Rented to Others—1, 2, 3, or 4 Families (HO 24 70)	Designed for insureds who own rental property not at the insured location; extends Coverage E—Personal Liability and Coverage F—Medical Payments to Others to one- to four-family residences owned by the insured and rented to others.
Personal Injury Coverage (HO 24 82)	Expands liability coverage by adding definition of personal injury and coverage for it. Personal injuries arise out of false arrest, detention, or imprisonment; malicious prosecution; invasion of privacy, wrongful eviction, or wrongful entry; libel or slander against a person or organization or disparaging acts against a person's or organization's goods, products, or services; libel or slander that violates a person's right of privacy.

[DA01001]

The agent may suggest Mark and Heather consider adding an Inflation Guard endorsement, which automatically increases the homeowners coverage amount annually. The endorsement is designed to help prevent underinsurance caused by economic inflation and rising replacement costs.

The agent may also suggest the Ordinance or Law—Increased Amount of Coverage endorsement. This endorsement would cover any additional repairs or upgrades that may have to be made after a fire in order to comply with current ordinances or laws.

SUMMARY

Individuals and families face a number of loss exposures in terms of the assets exposed to loss, the causes of loss to which property is exposed, and the financial consequences of loss. Assets exposed to loss can include both real property and personal property. Many causes of loss exist, including fire, theft, and collision, and they result in various financial consequences to property. These financial consequences include a reduction in value of property, increased expenses, and lost income.

Individuals and families have a variety of personal risk management needs related to their homes and personal liability. The ISO Homeowners program offers a selection of homeowners forms to meet these various needs. The forms vary according to the types of property eligible for coverage and type of coverage provided.

HO-3 Section I—Property Coverages contains four property coverages: Coverage A—Dwelling, Coverage B—Other Structures, Coverage C—Personal Property, and Coverage D—Loss of Use. Section I also includes twelve Additional Coverages, which provide limited coverage for various types of losses that would not otherwise be covered under Section I.

HO-3 provides open perils coverage for property described in Coverage A—Dwelling and Coverage B—Other Structures and named perils coverage for property described in Coverage C—Personal Property. Coverages A, B, and C are all subject to the Section I—Exclusions. Coverages A and B are also subject to several other exclusions that help to define the scope of open perils coverage.

HO-3 Section I—Conditions describes the eighteen major conditions applying to the property coverages that both the insured and the insurer must meet.

You should now be able to apply policy language to personal property losses to determine whether the losses are covered and, if so, the amount for which they are covered.

In addition to form HO-3, the ISO homeowners program includes five forms—HO-2 (Broad Form), HO-4 (Contents Broad Form), HO-5 (Comprehensive Form), HO-6 (Unit-Owners Form), and HO-8 (Modified Coverage Form)—that meet coverage needs or preferences that the HO-3 does not address.

Endorsements add or delete coverage, change definitions, or clarify the intent of insurance policies. These are common ISO endorsements for homeowners policies: Personal Property Replacement Cost Loss Settlement; Scheduled Personal Property; Inflation Guard; Earthquake; Assisted Living Care Coverage; Credit Card, Electronic Fund Transfer Card or Access Device; Forgery and Counterfeit Money Coverage—Increased Limit; Home Business Insurance (HOMEBIZ); Ordinance or Law—Increased Amount of Coverage; Limited Water Back-Up and Sump Discharge or Overflow Coverage; Supplemental Loss Assessment Coverage; Additional Residence Rented to Others—1, 2, 3, or 4 Families; and Personal Injury Coverage.

Direct Your Learning

2

Other Personal Lines Property Coverage

Educational Objectives

After learning the content of this assignment, you should be able to:

- Contrast the DP-3 policy with the HO-3 policy in regard to each of the following:
  - Types of property covered
  - Other coverages
  - Perils insured against
  - Exclusions and conditions
  - Coverage for liability and theft losses
- Given a case describing a dwelling claim, determine whether the Dwelling Property—Special Form (DP-3) policy would cover the claim and, if so, the amount the insurer would pay for the claim.
- Explain how the coverages under the HO-3 policy are modified by the Mobilehome Endorsement (MH 04 01) and other ISO endorsements unique to mobilehome coverage.
- Summarize the provisions of the NFIP General Property Form and the Residential Condominium Building Association Policy.
- Describe the operation of FAIR plans and beachfront and windstorm plans and the coverage they provide.
- Summarize the coverages provided by personal inland marine policies.
- Compare the coverages typically provided for watercraft under each of the following:
  - HO-3
  - Personal Auto Policy
  - Small boat policies
  - Boatowners and yacht policies

Outline

Other Personal Lines Property Coverage

2

DWELLING POLICIES

Because dwelling policies are used widely, particularly to insure rental dwellings, an understanding of the coverages provided by the DP-3 policy and how they differ from the HO-3 policy is important.

Some residences are not eligible for homeowners coverage for various reasons. Here are some of those reasons:

- The residence is not owner-occupied.
- The value of the dwelling is below the minimum limit for a homeowners policy.
- The residence does not otherwise meet an insurer's underwriting guidelines.

An insured might not want a homeowners policy for either or both of two reasons: The insured might not want or need the full range of homeowners coverages, and a homeowners policy might cost more than the insured is willing to pay.

A dwelling policy can be used to cover owner- and nonowner-occupied residences or to meet the needs of customers who do not want or need a homeowners policy. Although many differences exist between the dwelling and homeowners policies, among the most important differences is the fact that the unendorsed Insurance Services Office, Inc. (ISO) Dwelling Property 3—Special Form DP 00 03 (DP-3) does not provide any theft coverage for personal property or any liability coverages. However, both of these coverages can be added to the dwelling policy by an endorsement or a supplement.

Structures Eligible for Dwelling Policies

The HO-3 policy covers owner-occupied one- to four-family dwellings. Dwelling policies are designed principally for insuring one- to four-family dwellings, whether owner-occupied or tenant-occupied. However, dwelling policies may also be used for four other kinds of property and activities:

- A dwelling in the course of construction
- Mobile homes at a permanent location
- Houseboats, in some states
- Certain incidental business occupancies, if the businesses are operated by the owner-insured or by a tenant of the insured location

Coverages

The DP-3 offers property coverages on a dwelling and its contents that are similar to the coverages under Section I (property) of the HO-3 and other homeowners forms.

The dwelling form includes five coverages:

- Coverage A—Dwelling
- Coverage B—Other Structures
- Coverage C—Personal Property
- Coverage D—Fair Rental Value
- Coverage E—Additional Living Expense

Unlike the HO-3 policy, the dwelling policy does not automatically include all the property coverages. A limit for each desired coverage (dwelling, other structures, and personal property) must be shown on the Declarations page (with appropriate premium charges). Loss of use coverages (fair rental value and additional living expense), however, are automatically included in the DP-3.

Although a dwelling policy can be used for insuring only personal property with no dwelling or structures coverage, this is rarely done. The DP-3 form is more commonly used to cover only the dwelling and other structures (for example, to insure a house rented unfurnished to tenants) or to cover the dwelling, other structures, and personal property.

Coverage A—Dwelling

The DP-3 form provides coverage for the dwelling on the described location shown in the declarations and specifies that it must be used principally for dwelling purposes. The HO-3 form refers to the dwelling on the residence premises, including attached structures. The dwelling form also specifically states that, if not covered elsewhere in the policy, building equipment and outdoor equipment used for the service of the premises and located on the described location are covered. For example, if the insured owns a lawn mower kept in the garage of the insured dwelling and uses it to cut the grass at the insured location, the lawn mower would be included under Coverage A (if the insured did not purchase Coverage C—Personal Property). The remainder of the Coverage A language is similar in the dwelling and homeowners forms.

Coverage B—Other Structures

Although the dwelling and homeowners forms have some minor differences in their wording, their coverage for other structures is essentially the same. Structures set apart from the dwelling by clear space or connected to the dwelling by only a fence, utility line, or similar connection are defined as included under Coverage B. As in the HO-3 policy, Coverage B includes detached structures, such as garages and storage sheds, on the insured premises. Gravemarkers and mausoleums are specifically excluded under Other Structures in the DP-3 form, whereas the HO-3 policy provides up to $5,000 for gravemarkers as an additional coverage.

Coverage C—Personal Property

If Coverage C is selected, coverage under the dwelling form applies to personal property usual to the occupancy of a dwelling that is owned or used by the insured or resident family members. Coverage applies while the property is on the described location.

Unlike the homeowners form, the dwelling form has no special limits that apply to any specific type of personal property. For example, the homeowners form has special limits on theft losses to jewelry, furs, firearms, silverware, and similar types of property; the dwelling form has no such limits. Because the unendorsed dwelling form has no theft coverage, such theft limitations are not necessary. The homeowners policy has a special sublimit on money and related items, but the dwelling form excludes coverage for money altogether. The homeowners policy provides a special sublimit on watercraft (including their furnishings, equipment, and outboard motors), but the dwelling form excludes boats other than rowboats and canoes.

To cover personal property, the insured chooses a Coverage C limit in the dwelling form. If an insured is a landlord and has no personal property in the insured dwelling (or chooses not to insure personal property), he or she can choose to purchase only Coverage A under the DP-3. The HO-3 policy has no such option.

Coverage D—Fair Rental Value and Coverage E—Additional Living Expense

Coverages D and E in the DP-3 form correspond roughly to Coverage D—Loss of Use in the HO-3 form, which includes both fair rental value and additional living expense coverages. Coverage D covers the fair rental value of a property rented to others when it becomes unfit for its normal use because of a loss by a covered peril. Coverage E covers the increase in living expenses for the insured if the described property becomes unfit for its normal use because of a loss by a covered peril.

Other Coverages

Many of the other coverages provided in the dwelling policy correspond to the additional coverages in the homeowners policy, but there are some differences. Loss assessment coverage, which is included automatically (up to $1,000) in the homeowners policy, can be added to the dwelling policy by endorsement for an additional premium. The additional coverages in the homeowners policy for landlord's furnishings and for credit cards, transfer cards, forgery, and counterfeit money are not available in the dwelling policy.

Other Structures

The DP-3 form provides up to 10 percent of the Coverage A limit for Coverage B—Other Structures as outlined in the Other Coverages provision. This coverage is additional insurance and does not reduce the Coverage A limit for the same loss.

Debris Removal

The debris removal coverage of the DP-3 form is included in the limit that applies to the damaged property. In contrast, the HO-3 provides an additional 5 percent of the applicable coverage limit for debris removal if the amount to be paid for the damage to the property plus the debris removal expense exceeds the coverage limit for the damaged property. The debris removal coverage under the HO-3 also provides coverage for trees, shrubs, and plants, subject to sublimits. There is no debris removal coverage for trees, shrubs, and plants in the DP-3 form.

Improvements, Alterations, and Additions

The DP-3 form provides 10 percent of the Coverage C limit as additional insurance to cover a tenant's improvements, alterations, and additions for loss by a covered peril. No comparable coverage exists in the HO-3 form.

Worldwide Coverage

The DP-3 form provides up to 10 percent of the Coverage C limit for loss to the property covered under Coverage C, except rowboats and canoes, while that property is anywhere in the world. The HO-3 form provides worldwide coverage for personal property owned or used by an insured, with no limitation except that a 10 percent limitation applies to property usually located at a secondary residence of the insured.

Fair Rental Value and Additional Living Expense

The DP-3 form provides up to 20 percent of the Coverage A limit for losses under both Coverage D—Fair Rental Value and Coverage E—Additional Living Expense as outlined in the Other Coverages provision. This coverage is additional insurance and does not reduce the Coverage A limit for the same loss. Under the HO-3 form, the corresponding additional limit for loss of use is 30 percent of the Coverage A limit.

Reasonable Repairs

The DP-3 form, like the HO-3 form, provides coverage for the cost of reasonable repairs made after the occurrence of a covered loss solely to protect covered property from further damage. This coverage does not increase the limit of liability that applies to the covered property.

Property Removed

Under both the DP-3 and HO-3, covered property is protected if it is removed from the premises because it is endangered by an insured peril. Under both policies, this coverage applies to direct loss from any cause (as long as an insured peril necessitated the removal) for thirty days. In the dwelling form, as in the homeowners form, the limit for this coverage is the same as the limit for the property being moved.

Trees, Shrubs, and Other Plants

In both the HO-3 and the DP-3 forms, the maximum limit that can be applied (as an additional amount of insurance) to trees, shrubs, other plants, or lawns is 5 percent of the Coverage A limit. The limit for any one tree, plant, or shrub is $500, and only specified perils are covered. This coverage can be expanded by endorsement to include the perils of wind and hail.

Fire Department Service Charge

The DP-3 form, like the HO-3 form, will pay up to $500 for fire department service charges. Coverage is not provided if the property is located within the limits of the city, municipality, or protection district furnishing the fire department response. This coverage is additional insurance, and no deductible applies.

Collapse

The DP-3 form offers coverage for building collapse due to specified perils. As in the HO-3 form, coverage is for direct physical loss to covered property resulting from collapse caused by any of six perils:

- Coverage C—Personal Property perils
- Decay that is hidden from view
- Hidden insect or vermin damage, unless the insured is aware of the damage prior to the collapse
- Weight of contents, equipment, animals, or people
- Weight of rain collecting on a roof
- Use of defective materials or methods of construction

Collapse coverage does not increase the limit of liability that applies to the damaged covered property.

Glass or Safety Glazing Material

The DP-3 form provides coverage for breakage of glass or safety glazing material that is part of a building, storm door, or storm window, and for damage to covered property caused by breakage of such glass or safety glazing material. The coverage does not apply if the dwelling has been vacant for more than sixty consecutive days before the loss. This coverage does not increase the limit of liability that applies to the damaged property. Similar coverage is included in the HO-3 form.

Ordinance or Law

The DP-3 form provides coverage for increased costs the insured incurs because of the enforcement of any ordinance or law. If the insured has purchased Coverage A, ordinance or law coverage is provided up to 10 percent of the Coverage A limit. If there is no Coverage A limit, up to 10 percent of the Coverage B limit is provided for ordinance or law coverage. This coverage is additional insurance. Coverage under the HO-3 form is similar and provides up to 10 percent of Coverage A for ordinance or law coverage as additional insurance.

If the insured is a tenant at the described location, the limit applying to ordinance or law coverage is up to 10 percent of the limit that applies to improvements, alterations, and additions.

Perils Insured Against

Coverage A—Dwelling and Coverage B—Other Structures

The DP-3, like the HO-3, uses the special form approach and insures against "risk of direct loss to property" (as opposed to named perils coverage) under Coverage A—Dwelling and Coverage B—Other Structures. In both the DP-3 and the HO-3 forms, the coverage for direct physical loss to real property is determined by the causes of loss that are excluded. Those causes of loss that are not excluded are covered. For example, the DP-3 form excludes coverage for theft of any property that is not part of a covered building or structure. It also excludes loss caused by wind, hail, ice, snow, or sleet to outdoor radio and television antennas and aerials, and to trees, shrubs, other plants, or lawns. Other exclusions in the DP-3 are essentially the same as those in the HO-3.

Coverage C—Personal Property

Although the Coverage C named perils under the DP-3 form are similar to the named perils coverage in the HO-3 form, there are some differences. Theft of personal property is not covered under the DP-3, but coverage is provided for damage to covered property caused by burglars, unless the dwelling has been vacant for more than sixty days. For example, if burglars break down a door, damage a table, and steal a television, the damage to the door and the table would be covered, but the loss of the stolen TV would not be covered. The DP-3 specifically excludes pilferage, theft, burglary, and larceny under the peril of vandalism or malicious mischief.

The windstorm or hail coverage in the DP-3 also differs slightly from the HO-3. The DP-3 specifically excludes wind or hail damage to canoes and rowboats; the HO-3 covers such damage to watercraft and their trailers, furnishings, equipment, and outboard motors, but only while the items are inside a fully enclosed building.

Dwelling Policy General Exclusions

The general exclusions in the DP-3 track closely with the Section I exclusions in the HO-3. These exclusions include loss caused directly or indirectly by several perils or events:

- Ordinance or law, except as provided in the Other Coverages section
- Earth movement, such as an earthquake
- Water damage, such as flood and backup of sewers and drains
- Power failure that occurs off the described location
- Neglect on the part of the insured
- War
- Nuclear hazard
- Intentional loss
- Weather conditions that contribute to any of the preceding excluded causes of loss
- Acts or decisions of other persons, groups, organizations, or governmental bodies
- Faulty construction, planning, materials, or maintenance

Dwelling Policy Conditions

The DP-3 form contains a single section of conditions. Similar conditions are found in the HO-3 policy, but some HO-3 conditions apply only to Section I, while others apply to both Section I and Section II (liability). Because the DP-3 form has no Section II (liability) coverage, there is no need to specify the section to which the conditions apply. These conditions include the insured's duties after a loss, loss to a pair or set, other insurance, mortgage clause, and other similar conditions regarding the coverage. See the exhibit "Comparison of the HO-3 and the DP-3 Forms."

Coverage for Liability and Theft Losses

Although the ISO dwelling forms do not provide coverage for liability or theft losses, such coverages are available by adding a personal liability supplement and a theft endorsement.

Personal Liability Supplement

Liability coverage may be written as an addendum to the dwelling policy or as a separate policy using the personal liability supplement (DL 24 01). An

Comparison of the HO-3 and the DP-3 Forms

Coverage	HO-3	DP-3
A—Dwelling	Limit selected by insured	Same
	Replacement cost coverage if limit is at least 80% of replacement cost	Same
	Automatically included	Included only if limit selected and shown on Declarations page
B—Other Structures	10% of Coverage A	10% of Coverage A
	Automatically included	Provided in the Other Coverages section
	Replacement cost coverage if limit is at least 80% of replacement cost	Same
C—Personal Property	50% of Coverage A automatically included	Included only if limit selected and shown on Declarations page
	Worldwide coverage up to Coverage C limit	Worldwide coverage only up to 10% of Coverage C
	ACV (actual cash value) coverage	Same
D—Loss of Use	30% of Coverage A	Coverage D—Fair Rental Value and Coverage E—Additional Living Expense
	Automatically included	20% of Coverage A Provided in the Other Coverages section for both Coverage D and Coverage E
Additional/Other Coverages		
• Loss assessment	$1,000	None (can be added by endorsement)
• Credit card, electronic fund transfer card or access device, forgery and counterfeit money	$500	None
• Landlord's furnishings	$2,500 at residence	None included in the Other Coverages section, but if the dwelling is rented, the owner/landlord's furnishings are covered up to the Coverage C limit
• Debris removal	Additional 5% of limit of liability available	Included in limit of coverage
	Includes coverage for trees, shrubs, and plants, subject to a sublimit	No coverage for trees, shrubs, and plants
• Improvements, alterations, and additions	None	Tenant may use up to 10% of Coverage C (additional insurance)

• Reasonable repairs	Included in limit	Same
• Property removed	Covered up to 30 days from date of loss	Same
• Trees, shrubs, plants	5% of Coverage A, up to $500 per item for limited perils (not including wind or hail) Additional insurance	Same Additional insurance
• Fire dept. service charge	$500	Same
• Collapse	Covered for limited perils	Same
• Glass or safety glazing material	Covered	Covered
• Ordinance or law	10% of Coverage A	10% of Coverage A. If no Coverage A, 10% of Coverage B. If insured is tenant, 10% of improvements, alterations, and additions limit
Personal Property—Special Limits/ Exclusions	$200 for money $1,500 for securities and other documents $1,500 for watercraft	Money excluded Securities and documents excluded Watercraft excluded (except rowboats and canoes)
Perils Insured Against		
• Coverages A & B	Special-form coverage (risk of direct loss, subject to exclusions)	Same
• Coverage C	Named perils (broad form) Theft coverage included by endorsement	Same No theft coverage (theft can be added)
Section II—Liability		
• E—Personal Liability	Automatically included	None
• F—Medical Payments to Others	Automatically included	None Liability and medical payments can be added by purchase of personal liability supplement

This comparison is based on Insurance Services Office (ISO) forms. It can be used as a quick reference and as an easy method to compare the HO-3 and DP-3 policies. However, only the actual policy forms contain complete coverage information, and those forms should be used to determine coverage wording.

[DA05619]

insured who has both a homeowners policy on his or her residence and a dwelling policy on a rental dwelling also has the option of obtaining liability coverage for the rental dwelling by purchasing the homeowners additional residence rented to others endorsement (HO 24 70) for an additional premium.

The personal liability supplement provides Coverage L—Personal Liability and Coverage M—Medical Payments to Others. These coverages are similar in format and language to Coverage E—Personal Liability and Coverage F—Medical Payments to Others in Section II of the homeowners policy.

The exclusions and additional coverages in the personal liability supplement attached to the DP-3 are virtually the same as those applicable to Section II of the homeowners policy. The main difference is that the additional liability coverage for loss assessment provided (up to a limit of $1,000) in the HO-3 form is not provided in the personal liability supplement.

Residential Theft Coverage

An insured may choose between two endorsements to the dwelling form to provide theft coverage similar to that provided in the homeowners policy.

The first endorsement, the Broad Theft Coverage (DP 04 72) endorsement, provides coverage against the perils of theft, including attempted theft, and vandalism or malicious mischief as a result of theft or attempted theft on-premises and off-premises. Off-premises coverage is available only if the insured purchases on-premises coverage. The endorsement includes special limits similar to the sublimits included in the HO-3 form, such as those for money, jewelry, and firearms. See the exhibit "Broad Theft Coverage—Special Limits of Liability."

Broad Theft Coverage—Special Limits of Liability

Category	Limit
Money, bank notes, bullion, gold	$200
Securities, accounts, deeds	$1,500
Watercraft of all types, including their trailers	$1,500
Trailers or semitrailers, other than those used with watercraft	$1,500
Jewelry, watches, furs	$1,500
Firearms and related equipment	$2,500
Silverware, goldware, platinumware, and pewterware	$2,500

[DA05620]

The second endorsement, the Limited Theft Coverage (DP 04 73) endorsement, covers only on-premises theft, attempted theft, and vandalism or malicious mischief as a result of theft or attempted theft. The endorsement includes special limits only for watercraft and their trailers, trailers not used for watercraft, and firearms and related equipment. It does not cover off-premises theft.

DWELLING COVERAGE CASE STUDY

Knowing how to apply the Dwelling Property—Special Form (DP-3) dwelling policy to the facts of a case is an important skill. This case study can help the student begin to make the transition from knowing policy language to knowing how to apply policy language to losses.

This case helps the student to apply the Insurance Services Office, Inc. (ISO) DP-3 dwelling policy to a given set of facts. The unendorsed DP-3 policy covers the dwelling but does not include liability coverage.

Case Facts

Based on the facts presented in this case, will the property claim be covered? If so, what amount would the insurer pay for the claim?

Wally and Dawn are a young married couple who have just purchased their first home. They had been saving money for over a year so that they could make this purchase, and now their funds are limited. The three-bedroom home was a bargain but will require a lot of work over the next few years. Before obtaining insurance coverage for the home, Wally and Dawn received several quotes from different insurers. They discovered that the cost of an HO-3 homeowners policy was much higher than that of a DP-3 dwelling policy. Although the homeowners policy provided broader coverage, the couple decided to purchase the dwelling policy to save money. The policy does not include any endorsements.

About six months after Wally and Dawn obtained the policy, the home was damaged as a result of an electrical fire in the basement. Most of the fire damage was restricted to the basement, but there was smoke damage throughout the home. The total cost of home repairs was $35,000. The washer and dryer also needed to be replaced, and there was damage to some personal property stored in the basement, which amounted to a total actual cash value (ACV) of $2,350. Wally and Dawn could not live in the house for one month after the fire and rented an apartment for $725 for the month. Also, while the house was being repaired, a burglary occurred. During the night, someone broke in through the back door, and a television and some stereo equipment valued at $2,800 were stolen. The cost to repair the damage to the door and its framing was $3,150.

To confirm that the facts about an accident are accurate, insurers frequently rely on police reports, recorded statements from claimants and witnesses, and inspections of the premises where the loss occurred. See the exhibit "Case Facts."

Case Analysis Tools

To determine whether Wally and Dawn's DP-3 provides coverage for the damage to the home, the insurance or risk management professional should

Case Facts

Insureds	Wally and Dawn Jones
Types of policies and coverage limits	DP-3 Policy • Coverage A—Dwelling ($145,000 limit) • Coverage B—Other Structures (10 percent of Coverage A limit) • Coverage C—Personal Property ($25,000 limit) • Coverage E—Additional Living Expenses (20 percent of Coverage A limit) $500 deductible applies
Endorsements that affect the case	None
Other policy information	No other relevant information
Background	The insureds have complied with the policy conditions.

[DA05621]

have copies of the applicable policy forms. See the exhibit "Dwelling Fire Policy."

To determine whether a policy covers a loss, many insurance professionals apply the DICE method. ("DICE" is an acronym for categories of policy provisions: declarations, insuring agreement, conditions, and exclusions.) The DICE method has four steps:

1. Review of the declarations page to determine whether it covers the person or the property at the time of the loss
2. Review of the insuring agreement to determine whether it covers the loss
3. Review of policy conditions to determine compliance
4. Review of policy exclusions to determine whether they preclude coverage of the loss

Each of these four steps is used in every case. Other categories of policy provisions should be examined. For example, endorsements and terms defined in the policy should be reviewed in relation to the declarations, insuring agreement, exclusions, and conditions.

Dwelling Fire Policy

DWELLING FIRE POLICY

POLICYHOLDER (Named Insured) Wallace & Dawn Jones
32 Happy Lane
Anytown, USA 123456

POLICY NUMBER: ABC-DEF

POLICY PERIOD

Inception: March 5, 20XX

Expiration: March 5, 20XX

Policy period begins 12:01 A.M. standard time at the described location.

FIRST MORTGAGEE AND MAILING ADDRESS:

Anytown Bank & Trust
Main Street
Anytown, USA 12345

We will provide the insurance described in this policy in return for the premium and compliance with all applicable policy provisions.

COVERAGES	LIMIT
A—Dwelling	$145,000
B—Other Structures	Included
C—Personal Property	$ 25,000
D—Rental Value	Included
E—Additional Expense	Included

Deductible: $500.

CONSTRUCTION: Frame **NO. FAMILIES:** One **TYPE ROOF:** Approved

YEAR BUILT: 1948 **PROTECTION CLASS:** 6

POLICY PREMIUM: $ 987.00 **COUNTERSIGNATURE DATE:** March 1, 20XX

AGENT: J. Smith

Determination of Coverage

To examine the policy forms and determine whether coverage applies to the losses, the insurance professional can apply the DICE method, which involves four steps.

The first DICE step is to review the Declarations page to determine whether the individuals are covered and whether the incidents occurred during the policy period. In this case, Wally and Dawn are listed as named insureds on the Declarations page, and the losses occurred during the policy period.

The second DICE step is to determine whether the loss triggers coverage under the DP-3 dwelling policy. Coverage for the fire damage is triggered under the DP-3 policy for both Coverage A and Coverage C. For Coverage A, the perils insured against cover risk of direct physical loss to property, subject to exclusions. Because neither fire nor smoke is specifically excluded, the damage to the home is covered. See the exhibit "Perils Insured Against."

Perils Insured Against

PERILS INSURED AGAINST

A. Coverage A – Dwelling And Coverage B – Other Structures

1. We insure against risk of direct physical loss to property described in Coverages A and B.
2. We do not insure, however, for loss:
    a. Excluded under General Exclusions

For Coverage C—Personal Property, the perils of fire or lightning and the peril of smoke are both listed as covered perils, so the damaged washer, dryer, and other personal property are covered. See the exhibit "Coverage C—Personal Property."

The cost to rent an apartment would also be covered under Coverage E—Additional Living Expense. This coverage provides for "any necessary increase in living expenses" incurred to maintain a normal standard of living, as long as the loss is covered under the Coverage A or C perils. The peril must also cause the premises to be unfit for its normal use; in this case, the insurer has agreed that this is so. See the exhibit "Coverage E—Additional Living Expense."

The burglary loss of the television and stereo equipment is not covered because theft is not listed as one of the covered perils under Coverage C. The damage to the door, however, is covered under the "Damage by Burglars" peril, which covers damage to covered property that is caused by burglars. The wording of this peril specifically emphasizes that theft of property is not cov-

Coverage C—Personal Property

B. Coverage C – Personal Property

We insure for direct physical loss to the property described in Coverage C caused by a peril listed below unless the loss is excluded in the General Exclusions.

1. Fire Or Lightning …

7. Smoke

This peril means sudden and accidental damage from smoke, including the emission or puffback of smoke, soot, fumes or vapors from a boiler, furnace or related equipment.

This peril does not include loss caused by smoke from agricultural smudging or industrial operations.

Coverage E—Additional Living Expense

E. Coverage E – Additional Living Expense

1. If a loss to property described in Coverage A, B or C by a Peril Insured Against under this policy makes the Described Location unfit for its normal use, we cover any necessary increase in living expenses incurred by you so that your household can maintain its normal standard of living.

   Payment will be for the shortest time required to repair or replace the Described Location or, if you permanently relocate, the shortest time required for your household to settle elsewhere.

ered. Also, there is no coverage if the dwelling has been vacant for more than sixty days (however, a dwelling under construction is not considered vacant). In this case, the home was vacant, but only for thirty days. Furthermore, the home was under construction at the time of the loss, so coverage for the damage to the door will be covered. See the exhibit "Damage By Burglars."

The third DICE step is to determine whether all policy conditions have been met. Wally and Dawn have complied with all policy conditions, including promptly notifying the insurer of the loss. Also, the policy limits meet all insurance-to-value requirements as outlined in the DP-3 policy.

The fourth DICE step is to determine whether one or more exclusions preclude coverage that the insuring agreements have granted. In this case, none of the exclusions applies.

Damage By Burglars

9. **Damage By Burglars**
   a. This peril means damage to covered property caused by burglars.
   b. This peril does not include:
      (1) Theft of property; or
      (2) Damage caused by burglars to property on the Described Location if the dwelling has been vacant for more than 60 consecutive days immediately before the damage occurs. A dwelling being constructed is not considered vacant.

Determination of Amounts Payable

Determining the amount payable for a loss under the DP-3 policy involves analyzing the limit of liability available to pay losses.

Because fire and smoke are covered under the DP-3 policy and the insurance-to-value requirements have been met, the $35,000 damage to the home is covered in full. The cost of replacing the washer, dryer, and other personal property are also covered in full for the ACV of $2,350. Wally and Dawn will pay the $500 deductible for these losses one time unless the insurer determines that the fire loss and the burglary loss are two separate events. In that case, Wally and Dawn may have to pay a single $500 deductible for all losses related to the fire and then another $500 deductible for the burglary damage. The cost of renting an apartment for one month while the home was unfit for normal use will also be covered for $725 under Coverage E—Additional Living Expenses because this is less than the limit of 20 percent of the Coverage A limit. The cost to repair the damage caused by burglars will be paid in the amount of $3,150. The theft loss is not covered, so the $2,800 for the television and stereo equipment will not be paid. See the exhibit "Determination of Amounts Payable."

Determination of Amounts Payable

$35,000 damage to the home—Covered in full because the Coverage A limit is $145,000 and the insurance-to-value requirements have been met.

$2,350 actual cash value of replacing the washer, dryer, and other personal property—Covered in full because the Coverage C limit is $25,000.

$725 cost of renting an apartment for one month while the home was unfit for normal use—Covered in full under Coverage E—Additional Living Expenses because the amount is less than the limit of 20 percent of the Coverage A limit.

$3,150 cost to repair the damage caused by burglars—Covered in full under "Damage by Burglars" peril.

$2,800 cost of stolen television and stereo equipment—Not covered because theft is not listed as a covered peril for Coverage C.

Deductible—Wally and Dawn will pay the $500 deductible for these losses one time unless the insurer determines that the fire loss and the burglary loss are two separate events. In that case, Wally and Dawn may have to pay a single $500 deductible for all losses related to the fire and another $500 deductible for the burglary damage.

[DA05627]

MOBILEHOME COVERAGE

Mobile homes are generally less expensive than homes built on permanent foundations, making them a popular choice for seasonal or vacation homes and also providing a less costly option for home buyers.

Mobilehome owners often lease the land on which they place their home. Many mobilehome owners lease or own other structures as well. These factors and others create special needs to be addressed in mobilehome coverages.

Mobilehome coverage is provided through an endorsement that modifies provisions of the HO-3 policy (or similar policies). Additional mobilehome endorsements can be added to the policy to customize the coverage according to policyholders' needs.

Examining the provisions of Insurance Services Office, Inc. (ISO) mobilehome endorsements illustrates how these coverages modify the HO-3 policy to meet mobilehome owners' unique needs. Mobilehome exposures and coverages are examined here.

Mobilehome Exposures

The owners of mobile homes face the same exposures to loss that owners of conventional homes face, as well as vulnerability to additional exposures. A mobilehome owner might experience loss from one or more of several typical exposures:

- Damage to or destruction of the mobile home
- Damage to or destruction of other structures on the residence premises
- Damage to or destruction of personal property in the mobile home or in other structures
- Loss of use of the mobile home
- Liability loss because of bodily injury to others or damage to the property of others

For example, if a tornado struck a mobile home, the mobile home would likely be damaged or destroyed. Other structures on the premises, such as a garage or shed, might also sustain damage or be demolished. Personal property, such as clothing, detached furniture, dishes, tools, and toys from the mobile home and other structures might be destroyed or lost. Finally, the homeowner could suffer loss of use of the mobile home if the damage is extensive enough that the homeowner requires alternate housing until the mobile home is repaired or replaced.

Vulnerability to Additional Exposures

By definition, a mobile home is not permanently affixed to the land on which it is located. Most states consider mobile homes to be moveable property and not real estate. The exposure of mobile homes to some types of losses is greater than the exposure of homes built on permanent foundations.

Mobile homes are assembled in a factory and transported to their location in a complete or semicomplete condition. They are constructed of lighter materials than those used for homes built on permanent foundations, and special construction techniques are used. Because of their construction materials and loose foundation, mobile homes are particularly vulnerable to damage from windstorm, tornado, and earthquake.

Mobile homes' wheels are generally removed when the structure is set on blocks, piers, or masonry footings. When the mobile home is set in place, it should be tied down to anchors buried in the ground to prevent the unit from moving. Doing this helps protect it from being moved sideways or lifted off the ground in a windstorm, a vulnerability that results from the lightweight design. Some state codes require that mobile homes be tied down, and many insurers provide mobilehome coverage only if the structure is properly tied down.

Skirting material is often attached to the bottom of a mobile home to conceal the wheels, blocks, or piers, and tie-downs and give the appearance of a permanent structure. The skirting also reduces the buildup of debris underneath the mobile home and helps prevent damage that might subsequently result from this inherent vulnerability. For example, the skirting would prevent burning brush or leaves from blowing under the mobile home and causing fire damage.

Because mobile homes are frequently used as vacation homes, they may be located in recreational areas subject to greater loss exposure, such as in the mountains, beside a lake or river, or in heavily wooded areas. Compared with year-round residential mobile homes, the loss exposure of vacation mobile homes may be increased by the absence of services. For example, vacation areas often do not have full-time fire departments, and cellular and land-based telephone services may be limited in remote areas. Moreover, in these locations, the absence of nearby neighbors who could report a fire when the owner is away presents an increased exposure to fire and the possibility of greater severity when a loss occurs.

Other Property Exposure Considerations

The contents of mobile homes and other structures on the premises are usually similar to those in conventional dwellings, and they are subject to the same exposures. However, mobile homes often have built-in cabinets, appliances, and furniture, which are considered part of the mobile home rather than personal property. Additionally, an owner of a mobile home is subject to the same liability exposures as an owner of a conventional home.

Mobilehome Coverages

Many specialty insurers have developed policies for mobile homes, and the policies may also insure prefabricated, manufactured, or modular houses that are manufactured in one location and moved to their permanent location. ISO has developed special endorsements for insuring mobile homes.

ISO has designed an endorsement specifically for mobile homes, to be used with an HO-3 policy. According to ISO rules, mobilehome endorsements can also be used with an HO-2 policy. Mobilehome tenants may use the HO-4 policy without adding the mobilehome endorsement. A mobile home is eligible for coverage if it is designed for portability and year-round living. Typically, a mobile home must be at least ten feet wide and have an area of at least four hundred square feet to qualify for the mobilehome endorsement.

A mobilehome policy is created by attaching the Mobilehome Endorsement (MH 04 01) to a homeowners form and a Declarations page. As with all homeowners policies, other endorsements may be attached to modify the coverage. The mobilehome endorsement states that the insurance is subject to all applicable provisions of the homeowners form except as revised by the endorsement. The mobilehome policy modifies the HO-3 policy in several ways:

- Definitions—The definition of "residence premises" is changed in the mobilehome endorsement to mean the mobile home and other structures located on land owned or leased by the insured where the insured resides. This location must be shown as the residence premises on the declarations page.

- Section I—Property Coverages, Coverage A—Dwelling—This coverage applies to a mobile home used primarily as a private residence and to structures and utility tanks attached to the mobile home. It also applies to floor coverings, appliances, dressers, cabinets, and similar items that are permanently installed. In addition, coverage is provided for materials and supplies (located on or next to the residence premises) for construction, alteration, or repair of the mobile home or other structures on that premises.
- Section I—Property Coverages, Coverage B—Other Structures—The liability coverage limit for other structures on the premises is a maximum of 10 percent of the limit that applies to Coverage A, with a minimum limit of $2,000.
- Section I—Property Coverages, Additional Coverages—An extra additional coverage provided in the mobilehome endorsement is unique for mobile homes. This "property removed" coverage applies if the mobile home is endangered by an insured peril, requiring removal to avoid damage, and provides up to $500 (with no deductible) for reasonable expenses incurred by the policyholder for removal and return of the entire mobile home. The mobilehome endorsement removes the ordinance or law additional coverage that is provided by the HO-3; however, it may be restored by another endorsement.
- Section I—Conditions, Loss Settlement—According to the loss settlement condition in the mobilehome endorsement, carpeting and appliances are not included as property to be valued on the basis of actual cash value (ACV). Therefore, such property is included in Coverage A, and—if the required amount of insurance is met— replacement cost coverage applies.
- Section I—Conditions, Loss to a Pair or Set—Additional coverage is added to repair or replace damaged parts of a series of panels to match the remainder of the panels as closely as possible or to provide an acceptable decorative effect. However, the coverage does not guarantee that replacements will be available, and the insurer is not required to pay for repair or replacement of the entire series of pieces or panels.
- Section I—Conditions, Mortgage Clause—This provision modifies the word "mortgagee" in the policy to include a lienholder (a lending institution that holds title to the mobile home).

The mobilehome endorsement amends the homeowners policy in regard to Section I—Property Coverages. The endorsement does not amend Section II—Liability Coverages. Therefore, the liability coverage under a mobilehome policy is the same as the liability coverage under a homeowners policy. However, because the endorsement changes the definition of "residence premises," any reference to the insured location in Section II would apply to the mobile home and other structures at the location shown on the declarations page.

A mobilehome policy can be endorsed with many of the typical homeowners endorsements. Five endorsements are available only with the mobilehome policy:

- Actual Cash Value Mobilehome endorsement (MH 04 02)—This endorsement changes the loss settlement terms on the mobile home and other structures to apply an ACV basis rather than a replacement cost basis. Because carpeting and appliances are included as part of the mobile home (Coverage A), losses to such property would also be settled on an ACV basis. This endorsement is typically used by an insurer that prefers not to provide replacement cost coverage on the mobile home—for example, because the mobile home is old.
- Transportation/Permission to Move endorsement (MH 04 03)—This endorsement provides coverage for perils of transportation (collision, upset, stranding, or sinking) and coverage for the mobile home and other structures at the new location anywhere in the United States or Canada for a period of thirty days from the effective date of the endorsement. Losses are subject to a transportation peril deductible specified in the endorsement or elsewhere in the policy.
- Mobilehome Lienholder's Single Interest endorsement (MH 04 04)—This endorsement may be required by a lienholder. It provides coverage only to the lienholder for collision and upset transportation exposures, subject to numerous recovery conditions. It also provides coverage to the lienholder for any loss resulting from the owner's conversion, embezzlement, or secretion (concealment) of the mobile home.
- Property Removed Increased Limit endorsement (MH 04 06)—This endorsement allows the policyholder to increase the $500 limit, provided as an additional coverage under the ISO Mobilehome Endorsement (MH 04 01), for removing a mobile home that is endangered by an insured peril. Removal costs for a mobile home could easily exceed $500. This endorsement enables the policyholder to recover a greater share of the removal cost and encourages the policyholder to remove the property, when necessary, to avoid damage.
- Ordinance or Law Coverage endorsement (MH 04 08)—This endorsement enables the mobilehome policyholder to add ordinance or law coverage for an amount equal to a specified percentage of the Coverage A limit. The provisions of this endorsement are virtually identical to those in the Ordinance or Law additional coverage provision in the homeowners policy.

NFIP GENERAL PROPERTY FORM

Flood and earthquake are perils with catastrophic loss potential and thus are more difficult to insure than many other causes of property loss. This section examines the National Flood Insurance Program (NFIP) Standard Flood Insurance used in combination with, or instead of, standard commercial property forms.

The NFIP Standard Flood Insurance Policy comes in three distinct forms: (1) General Property Form, (2) Residential Condominium Building Association Policy (RCBAP), and (3) Dwelling Form. The General Property Form is used to insure most commercial buildings and contents.

General Property Form

The version of the National Flood Insurance Program (NFIP) Standard Flood Insurance Policy that is used for insuring commercial buildings and contents.

The **General Property Form** differs from standard commercial property coverage forms in many respects. Two fundamental differences are that the General Property Form has no coinsurance provision and cannot be written for a blanket limit. Each building and its contents must be insured for separate limits. Furthermore, the General Property Form covers on an actual cash value (ACV) basis with no option for replacement cost.

NFIP Definition of Flood

The General Property Form covers direct physical loss caused by "flood" at the premises described in the application and declarations form attached to the policy.

This is the NFIP definition of flood:

> Flood, as used in this flood insurance policy, means:
>
> 1. A general and temporary condition of partial or complete inundation of two or more acres of normally dry land area or of two or more properties (at least one of which is your property) from:
>
> a. Overflow of inland or tidal waters;
>
> b. Unusual and rapid accumulation or runoff of surface waters from any source;
>
> c. Mudflow.
>
> 2. Collapse or subsidence of land along the shore of a lake or similar body of water as a result of erosion or undermining caused by waves or currents of water exceeding anticipated cyclical levels that result in a flood as defined in A.1.a. above.

The policy definition of mudflow, which is used in the definition of flood, is this:

> Mudflow. A river of liquid and flowing mud on the surfaces of normally dry land areas, as when earth is carried by a current of water. Other earth movements, such as landslide, slope failure, or a saturated soil mass moving by liquidity down a slope, are not mudflows.

Especially after Hurricane Katrina devastated New Orleans and the Gulf Coast in 2005, it is natural to think of flooding as associated with rain and windstorms. The NFIP definition, however, includes more than that. Item 1.b. of the definition covers accumulation or runoff of surface waters from any source.

One of the most devastating floods in U.S. history occurred in Johnstown, Pennsylvania, in 1899 when failure of a dam unleashed 20 million tons of water, resulting in a flood that killed more than 2,200 people. This type of event meets the NFIP definition of flood.

Losses Excluded

The policy divides losses that are not covered into four groups.

The flood policy covers direct physical loss only, and it thus contains several exclusions aimed at eliminating coverage for loss of use, loss of income, most additional expenses (other than those specifically covered), the cost of complying with any ordinance or law (except for the Increased Cost of Compliance coverage discussed subsequently), and any other type of economic loss.

The policy does not cover any loss directly or indirectly caused by a flood already in progress when the policy period begins or the coverage is increased.

The policy does not cover loss caused directly by earth movement, including earthquake, landslide, land subsidence, and gradual erosion. Destabilization or movement of land resulting from accumulation of water in subsurface land areas is also excluded. However, losses from mudflow and subsidence as a result of erosion that are included in the definition of flood are covered.

The flood policy excludes a long list of perils, including pressure of weight or ice; rain, snow, sleet, hail, or water spray; theft, fire, explosion, wind, or windstorm; or any deliberate act by the insured to cause a loss. Flood (as defined in the policy) that results from one of the excluded perils, however, is covered. For example, rain or melting snow often causes flood damage. The exclusion of rain or snow does not eliminate coverage for loss caused by the resulting flooding. Coverage is excluded for water, moisture, mildew, or mold damage caused by the policyholder's failure to inspect and maintain the insured property after the flood waters recede.

Property Covered

The Property Covered section of the policy contains these coverages:

- Coverage A—Building Property
- Coverage B—Personal Property
- Coverage C—Other Coverages
- Coverage D—Increased Cost of Compliance

Because these coverages are subject to many detailed provisions, they are only summarized here.

For purposes of Coverage A—Building Property, the General Property Form specifically defines "building" as a structure with two or more outside rigid walls and a fully secured roof that is affixed to a permanent site.

The flood policy's requirement of two or more outside walls can be a significant difference from most commercial property policies.

Many structures that would be considered buildings under most commercial property policies (for example, an open-sided parking garage) would not be included within the flood policy definition of building.

The NFIP definition of building also includes a manufactured (mobile) home on a permanent foundation; or a travel trailer without wheels and affixed to a permanent foundation, if the structure is regulated under the community's floodplain management and building ordinances or laws.

Special anchoring requirements apply to manufactured homes or travel trailers that are located in special flood hazard areas.

In addition to covering buildings at described locations, Coverage A—Building Property covers these items, subject to provisions that are generally more restrictive than those found in commercial property policies:

- Additions and extensions to the building that are attached to and in contact with the building by means of a rigid exterior wall, a solid load-bearing interior wall, a stairway, an elevated walkway, or a roof.
- A long list of specific types of fixtures, machinery, and equipment.
- Materials and supplies to be used for construction, alteration, or repair of the insured building. Such items are covered only if they are stored in a fully enclosed building at the described location or on an adjacent property.
- A building under construction, alteration, or repair at the described location. The flood policy does not provide any automatic coverage for a building being constructed at a location that is not described in the policy.

Coverage B—Personal Property covers two categories: household personal property and other than household personal property. The second category, which is generally applicable to commercial property, includes these items:

- Furniture and fixtures
- Machinery and equipment
- Stock (defined to include merchandise, raw materials, and in-process or finished goods)
- Other personal property owned by the insured and used in the insured's business

Coverage B does not include personal property of others. A $2,500 aggregate limit applies to certain valuable items, including fine arts, collectibles, jewelry, and furs. If more insurance is desired for such items, they can usually be insured against flood under an inland marine policy.

If the insured is a tenant, up to 10 percent of the amount of insurance on personal property may be applied to cover improvements made or acquired by the insured as a tenant. (In contrast, the Building and Personal Property Coverage Form has no sublimit on improvements and betterments.) Condominium unit owners may apply up to 10 percent of the amount of their personal property insurance to interior walls, floors, and ceilings not covered by the association's master policy.

When a policy covers both building and personal property, certain items that might be considered as either building or personal property are covered as building only. These items include many types of building service equipment, such as stoves, ranges, and refrigerators. This approach contrasts with standard commercial property forms, which give the insured the option of making claim for such property as either building or business personal property.

Coverage C—Other Coverages includes three insuring agreements:

- Debris Removal
- Loss Avoidance Measures
- Pollution Damage

Debris Removal coverage has a significant difference from debris removal coverage under standard commercial property forms. In addition to covering removal of debris of covered property, the flood policy covers removal of debris of other property (such as mud or debris of other buildings) that floats into or onto covered property during a flood. The flood policy covers the cost to remove debris of covered property from both the insured premises and from other locations to which the debris might float during flooding.

Another difference is that the flood policy does not include either the 25 percent of loss sublimit or the $10,000 additional coverage for debris removal found in most commercial property forms. The absence of the 25 percent sublimit means that the entire policy amount can be used for debris removal. However, that would not leave any policy limit available for damage to insured property.

Under Loss Avoidance Measures, the NFIP covers reasonable expenses up to $1,000 for the cost of sandbags, other supplies, and labor to protect the building from imminent flooding. The insurer will reimburse the insured for these expenses even if the flood does not reach the covered property, as long as general flooding occurs in the area.

A separate $1,000 limit applies to the cost to remove covered property to a safer location when the danger of flooding is imminent. When covered property—either building property or personal property—is moved to a safer location, the policy will cover the property for up to forty-five days while in a fully enclosed building at that location.

Neither of the $1,000 sublimits increases the limit of insurance. The deductible does not apply to either type of expenses incurred for protective measures.

Under Pollution Damage, the NFIP pays up to $10,000 for damage to the covered property caused by the discharge, seepage, migration, release, or escape of pollutants as a result of a flood. This additional coverage does not increase the limit of insurance on building or personal property, nor does it cover testing or monitoring of pollutants unless required by law or ordinance.

Increased Cost of Compliance (ICC) pays up to $30,000 for the cost to comply with state or local floodplain management laws or ordinances affecting the repair or reconstruction of a flood-damaged structure. Specific compliance actions that are eligible for coverage are elevation, floodproofing, relocation, and demolition of the covered structure.

ICC coverage applies only to policies with building coverage. The $30,000 limit is an additional amount of insurance, but the total loss payment may not exceed the maximum amount of insurance available per building under the NFIP, which is $500,000 for commercial properties. The policy contains a complex set of eligibility requirements for ICC coverage.

ICC coverage is quite different from the ordinance or law coverage that can be added to commercial property policies. ICC coverage is limited to local floodplain management laws or ordinances; it covers only specific compliance activities; and it is limited to loss from a single peril, flood.

The General Property Form excludes a long list of various types of property, such as these:

- Property not inside the fully enclosed building.
- Property located in, on, or over water.
- Open structures.
- Vehicles other than a manufactured home or a travel trailer affixed to a permanent foundation in accordance with local floodplain regulations. Coverage also applies to self-propelled vehicles used to service the premises or to provide mobility for handicapped persons, provided the vehicles are inside a described building when they are damaged by flooding.
- Underground structures.
- Buildings and their contents if more than 49 percent of the ACV of the building is below ground unless the lowest level is above the base flood elevation.
- Property not eligible for flood insurance under the Coastal Barrier Resources Act and the Coastal Barrier Improvement Act of 1990.

Property in a basement is limited to building service equipment, foundation walls supporting the building, and the cost for drywall construction excluding finishing and taping. A basement is defined as any area of the building, having its floor below ground level (subgrade) on all sides. Therefore, the first floor of a building that is six inches below grade on all sides is considered a basement for NFIP purposes.

Many of the other types of excluded property are similar to property excluded in the Building and Personal Property Coverage Form, such as accounts, bills, and retaining walls.

Other Insurance

The maximum coverage limits available under NFIP rules are not adequate for many organizations. Consequently, it is not unusual for an organization to buy coverage from the NFIP and also buy additional flood insurance from a commercial insurer. When commercial insurers provide flood insurance, they often stipulate that their flood insurance will apply in excess of the maximum limits available from the NFIP. The NFIP Other Insurance provision anticipates this practice. If flood insurance other than NFIP insurance covers the loss, the NFIP policy will pay its share, based on these rules:

- The NFIP policy will pay its pro rata share of the loss based on the total amount of insurance, unless the other flood insurance has a provision stating that it is excess insurance. If the other insurance has such a provision, the NFIP policy will be primary.
- If the other insurance policy does not state that it is excess to the NFIP policy, the NFIP policy will be primary (but subject to its own deductible) up to the deductible in the other flood coverage. Once the deductible is reached, the NFIP policy will share the remaining loss proportionately based on the amounts of insurance.

Deductibles

Deductibles apply separately to building property and personal property insured under the General Property Form. Therefore, if the policy has a $1,000 deductible and the building and contents are both damaged, the insured will retain up to $2,000 per loss.

No deductible applies to the loss avoidance measures covered under Coverage C or to Coverage D—Increased Cost of Compliance. For minimum deductible amounts and credits for increased deductibles, see the NFIP Flood Insurance Manual.

Residential Condominium Building Association Policy

The RCBAP is used for insuring residential condominium buildings, as well as contents that are owned either by the unit owners in common or by the condominium association solely.

A residential building is one in which at least 75 percent of the floor area is occupied for residential purposes. Nonresidential condominiums can be insured under the General Property Form.

These characteristics of the RCBAP distinguish it from the General Property Form:

- A higher limit of insurance. The limit can be equal to $250,000 times the number of units in the building. For example, a high-rise condominium building with thirty units could obtain as much as $7,500,000 of insurance. The maximum limit on contents is $100,000 per building. (Unit owners can purchase separate NFIP policies covering the contents in their own units.)
- Replacement cost coverage on building property.
- An 80 percent coinsurance requirement based on either the replacement cost of the building or the maximum amount available under the NFIP, whichever is lower.

The RCBAP Other Insurance clause states that if a flood insurance policy in the name of a unit owner covers the same loss as the condominium association policy, then the condominium association policy will be primary and the unit owner's policy will be excess.

Because the maximum amount of insurance available under the RCBAP is the limit per building times the number of units, most condominium associations will not need any additional flood insurance.

If additional coverage is needed, it can be obtained in either of two ways: If each unit owner obtains the additional insurance through the NFIP, problems with other insurance will be avoided. If a commercial insurer provides the additional coverage, careful coordination with NFIP coverage is required to be sure that the total amount collectible will meet the insured's expectations.

FAIR AND BEACHFRONT AND WINDSTORM PLANS

Urban riots in the 1960s and windstorms affecting increasingly popular coastal communities have resulted in excessive property damage and, consequently, restricted insurance availability. State governments have therefore been prompted to develop programs that enable homeowners to purchase insurance for urban and coastal properties that are not insurable in the voluntary insurance market.

Most residences are insured under either a homeowners or a dwelling policy provided by a private insurer in the voluntary market, through which organizations willingly insure properties with average and below-average exposure to losses. However, insurers are reluctant to insure some residential dwellings that have greater-than-average exposure to losses. Examples of such homes include those in urban and coastal areas that are exposed to windstorm losses. Several government plans are available to insure such homes, which previously were uninsurable or were insurable only through the nonstandard market at very high premiums. (The nonstandard market is composed of organizations that insure properties with above-average exposure to losses.)

Examining two types of insurance plans, Fair Access to Insurance Requirements (FAIR) plans and beachfront and windstorm plans, illustrates how state governments have responded to the needs of homeowners who have difficulty insuring properties that face greater-than-average exposure to losses. A review of each of these plans focuses on the purposes and operations of the plan as well as the property that is eligible and the coverages available under the plan.

FAIR Plans

FAIR plans make standard lines of property insurance available for exposures located in areas underserved by the voluntary market. Participating private insurers and state insurance authorities coordinate efforts to provide such coverage. Each state with a FAIR plan has enacted its own legislation in response to local market needs, so the coverage provided and the methods of operation vary considerably.

Purpose and Operation

Lenders usually will not extend credit for the purchase of property unless the owner can obtain adequate property insurance coverages. FAIR plans make insurance coverage available when insurers in the voluntary market cannot profitably provide coverage at a rate that is reasonable for policyholders and provide the needed support for credit. Urban areas that are susceptible to damage caused by riots and civil commotion pose greater-than-average risk of loss for insurers in the voluntary market and are candidates for state-run FAIR plans. Some FAIR plans provide certain coverages for owners of coastal properties that pose greater-than-average exposure to windstorm damage. The potential hazard of brush fires in some wooded, suburban areas may also pose greater-than-average risk for insurers; consequently, some FAIR plans provide coverage for homes located in hazardous brush areas.

A property owner who is unable to obtain basic property insurance in the voluntary market can apply for insurance to the state's FAIR plan through

Syndicate
A group of insurers or reinsurers involved in joint underwriting to insure major risks that are beyond the capacity of a single insurer or reinsurer; each syndicate member accepts predetermined shares of premiums, losses, expenses, and profits.

an authorized insurance agent or broker. The FAIR plan might operate as a policy-issuing **syndicate**, in which the plan issues the policies and the plan's staff handles underwriting, processing, and possibly claim handling. In several states, the FAIR plan contracts with one or more voluntary insurers to act as servicing organizations. For a percentage of premium, these insurers perform underwriting, policyholder service, and claim handling functions. In the majority of plans, all licensed property insurers are required to share payment for plan losses in proportion to their share of property insurance premiums collected within the state.

Eligible Property

To be eligible for FAIR plan coverage, a property must be ineligible for coverage in the voluntary market, and the policyholder must have the property inspected by the FAIR plan administrator. Only property that meets the FAIR plan inspection criteria can be insured through the program. If the property fails to meet the basic safety levels (such as older houses in poor repair), owners can be required to make improvements as a condition for obtaining insurance. If the problems are not corrected, the state can deny insurance, provided the exposures are not related to the neighborhood location or to hazardous environmental conditions that are beyond the owner's control (such as a location next to a fireworks factory).

Under most FAIR plans, five types of exposures are considered uninsurable:

- Property that is vacant or open to trespass
- Property that is poorly maintained or that has unrepaired fire damage
- Property that is subject to unacceptable physical hazards, such as poor housekeeping or storage of flammable materials
- Property that violates a law or public policy, such as a condemned building (one that is considered unfit for human habitation)
- In some states, property that was not built in accordance with building and safety codes

Coverages

Some state FAIR plans provide limited homeowners coverage; however, most plans provide coverage only for fire and a limited number of perils, which often include vandalism, riot, and windstorm. Available limits of insurance and mandatory deductibles vary widely among plans.

Difference in conditions (DIC) policy, or DIC insurance
Policy that covers on an "all-risks" basis to fill gaps in the insured's commercial property coverage, especially gaps in flood and earthquake coverage.

When a policyholder wants greater coverage than that offered by the FAIR plan (such as when an expensive suburban home is written in the FAIR plan because it is located in a wooded area), a specialty insurer can write a **difference in conditions (DIC) policy**. This additional policy can cover risks of direct loss while excluding fire and the other perils covered under the FAIR plan policy. Because fire is the primary loss exposure for these suburban properties and FAIR plans provide coverage for that exposure, private insurers are willing to provide coverage for other perils.

Beachfront and Windstorm Plans

Properties located along the Atlantic and Gulf Coasts are especially vulnerable to windstorm loss. Serious winter storms can strike from the mid-Atlantic states northward, and the southern Atlantic and Gulf Coast states are subject to damage from hurricanes. Hurricanes in Florida and Hawaii have resulted in costly wind damage. Beginning in the late 1960s and beyond, insurers in the voluntary market withdrew from writing property coverage in coastal areas. Because these properties were uninsurable, numerous coastal states responded by developing beachfront and windstorm plans. Use of these plans and FAIR plans providing windstorm coverages has increased with the popularity and value of coastal properties.

Purpose and Operation

Beachfront and windstorm plans are similar to FAIR plans in that they make insurance coverage available for properties with greater-than-average exposure to loss and provide the needed support for credit. Most beachfront and windstorm plans provide insurance coverage for windstorm and hail losses that cannot be obtained in the voluntary market. Under these plans, losses from tidal water are generally excluded and should be covered under a flood insurance policy.

The operation of beachfront and windstorm plans is similar to that of FAIR plans. Some states that offer beachfront and windstorm plans operate using a single servicing organization that provides the underwriting, policyholder services, and claim handling services. Others operate as policy-issuing syndicates in which the plan issues the policies and the plan's staff provides services. In all plans, insurers that write property coverages in that state are required to share in plan losses in proportion to their share of state property insurance premiums.

Eligible Property

Properties eligible for coverage under beachfront and windstorm plans must be ineligible for coverage in the voluntary market and must be located in designated coastal areas. Furthermore, in some states, they must be located within a certain distance of the shoreline. Owners of property in coastal areas can obtain coverage for most real and personal property through these plans. Eligibility for coverage under each plan requires that buildings constructed or rebuilt after a specified date conform to an applicable building code. In addition to dwellings and other residential buildings, mobilehomes may be eligible if they meet certain construction and tie-down requirements.

As with FAIR plans, beachfront and windstorm plans will not insure certain types of property:

- Property that is poorly maintained or that has unrepaired damage
- Property that is subject to poor housekeeping
- Property that violates a law or public policy

Coverages

The perils insured against in beachfront and windstorm plans vary by state, but many such plans provide only windstorm and hail coverage. In those states, policyholders must obtain other property coverages through the voluntary insurance market or other nonstandard markets. A few states offer broader property coverages through the plans. The maximum limits of insurance available, as well as deductibles, vary among states. State plans generally contain a provision that no application for new coverage or increase in limits will be accepted when a hurricane has formed within a certain distance of the beach area where the property is located.

In recent years, some states have merged their FAIR and beachfront and windstorm plans as the popularity of coastal properties and these plans has grown. Florida and Louisiana have merged their FAIR and windstorm plans to create state-run property insurance companies: Florida Citizens Property Insurance Company (CPIC) and Louisiana Citizens Property Insurance Corporation (Louisiana Citizens), respectively. These state plans provide coverage for a range of exposures throughout the state; however, the primary loss exposure is beachfront windstorms.

INLAND MARINE FLOATERS

A homeowners policy may not provide adequate insurance for some types of personal property. Often, such coverage needs can be met with a personal inland marine policy.

Inland marine insurance is designed to cover property that has special value or that frequently moves ("floats") from one location to another. Although these types of personal property are covered under a homeowners policy, they are usually subject to certain limitations. Examples of such property include jewelry, furs, fine arts, silverware, cameras, stamp and coin collections, clothes and luggage, sports equipment, and musical instruments.

Inland marine insurance
Insurance that covers many different classes of property that typically involve an element of transportation.

Insurance buyers and practitioners often refer to personal inland marine policies as floaters, but the newest Insurance Services Office, Inc. (ISO) personal inland marine coverage forms (2002) no longer use that term.

Characteristics and Components

The restrictive nature of some personal property coverages under a homeowners policy creates the need for personal inland marine policies, which can provide higher limits of insurance for losses of a particular type or that occur at a particular location. For example, homeowners coverage for theft of jewelry is frequently limited to $1,500 or less, homeowners coverage for coins and medals is limited to $200, and homeowners coverage is limited to $1,000 or less for personal property that is usually located at an insured's premises other than the **residence premises**.

Residence premises

The place where the insured resides as identified in the policy declarations.

Often, individuals who own these types of property insure them by adding an endorsement to the homeowners policy. Examples can illustrate some of the reasons people may prefer to obtain coverage under a separate personal inland marine policy:

- A couple owns highly valued paintings and sculptures, and their insurer is reluctant to provide the requested amount of coverage by endorsement to their homeowners policy.
- To insure his collection of costly cameras and lenses, an amateur photographer needs customized coverage that his homeowners policy cannot offer.
- A retired person owns valuable jewelry or golf equipment but lives in a retirement home and has no homeowners policy.
- A couple want to keep their homeowners premium separate from the premium on jewelry or collectibles because the homeowners premium is paid together with their mortgage payment.

Although personal inland marine insurance can be customized to meet a variety of coverage needs, personal inland marine policies share these general characteristics:

- The coverage is tailored to the specific type of property to be insured, such as jewelry, cameras, or musical instruments.
- The insured may select the appropriate policy limits.
- Policies are often written without a deductible.
- Most policies insure property worldwide with special form coverage (open perils), subject to exclusions.

Open Perils Coverage

Special form (open perils) coverage was formerly known as "all risks of physical loss or damage," but as a result of expansive court decisions, the word "all" was dropped.

[DA00845]

In addition to the shared characteristics, personal inland marine policies have a shared structure consisting of three components:

- Declarations page
- Common Policy Provisions
- Coverage form

The Declarations page lists the named insured, the policy period, the premium, any deductible, any forms attached, and other options. Together with the Declarations page, the Common Policy Provisions and a coverage form complete the policy.

Common Policy Provisions

The Common Policy Provisions of the Insurance Services Office, Inc. (ISO) personal inland marine policy include an insuring agreement, definitions, exclusions, and conditions. (Each personal inland marine policy also contains other conditions and exclusions that are listed in the particular coverage form selected.)

The insuring agreement states that the insurer is providing the insurance described in the policy in return for the premium paid by the insured and the insured's compliance with policy provisions.

The Definitions section describes which terms in the policy refer to the insured and which refer to the insurer.

The Common Policy Provisions exclude coverage for losses caused directly or indirectly by several perils:

- War
- Nuclear hazard
- Governmental action (such as property seized by a public authority)
- Intentional loss
- Neglect

The Conditions section of the Common Policy Provisions specifies that insured property may have scheduled coverage by which articles or items are specifically listed. With certain exceptions, the amount paid for a covered loss is the least of four amounts:

- The actual cash value of the insured property at the time of loss or damage
- The amount for which the insured could reasonably be expected to have the property repaired to its condition immediately before loss

- The amount for which the insured could reasonably be expected to replace the property with property substantially identical to the lost or damaged article
- The amount of insurance stated in the policy

The Conditions section of the Common Policy Provisions also specifies that insured property may have unscheduled coverage by which articles are covered on a **blanket basis**, such as stamps or coins in a collection. Separate loss settlement conditions apply to unscheduled property, with limitations on an absolute dollar amount (such as $250 per any one stamp or coin) and limitations determined by the proportion of the loss amount to the amount of blanket insurance provided.

Blanket basis

A basis for insuring all items within a single amount of insurance without specifically identifying each item.

A personal inland marine policy generally extends coverage to the named insured and members of the insured's family living in the same household.

Coverages

In the ISO personal inland marine program, two types of coverage forms are available: specialized and general.

Specialized forms are used to cover a single category of personal property, such as outboard motors and boats, fine arts, cameras, or motorized golf carts. In addition to the wide variety of specialized ISO forms, insurers often offer their own versions of these forms, making personal inland marine a highly customized line of business.

General forms are broader and generic in nature. These three general forms are commonly used to provide coverage on a single form for many kinds of personal property:

- Personal Articles Standard Loss Settlement Form
- Personal Property Form
- Personal Effects Form

Personal Articles Standard Loss Settlement Form

The Personal Articles Standard Loss Settlement Form provides special form coverage for any of several classes of personal property, including jewelry, furs, cameras, musical instruments, silverware, golfer's equipment, fine arts, and stamp and coin collections. A specific amount of insurance is shown in the policy for each class of property or for each specific article. (An agreed value version of the endorsement is also available.)

In addition to the exclusions listed in the Common Policy Provisions, the Personal Articles Standard Loss Settlement Form excludes losses caused by wear and tear, deterioration, **inherent vice**, or insects or vermin.

Inherent vice

A quality of or condition within a particular type of property that tends to make the property destroy itself.

Additional exclusions apply to fine arts. The Personal Articles Standard Loss Settlement Form excludes coverage for breakage of fragile articles unless the breakage is caused by fire or lightning; explosion, aircraft, or collision; windstorm, earthquake, or flood; malicious damage or theft; or derailment or overturn of a conveyance.

Personal Property Form

The Personal Property Form provides special form coverage on unscheduled personal property owned or used by the insured and normally kept at the insured's residence. The form also provides worldwide coverage on the same property when it is temporarily away from the residence premises. The Personal Property Form can be used to insure thirteen classes of unscheduled personal property. Coverage applies when a separate amount of insurance is shown for any of these classes:

- Silverware
- Clothing
- Draperies and rugs
- Electronic equipment and musical instruments
- Objects of art
- China and glassware
- Cameras
- Sports equipment and supplies
- Major appliances
- Bedding and linen
- Furniture
- Professional personal property and all other personal property
- Building additions and alterations

The total amount of insurance in each category is the maximum limit of recovery for any single loss to property in that category. The total amount for the thirteen categories is the total policy limit. Many of the exclusions that apply in the Personal Articles Standard Loss Settlement Form also apply to the Personal Property Form.

Personal Effects Form

The Personal Effects Form is designed for frequent travelers. It provides special form coverage on personal property such as luggage, clothes, cameras, and sports equipment normally worn or carried by tourists and travelers. The form covers property worldwide, but only while the property is away from the insured's permanent residence. **Personal effects** are not covered when in storage. Many of the exclusions that apply in the Personal Articles Standard Loss Settlement Form and the Personal Property Form also apply to the Personal Effects Form.

Personal effects
Personal property items owned by individuals that are personal in nature, such as jewelry, clothes, wallets, or purses.

The Personal Effects Form specifically excludes these types of property:

- Accounts, bills, currency, deeds, securities, passports
- Animals
- Artificial teeth or limbs
- Contact lenses
- Bicycles, hovercraft, motors, motor vehicles, watercraft
- Household furniture
- Merchandise for sale or exhibition
- Physicians and surgeons instruments
- Salesperson's samples
- Theatrical property
- Contraband property in the course of illegal transport or trade

Because the homeowners policy covers personal property worldwide, most homeowners do not see any need to purchase coverage under an inland marine Personal Effects Form. Coverage is occasionally sold to those who are ineligible for homeowners policies or to travelers who want the broadest possible protection on their luggage and other personal effects.

PERSONAL WATERCRAFT INSURANCE

Many individuals and families own personal watercraft. Personal watercraft can vary from a small rowboat to a houseboat to a large ocean-going yacht. A variety of insurance policies are available to meet an insured's specific personal watercraft coverage needs.

The loss exposures associated with the ownership and operation of watercraft are many and varied. For example, one individual might own a small flat-bottomed fishing boat with a low horsepower motor and trailer, used only on inland lakes, while another family owns a large boat with twin outboard motors that they use on coastal waters. One individual may believe that the watercraft coverage provided by his homeowners policy and Personal Auto Policy (PAP) is adequate; another may believe that a small boat policy or boatowners or yacht policy is required.

Personal watercraft insurance, found under a variety of policies and coverage forms, is available to meet the insuring requirements of these individuals and families.

Personal watercraft includes small rowboats, canoes, outboard and inboard motorboats, sailboats, houseboats, and power yachts. The types of loss exposures and hazards arising from the ownership and operation of personal watercraft can help determine the appropriate type of insurance contract to treat the loss exposures.

Because watercraft are used on bodies of water for recreational purposes and few restrictions apply to their operation, certain personal insurance policies limit or restrict coverage. Watercraft property and liability loss exposures are not intended to be covered by homeowners and auto policies; therefore, other coverage forms are designed specifically to address watercraft loss exposures.

These personal insurance policies provide watercraft or watercraft-related coverage:

- HO-3
- PAP
- Small boat policies
- Boatowners and yacht policies

HO-3 Watercraft Coverage

Property and liability coverage for watercraft and related equipment is available under the HO-3. However, this coverage is limited by exclusions. Insurance professionals and insureds should be aware of these exclusions and policy limitations to ensure that the scope of the coverage provided adequately meets the insured's risk management requirements. If the homeowners watercraft coverage does not suffice, boatowners insurance or yacht insurance may be an appropriate alternative.

The HO-3 Section I—Property Coverages provides limited physical damage coverage under the homeowners policy that may be adequate for rowboats, canoes, and small outboard boats. Section I watercraft physical damage coverage includes these provisions:

- A $1,500 limit applies to watercraft, including trailers, furnishings, equipment. (For example, an insured's $800 kayak is fully covered for physical damage loss.)
- Coverage is provided on a named-perils-only basis. (The insured's kayak is covered only for the HO-3 Section I perils, not for **perils of the sea**.)
- Windstorm coverage applies (up to the $1,500 limit) only when the craft is inside a fully enclosed building.
- Theft coverage does not apply to the boat and motor when away from the residence premises; accessories, trailers, and other boating personal property are excluded from this coverage. (For example, the insured's kayak would not be covered if it is stolen from the roof of the insureds' car while the insureds are traveling.)

Perils of the sea
Accidental causes of loss that are peculiar to the sea and other bodies of water.

The liability section of the homeowners policy includes a detailed watercraft exclusion focusing on craft of certain size and length. HO-3 Section II watercraft liability coverage, by virtue of the scope of the exclusion, covers only certain limited watercraft loss exposures:

- All watercraft not powered, except sailing vessels twenty-six feet or more in length. Therefore, catamarans, sailboards, canoes, rowboats, and smaller sailboats (without auxiliary power) are covered.
- All inboard, inboard-outdrive, and sailing vessels not owned or rented by an insured. Therefore, any boat borrowed or operated on behalf of an insured is covered. For example, a forty-two-foot-long sailboat, if borrowed by the insured, would be covered for liability under the homeowners policy. The same boat, if rented or owned, would be excluded.
- All inboard and inboard-outdrive boats of fifty horsepower or less, rented to an insured.
- All sailing vessels with auxiliary power, if less than twenty-six feet long.
- All boats powered by an outboard motor or motors, unless the motor both exceeds twenty-five horsepower and was owned by an insured at policy inception. For example, a boat powered by a fifty-horsepower outboard motor and purchased by the insured during the homeowners policy period would be covered for liability until the renewal date.

The homeowners forms limit the watercraft covered under Section II—Liability coverages according to the type and length of the watercraft and the horsepower of the motor or motors. However, liability coverage for an otherwise excluded watercraft can be covered under Section II by attaching a Watercraft endorsement (HO 24 75) specifically scheduling the watercraft (boat and motor) for liability coverage.

Personal Auto Policy Watercraft Coverage

The PAP does not provide physical damage or liability coverage for watercraft, motors, or watercraft-related equipment. However, physical damage loss to a boat trailer is covered if the trailer is described on the PAP declarations page. For example, if the insured has other than collision coverage on a boat trailer and the trailer is stolen, the PAP provides coverage. Also, a boat trailer the insured owns is covered for liability (regardless of whether it is described on the declarations page) if it is designed to be pulled by a private passenger auto, pickup, or van. The PAP also covers nonowned trailers under Part D—Coverage for Damage to Your Auto to a limit of $1,500. Therefore, any boat trailer the insured may rent or borrow could be covered under the PAP for auto-related loss exposures.

If an insured has the use of any nonowned watercraft trailers that exceed $1,500 in value, or if the insured has any watercraft (which are excluded under the PAP), the appropriate coverage for such loss exposures can be provided under a small boat policy or boatowners or yacht policy.

Small Boat Policies

Because of the watercraft coverage limitations and exclusions in the homeowners and personal auto policies, boat owners usually opt to address the property and liability loss exposures related to their ownership and operation of watercraft by obtaining more comprehensive and appropriate coverage.

Small boat policies are designed to cover boats up to a certain size (such as twenty-six feet in length). Many insurers have developed such policies, which have various names (often with a nautical theme). Although small boat policies are not standard, they have certain common features regarding covered property, covered perils, and policy exclusions. See the exhibit "Personal Watercraft Coverage."

Personal Watercraft Coverage

Some types of small watercraft may not be classified as small boats and thus are not covered (on a minimal basis) under a homeowners policy or PAP or eligible for standard small boat insurance. Personal watercraft include high-speed, single-engine inboard-powered craft, such as Jet Skis, WaveRunners, and Sea-Doos. They are no more than sixteen feet in length and use a water-jet pump as their primary propulsion source. Specialty insurers provide personal watercraft coverage to insure these types of risks.

Loss exposures related to these personal watercraft result from high performance and handling characteristics associated with their speed, power, and size, as well as from minimal operator and passenger protection because of the exposed nature of carriage. Additionally, operators and owners increasingly use personal watercraft for passenger float-towing or waterskiing, which pose additional loss exposures. For example, an individual with a Jet Ski may use a tow rope to tow several of his friends through the water on an inflated inner tube. He can be held liable for any injuries his friends suffer while being towed.

Coverages commonly provided by personal watercraft coverage include these:

- Physical damage coverage
- Liability coverage
- Medical payments coverage
- Trailer coverage
- Additional coverage options—uninsured boater, nonowned watercraft liability, and emergency towing

[DA00846]

A small boat policy may cover the boat, motor, equipment, and trailer. Most small boat policies are written on an actual cash value (ACV) basis and contain a deductible, such as $100, $250, or more.

A small boat policy can be written to provide named perils or special form ("all-risks") coverage. Most small boat policies are of the special form type and cover all direct physical losses to covered watercraft except losses that are specifically excluded. Typical property loss exposures covered under a small boat policy could include damage to the boat as a result of a collision with another object, theft of the boat's motor or equipment, lightning damage to the boat's electrical and navigational equipment, and wind damage to a sail.

Generally, a small boat policy includes liability insurance for bodily injury, loss of life, illness, and property damage to third parties arising out of the ownership, maintenance, or use of the boat. Medical payments coverage is typically included for any insured person who sustains bodily injury while in, upon, boarding, or leaving the boat. Liability loss exposures covered under a small boat policy can include bodily injury liability for injuries sustained by passengers when a boat collides with a dock, property damage liability for damage to the dock resulting from the collision, and liability for medical payments to a patron on the dock who sustains a minor leg injury as a result of the collision.

These major exclusions are commonly found in small boat policies:

- General risks of direct loss—There is no coverage for loss caused by wear and tear, gradual deterioration, vermin and marine life, rust and corrosion, inherent vice, latent defect, mechanical breakdown, or extremes of temperature.
- Repair or service—Loss or damage from refinishing, renovating, or repair is not covered.
- Business pursuits—Coverage is excluded if the boat is used to carry passengers for compensation, if the boat or insured property is rented to others, or if the covered property is being operated in any official race or speed contest. For example, if an insured owns a small motorboat, coverage is excluded for the boat if he engages in official motorboat racing contests.

Boatowners and Yacht Policies

Many insurers have developed special boatowners package policies for boats up to a certain length, such as twenty-six feet. Larger boats are usually written under yacht policies. Both types of policies combine physical damage, liability, and medical payments coverage in one policy and typically include perils of the sea coverage. Other coverages are also frequently added to the policy, either by automatic inclusion or by endorsement. Although boatowners and yacht policies have no standard rules or forms, they contain certain common features, including warranties, persons insured, physical damage coverage, liability coverage, medical payments coverage, and other coverages.

Personal watercraft insurance generally contains several **warranties**. If a warranty is violated, higher premiums may be required, or the coverages may not apply, depending on the warranty. These are the major personal watercraft insurance warranties:

Warranty
A promise made by an insured that guarantees compliance with the insurer's conditions.

- Pleasure use—The insured warrants that the boat will be used only for private, pleasure purposes and will not be hired or chartered unless the insurer approves. For example, an insured with a boatowners policy could jeopardize his coverage if he routinely charters his boat for deep-sea fishing trips.

- Seaworthiness—The insured warrants that the boat is in a seaworthy condition. For example, an insured who fails to properly maintain his boat in order to maintain its seaworthiness could jeopardize his coverage.
- Lay-up period—The insured warrants that the boat will not be in operation during certain periods, such as during the winter months. The lay-up period is usually shown on the declarations page. For example, an insured may have a lay-up period from November 1 to April 1 of each policy year.
- Navigational limits—These warranties limit the use of the vessel to a certain geographical area (for example, inland waterways, and coastal areas only). Navigation limits are stated on the declarations page of the policy. For example, if an insured wishes to operate outside the stated navigational limits, permission must be obtained from the insurer (and an additional premium may be charged) for coverage to apply.

The insured includes those named on the declarations page, resident relatives of the household, and persons under the age of twenty-one in the insured's care. The insured's paid captain and crew are also considered insureds. Other persons or organizations using the boat without a charge are covered provided the named insured gives permission. For example, an insured may lend her boat to a local youth organization for a day on the water. The organization would be considered insureds under a typical boatowners or yacht policy.

Hull insurance
Insurance that covers physical damage to vessels, including their machinery and fuel but not their cargo.

Boatowners and yacht policies contain physical damage coverage (also called **hull insurance**) on either a named perils or a special form basis covering the boat or "hull," equipment, accessories, motor, and trailer. Because a special form policy covering risks of direct physical loss or damage is broader than a named perils policy, the coverages provided by insurers for watercraft hull coverage can vary greatly.

Certain property damage exclusions are commonly found in boatowners and yacht policies:

- Wear and tear, gradual deterioration, rust, corrosion, mold, wet or dry rot, marring, denting, scratching, inherent vice, latent or physical defect, insects, animal or marine life, weathering, and dampness of atmosphere. For example, the coverage is not designed to protect against lack of routine maintenance and the products of age and weathering.
- Mechanical breakdown or faulty manufacturing, unless the loss was caused by fire or explosion.
- Freezing and thawing of ice, unless the insured has taken reasonable care to protect the property. For example, an insured could install a circulating water system to keep the water from freezing around the boat in icy conditions.

- Loss that occurs while the boat is used in any official race or speed contest. However, most watercraft policies do not exclude sailboat racing.
- Intentional loss caused by an insured.
- War, nuclear hazard, and radioactive contamination.

Boatowners and yacht policies can be written on either a replacement cost basis or an ACV basis. Because replacement cost coverage offers better protection for the insured than coverage on an ACV basis, this difference in valuation is important in any comparison of boat policies. Yachts are typically insured on an agreed value basis. Agreed value means that in the event of a total loss, the insurer pays the insured the full amount stated in the policy declarations as the total, or agreed, value of the hull. Small boats are usually written with a $100 to $250 deductible. Medium to large boats often carry a deductible equal to 1 percent to 10 percent of the insured value of the watercraft.

Basic watercraft liability policies typically cover only bodily injury and property damage perils related to the operation of watercraft. In addition, boatowners and yacht policies typically include a form of liability coverage called **protection and indemnity (P&I) insurance**. P&I is a broader form of bodily injury and property damage coverage that protects an insured against bodily injury and property damage liability arising from the ownership, maintenance, or use of the boat, and also against crew injuries, wreck removal, and negligence for an unseaworthy vessel. Defense costs arising from any claim, including suits from third parties, are also covered.

Protection and indemnity (P&I) insurance
Insurance that covers shipowners against various liability claims due to operating the insured vessel.

This list represents most of the exclusions that insurers include in boatowners and yacht policies:

- Intentional injury or illegal activities.
- Renting the watercraft to others or carrying persons or property for a fee without the insurer's permission.
- Liability arising out of water-skiing, parasailing (a sport using a type of parachute to sail through the air while being towed by a powerboat), or other airborne or experimental devices.
- Using watercraft (except sailboats in some policies) in any official race or speed test.
- Losses covered by a workers compensation or similar law. (For example, any of the insured's employees who are injured in the course of their duties—such as a captain injured while preparing a boat for a sail—and who should otherwise be covered by workers compensation or a similar law are excluded from coverage.)
- Bodily injury or property damage arising out of transportation of the boat on land. (Coverage can be included with the payment of an additional premium.)
- Liability assumed under a contract.

- Injury to an employee if the employee's work involves operation or maintenance of the watercraft (unless otherwise covered by the P&I coverage).
- Business use.
- Discharge or escape of pollutants unless sudden or accidental. (For example, coverage would not apply to a yacht that is slowly leaking diesel fuel into the water where it is docked, causing possible pollution damage.)
- War, insurrection, rebellion, and nuclear perils.

Medical payments coverage under boatowners and yacht insurance policies includes coverage for such bodily-injury related expenses as medical, surgical, x-ray, dental, ambulance, hospital, professional nursing, and funeral services; and for first aid rendered at the time of the accident. An insured does not have to be at fault for the coverage to apply. Coverage is usually limited to a maximum of $1,000 to $5,000 per person per occurrence, although this can be increased for an additional premium.

Covered persons include the insured, family members, or any other person (except employees of the insured, trespassers, and racing participants) while in, upon, boarding, or leaving the covered watercraft. Therefore, medical payments coverage in boat policies is similar to that provided in personal auto policies because it covers the insured and family members. In contrast, medical payments coverage in homeowners policies does not cover the insured or resident family members (and is thus named "medical payments to others").

Additional coverages may be added to or provided in boatowners and yacht policies:

Uninsured boaters coverage
Coverage for the insured's bodily injury incurred in a boating accident caused by another boat's owner or operator who is uninsured and who is legally responsible for the injury; similar to the PAP's uninsured motorists coverage.

United States Longshore and Harbor Workers' Compensation Act (LHWCA)
A federal statute that eliminates the right of most maritime workers (other than crew members of vessels) to sue their employers and, in return, requires such employers to provide injured or ill workers with benefits like those provided by state workers compensation statutes.

- **Uninsured boaters coverage** may be offered by endorsement or as a coverage option by insurers to boatowners. Coverage is structured similarly to the uninsured motorists coverage found in the PAP, with certain limitations and restrictions specific to the scope of watercraft loss exposures. For example, uninsured boaters coverage typically excludes bodily injury caused by an individual's occupying or being struck by any watercraft owned by the insured or by any family member insured under the policy.
- The insured's liability for injury to maritime workers (except crew members) injured in the course of employment who are covered under the **United States Longshore and Harbor Workers' Compensation Act** and for which the insured might be held responsible may be included under watercraft liability coverage.
- The legal obligation of the insured to remove a wrecked or sunken vessel following a loss may be included in a boatowners or yacht policy.
- Bodily injury or property damage arising out of transportation of the boat on land can usually be included in a boatowners or yacht policy for an additional premium.
- Damage to or loss of the insured's personal effects, for a limited amount, may be included in a boatowners or yacht policy. Personal effects coverage applies to property not intended for the normal operation of the boat,

such as an insured's portable television, stereo, camera, or other personal items.

- The cost of commercial towing and assistance, for a limited amount, may be included in or added to the policy.
- Hurricane protection coverage may be available by endorsement to reimburse boatowners for the costs of removing their watercraft from the water if a hurricane is approaching or to cover the costs of moving the boat to a safe harbor because of an approaching storm. For example, if a hurricane is approaching the marina area where an insured's boat is docked, hurricane protection coverage would reimburse the insured the costs of hiring a professional to move the boat to a safe location, on the basis that the cost of doing so would be significantly less than the potential total loss of the boat in the hurricane.

SUMMARY

Homeowners policies are a common type of residential insurance. Not all residences, however, are eligible for homeowners coverage, and not all insureds want or need a homeowners policy. For these residences and customers, a dwelling policy may be more appropriate. Dwelling policies may be written for one- to four-family owner- or tenant-occupied dwellings, dwellings under construction, or mobile homes at a permanent location.

Knowing how to apply the dwelling policy to the facts of a case is a critical skill. The first stage in this process is determining whether a loss is covered, and, if so, the second stage involves determining how much an insurer should pay for the loss.

ISO provides a mobilehome endorsement for homeowners policies to create a policy that covers typical homeowners exposures along with unique exposures and considerations associated with mobile homes. The mobilehome endorsement replaces definitions; modifies some coverages; and adds coverages, conditions, and a clause that meet the needs of mobilehome owners and their insurers. Five additional ISO mobilehome endorsements may be used to further modify the policy.

Most commercial buildings are insured under the Standard Flood Insurance Policy—General Property Form. The policy covers, on an ACV basis only, loss to covered building property and contents caused by flood, according to the NFIP definition. Residential condominium buildings are insured under the NFIP's Residential Condominium Building Association Policy.

Fair Access to Insurance Requirements (FAIR) plans and beachfront and windstorm plans are provided by private insurers coordinating with state insurance authorities to provide insurance for properties with greater-than-average exposures to loss in areas underserved by the voluntary market. Property under both types of plans must meet state-specified eligibility requirements, and coverages under the plans usually correlate with the plan's purpose. FAIR plans for urban properties cover fire and a limited number of other perils, whereas beachfront and windstorm plans typically cover windstorm and hail. However, in recent years, the distinction has blurred, and some states have merged their plans.

Inland marine insurance is designed to cover property that has special value or that frequently moves ("floats") from one location to another. Commonly used personal inland marine forms include the Personal Articles Standard Loss Settlement Form, the Personal Property Form, and the Personal Effects Form. Personal inland marine insurance can be used to provide coverage for personal property in circumstances when homeowners policy coverage is not available or is too restrictive.

Personal watercraft insurance covers a variety of watercraft, from small rowboats and canoes to houseboats and large yachts. Loss exposures for such watercraft vary and can help insurance professionals determine the appropriate insurance policy or policies for a specific watercraft, whether an HO-3, a PAP, a small boat policy, or a boatowners or yacht policy.

Direct Your Learning

3

Commercial Property Insurance, Part I

Educational Objectives

After learning the content of this assignment, you should be able to:

- Describe commercial property insurance in terms of these elements:
  - The major categories of loss exposures that can be covered
  - The components of a commercial property coverage part
- Determine whether a described item of property qualifies as Covered Property under one or more of these categories in the Building and Personal Property Coverage Form:
  - Building
  - Your Business Personal Property
  - Personal Property of Others
- Determine which of the additional coverages and coverage extensions of the Building and Personal Property Coverage Form (BPP) apply to a described loss.
- Determine whether the cause of a described loss is a covered cause of loss under either the Causes of Loss—Basic Form or the Causes of Loss—Broad Form.
- Determine whether the cause of a described loss is a Covered Cause of Loss under the Causes of Loss—Special Form.
- Apply the Limits of Insurance and Deductible provisions of the Building and Personal Property Coverage Form to a described loss.

Outline

Commercial Property Insurance, Part I

3

OVERVIEW OF COMMERCIAL PROPERTY INSURANCE

Almost all businesses, including not-for-profit and governmental organizations, face potentially devastating losses associated with commercial property ownership. Purchase of a commercial package policy's commercial property coverage is one method businesses may use to transfer the risks associated with such potential losses.

Commercial property loss exposures may be analyzed according to three components:

- Types of property
- Causes of loss to property
- Financial consequences of property losses

The commercial property coverage part is a common example of insurance policy provisions that cover commercial property loss exposures.

Commercial Property Loss Exposures

The three components used to analyze property loss exposures allow for identification of the exposures in specific terms. For example, they may refer to a building exposure (type of property), a windstorm exposure (cause of loss), or a loss of business income exposure (financial consequence). Similarly, they could identify a property loss exposure in terms of two or even all three of these elements, such as a building fire exposure or loss of business income resulting from breakdown of a production machine.

Types of Property

Property is any item with value. Individuals, families, and organizations own and use property, depend on it as a source of income or services, and rely on its value. Property can decline in value—or even become worthless—if it is lost, damaged, or destroyed. Any item of property can be classified as either real property or personal property.

Examples of real property, in addition to land, are buildings, driveways, sidewalks, underground piping, and radio transmission towers. Property that is permanently attached to a structure, such as built-in appliances or paneling, is also generally considered part of the structure. For example, most buildings also include plumbing, wiring, and heating and air conditioning equipment. Similarly, a high-rise building usually has elevators and may have specially designed platforms, hoists, and tracks used by window washers. Such equipment is considered part of the building.

All property that is not real property is personal property. Examples of personal property include vehicles, merchandise, furniture, tools, clothing, and oil while being transported through an underground pipeline. For insurance purposes, personal property falls into these classifications:

- Contents—Property insurance policies typically use the term "personal property" to refer to the contents of a building (for example, office furniture, machinery and equipment, and stock such as completed products in inventory), rather than "contents," because the property often is covered even when it is not literally contained in the building. Policies generally use the term "business personal property" to refer to the contents of a commercial building. Contents also include personal property of others that is in the insured's care, custody, or control; this property is covered by the Personal Property of Others provision in commercial property coverage forms.
- Property in transit—Most businesses ship property to others (such as merchandise) or receive property from others (such as raw materials or supplies). Property in transit can be transported by a variety of means, for any length of time, and over various distances on the owner's own vehicles or by a transportation company. A commercial property policy may provide some coverage for property in transit, but it is often inadequate for insureds with significant transit exposures. A firm that needs broader coverage for property in transit can purchase separate cargo insurance.
- Property in the possession of others—In many situations, an organization may place its property in the temporary possession of others for processing, cleaning, repairing, adjusting, storing, exhibiting, or selling. Because the probability of loss at the temporary location could differ greatly from the probability of loss at the owner's location, building and contents insurance policies usually provide only a nominal amount of insurance for property at other locations. Like property in transit, property in the possession of others can be insured for its full value under specialized policies designed for that purpose.
- "Floating" property—Many businesses own property that normally does not remain at a fixed work site or that is in transit between work sites (for example, a wedding photographer's cameras and a building contractor's tools and mobile equipment). Such property is often referred to as "floating" property. Insurance for floating property is available under specialized inland marine policies called "floaters."

Causes of Loss to Property

The potential causes of loss to property are another important aspect of property loss exposures. A cause of loss (for example, fire or vandalism) adversely affects property and leaves it in an altered state. Some causes of loss do not alter the property itself but do affect a person's ability to possess or use the property. For example, property lost or stolen may still be used, but not by its rightful owner.

Buildings and personal property are subject to many potential causes of loss. For most insureds, fire is the cause of loss that poses the greatest risk of a large or even total property loss. Windstorms, such as hurricanes and tornadoes; flood; earthquake; terrorism; and war also pose potentially catastrophic exposures for insurers and insureds.

Financial Consequences of Property Losses

Financial consequences are the third and final important aspect of property loss exposures. The adverse financial consequences of a property loss may include a reduction in the value of the property, lost income, and/or extra expenses.

When a property loss occurs, the property's value is reduced. This reduction in value can be measured in different ways. Property that must be replaced has no remaining worth, unless some salvageable items can be sold. If the property can be repaired or restored, the reduction in value can be measured by the cost of the repair or restoration. For example, if a fence worth $7,000 is damaged by a falling tree and the fence owner has to pay $2,000 to have the damage repaired, the fence owner has incurred a partial loss that reduces the value of the fence by $2,000.

A business may lose income as a result of a property loss. When property is damaged, income might be lost because the property cannot be used until it is repaired, restored, or replaced. For example, when a business suffers a serious fire, it might have to close until repairs to the building are made and personal property is replaced. The resulting loss of income occurs over time. As another example, the owner of a rental property faces rental income loss if the property is damaged and temporarily unavailable for rent. The owner would probably continue to incur some expenses, such as mortgage payments and taxes, but would not receive the rent that helped pay those expenses.

For a business to determine the extent of a property loss exposure, it must consider the extra expenses that the loss of the property would require. When property is damaged, the property itself declines in value, and the owner or other affected party suffers a corresponding loss. In addition, the owner or other user of that property might incur extra expenses in acquiring a temporary substitute or in temporarily maintaining the damaged property in a usable condition. For example, when a store's premises are damaged, the owners might have to rent temporary space at considerably greater expense than their normal rent.

Components of a Commercial Property Coverage Part

Commercial property coverage part

Commercial package policy (CPP) coverage component that provides a broad range of coverages to "middle-market" or larger firms to insure buildings and business personal property.

Commercial package policy (CPP)

Policy that covers two or more lines of business by combining ISO's commercial lines coverage parts.

Monoline policy

Policy that covers only one line of business.

Package modification factors

Factors that are applied to the regular policy premiums for certain coverage parts of a CPP that includes both property and liability coverages, resulting in premium discounts for those coverage parts.

Commercial property declarations page

A required commercial property coverage part component that provides basic information about the policyholder and the insurance provided.

Commercial property loss exposures can be insured under a **commercial property coverage part**, which consists of five components:

- Commercial property declarations
- One or more commercial property coverage forms
- One or more causes of loss forms
- Commercial Property Conditions
- Any applicable endorsements

The commercial property coverage part is a component of the **commercial package policy (CPP)** program of Insurance Services Office, Inc. (ISO). A commercial property coverage part can be one of the two or more coverage parts included in a CPP. It can also be the single coverage part included in a **monoline policy** under ISO procedures.

An important element of the CPP program is the package discount the insured may receive. The premium for a CPP is initially determined as if each coverage part were being issued as a monoline policy. If a CPP includes both property coverage and liability coverage, the premiums for certain coverage parts are multiplied by **package modification factors**, resulting in premium discounts. These discounts are justified by the greater efficiency of issuing a single package policy instead of several monoline policies.

Commercial Property Declarations

A **commercial property declarations page** contains information that pertains specifically to property insurance:

- A description of the property insured
- The kinds and amounts of coverage provided and the covered causes of loss (basic, broad, or special)
- A list of mortgagees, if any
- The deductible amount
- A list of the property coverage forms and endorsements attached to the policy
- The applicable coinsurance percentage(s)
- Any optional coverages

Supplemental declarations can be added as needed on a separate page. For example, if an insured fast-food franchise cannot list all of its locations on the declarations page, it may add a supplemental schedule to show them.

Commercial Property Coverage Forms

The CPP program includes several different **commercial property coverage forms**. A commercial property coverage form typically contains these elements:

- Insuring agreement
- Delineation of the property covered and not covered
- Additional coverages and coverage extensions
- Provisions and definitions that apply only to that coverage form

A commercial property coverage part often includes more than one commercial property coverage form. Typically, one coverage form insures the insured's buildings and/or personal property, and another coverage form insures business income and/or extra expense.

A commonly used commercial property coverage form is the Building and Personal Property Coverage Form, also referred to as the BPP, which can be used to insure buildings, business personal property of the insured, and personal property of others in the insured's custody. Additional personal property coverage forms are available for insuring buildings and/or personal property in several special situations, such as buildings under construction, condominium association property, and condominium commercial unit owners' property. Commercial property coverage forms are also available for insuring loss of business income and/or extra expense.

Commercial property coverage form

A commercial property coverage part component that can be any of several commercial property forms containing an insuring agreement and related provisions.

Causes of Loss Forms

The three types of **causes of loss forms**—Basic, Broad, and Special—allow the insured to select, or the underwriter to offer, a range of covered perils.

A commercial property coverage part may contain more than one causes of loss form. One causes of loss form (such as the Special Form) may apply to buildings, while another (such as the Broad Form) may apply to personal property.

The commercial property declarations indicate which form applies to each type of property at each location. It is generally the underwriter's reluctance to provide the broader coverages for certain types of property that results in the use of different causes of loss forms in the same policy. Such instances are infrequent, however.

Causes of loss form

A required component of the commercial property coverage part that specifies perils covered.

Commercial Property Conditions

The **Commercial Property Conditions** are a required component of the commercial property coverage part that contains conditions applicable to all commercial property coverage forms. They are printed as a separate form and apply to all coverage forms included in a commercial property coverage part unless a coverage form contains a condition to the contrary. Like the

Commercial Property Conditions

A required component of the commercial property coverage part that contains conditions applicable to all commercial property coverage forms.

Common Policy Conditions, the Commercial Property Conditions do not require reiteration in each coverage form.

Endorsements

Many endorsements are available to tailor commercial property coverage to meet the specialized needs of particular insureds or to eliminate exposures that underwriters are not willing to insure.

BPP COVERED PROPERTY

The main insuring agreement of the Building and Personal Property Coverage Form (BPP) states that the insurer will pay for direct physical loss of or damage to Covered Property at the described premises caused by or resulting from any Covered Cause of Loss. Determining whether property qualifies as Covered Property is therefore an essential step in deciding whether the BPP covers a loss.

The BPP can cover any combination of three broad categories of property:

- Building
- Your Business Personal Property
- Personal Property of Others

Coverage can be provided on any combination of these categories. The insured's selection of categories is indicated on the commercial property declarations page by entering a limit of insurance for each chosen category of covered property.

If there is no entry for one of the categories of covered property (for example, Building), then no coverage applies to that category, even if the insured owns property fitting that category. The Property Not Covered section of the BPP specifies property that is not covered and therefore works in tandem with the Covered Property section to describe what property is covered by the BPP.

Categories of Covered Property

Understanding how the BPP defines each of the three categories of Covered Property is essential to determining whether it covers a particular loss.

Building

The policy covers buildings or structures listed and described in the declarations.

The BPP's definition of Building also includes these elements:

- Completed additions to covered buildings
- Fixtures (including outdoor fixtures)

- Permanently installed machinery and equipment
- Personal property owned by the insured and used to maintain or service the building or its premises (for example, fire extinguishing equipment; outdoor furniture; floor coverings; and equipment for refrigeration, ventilation, cooking, dishwashing, or laundering)

In addition, if they are not otherwise insured, the building description covers additions, alterations, or repairs in progress, including materials, equipment, and supplies used in connection with such work. However, such materials, equipment, and supplies are covered only if they are located within 100 feet of the described premises.

Fixtures are items attached to a building or to the land, usually in such a way that they cannot easily be removed, such as plumbing and electrical fixtures. Outdoor fixtures include items outside the building but attached to the land, such as light poles and flagpoles.

Fixtures are real property. The term "fixtures" is broad enough to include fences and outdoor signs, but coverage for these items is specifically excluded or limited.

Your Business Personal Property

Your Business Personal Property covers personal property owned by the insured and used in the insured's business. Except for an extension that provides limited coverage for property while away from the insured premises, coverage applies only when the property is located in or on the described Building or in the open (or in a vehicle) within 100 feet of the building or structure or within 100 feet of the described premises, whichever distance is greater.

Your Business Personal Property includes furniture and fixtures, machinery and equipment, stock, and all other personal property owned by the insured and used in the insured's business, except those items excluded under the Property Not Covered section.

The form defines stock as "merchandise held in storage or for sale, raw materials and in-process or finished goods, including supplies used in their packing or shipping." Your Business Personal Property also includes labor, materials, or services furnished by the insured on personal property of others.

The insured's interest in improvements and betterments is also insured as Your Business Personal Property, even though improvements and betterments are actually a part of the building and are technically real property. For example, a restaurant that rents space in a commercial building might install elaborate wall and ceiling treatments that could not be removed when the lease is terminated.

It is common for some commercial tenants to spend $1 million or more upgrading their premises. It is important to consider the insurable value of improvements and betterments when setting the amount of insurance that a tenant should carry; ignoring improvements and betterments can result in severe underinsurance difficulties when a loss occurs.

Your Business Personal Property also includes leased personal property for which the named insured has a contractual responsibility to procure coverage. An example of such property is phone or computer equipment leased by the insured under an agreement requiring the insured to purchase insurance on the equipment.

Personal Property of Others

This coverage is designed to protect the insured against loss of or damage to the personal property of others while such property is in the custody of the insured. It is an important coverage for businesses (bailees) that have customers' property in their custody, such as laundries, dry cleaners, appliance repair shops, and furniture upholstery shops.

The BPP covers such property only while it is in the insured's care, custody, or control and in or on the building described in the declarations or within 100 feet of the building or structure or within 100 feet of the described premises, whichever distance is greater. Coverage applies regardless of whether the insured is legally responsible for the damage.

Even if the insured does not buy coverage for personal property of others (as indicated by an amount of insurance being shown for that category on the declarations page), the BPP still provides a coverage extension for personal property of others, which is limited to $2,500 at each insured location.

Property Not Covered

The BPP's Property Not Covered section lists several classes of property or kinds of property losses that do not qualify as covered property. Therefore, the Covered Property section and the Property Not Covered section must be read together when determining whether a specific kind of property is insured.

There are several reasons for excluding some kinds of property from coverage:

- Some kinds of property, such as smuggled goods being held for sale, are illegal to insure.
- Some property may be much less susceptible to loss by most of the perils insured against. Examples include building foundations below the lowest basement floor or the surface of the ground, retaining walls that are not part of a building, and underground pipes.
- Some kinds of property are excluded because they can be insured more advantageously under other forms. For example, insurers generally prefer to cover money, securities, automobiles, and aircraft under other policies.

By endorsement, insurance can be made available for almost all of the items listed in the Property Not Covered section. Only contraband or property in the course of illegal transportation or trade is totally uninsurable.

Property otherwise insured is not totally excluded. The BPP covers such property, but only in excess of the other insurance.

For example, assume that a computer system valued at $150,000 is insured under the general category of business personal property in a BPP and is also insured for $100,000 under a separate electronic data processing (EDP) equipment policy issued by a different insurer. If the computer system is totally destroyed by fire, a cause of loss insured under both policies, the insurer that issued the EDP policy must pay its limit ($100,000). The insurer that issued the BPP would then pay the difference between the limit of the EDP policy and the amount of loss otherwise payable under the BPP.

Marketing Tip—Typically, property is excluded from a policy because it is considered uninsurable (such as land and water) or because the loss exposures require careful underwriting (such as bridges, piers, wharves, or docks) beyond that which is contemplated by a standard form. Additionally, under the BPP, items such as foundations or pilings and underground pipes and flues are excluded from building and personal property coverage to reduce the amount of insurance needed to satisfy the coinsurance clause.

Coverage for some excluded items can be added back to the BPP, although doing so increases the amount of insurance needed (and therefore the coinsurance required). Producers can endorse the policy to provide coverage for those items and should help the insured determine the need for coverage. Even though the probability of loss to items such as excavations, foundations below ground, and underground pipes is very low, they are susceptible to serious loss from such perils as explosion and water damage. Should a loss occur, the insured will appreciate the coverage.

Exceptions provide coverage under certain circumstances for some types of property not covered. For example, animals are not covered unless they are owned by others and boarded by the insured or held as stock, as in a pet shop. Similarly, some coverage is provided for vehicles or self-propelled machines.

Apply Your Knowledge

A business owns an office building and insures it under a BPP covering only the Building as defined in the policy. Would equipment that the business owns and uses to clean and maintain the building be Covered Property under its BPP?

Feedback: Yes, the equipment would be Covered Property under the BPP, because the definition of Building includes personal property owned by the insured and used to maintain or service the building or its premises.

A business owns a building insured under a BPP, with coverage indicated for the Building and Your Business Personal Property as defined in the policy. Would merchandise that the business owns and displays at a trade show held in a different city qualify as Covered Property under its BPP?

Feedback: No. The insured's merchandise meets the BPP's definition of stock, and stock is one of the types of property listed under Your Business Personal Property. However, while located in another city, the merchandise does not meet the requirement that the property must be located in or on the described building or in the open (or in a vehicle) within 100 feet of the insured's building or the described premises.

Therefore, the merchandise is not Covered Property while located at the trade show. (However, a coverage extenson in a later section of the BPP provides limited coverage for this loss exposure.)

BPP ADDITIONAL COVERAGES AND COVERAGE EXTENSIONS

The Building and Personal Property Coverage Form, also referred to as the BPP, includes additional coverages and coverage extensions that provide several enhancements of its basic coverage.

The BPP provides several supplemental coverages in addition to the basic coverages for buildings, the insured's business personal property, and the property of others. These supplemental coverages are described under two subheadings: Additional Coverages and Coverage Extensions. See the exhibit "BPP Additional Coverages and Coverage Extensions: Special Limits."

Additional Coverages

These are the six additional coverages in the BPP:

- Debris Removal
- Preservation of Property
- Fire Department Service Charge
- Pollutant Cleanup and Removal
- Increased Cost of Construction
- Electronic Data

Debris Removal

Following a loss, large amounts of debris may remain on the premises, and the cost of removing the debris may be substantial. The Debris Removal

> **BPP Additional Coverages and Coverage Extensions: Special Limits**
>
> All of the BPP's additional coverages and coverage extensions, except Preservation of Property, are subject to special dollar limits. In many cases, these limits result in insufficient coverage. For example, the limit for the Pollutant Cleanup and Removal additional coverage is $10,000 per policy year. Because losses related to pollutant cleanup can be extensive, this limit often proves inadequate for policyholders. Similarly, the Electronic Data additional coverage limit is $2,500 per policy year, a limit that does not adequately address the potentially catastrophic effects of losses related to electronic data.
>
> The limits for many of the BPP's additional coverages and coverage extensions can be increased by showing a higher limit in the declarations, adding an appropriate coverage endorsement, or buying another type of policy to supplement the BPP. However, many insurers will not provide higher limits under the BPP for the Pollutant Cleanup and Removal or the Electronic Data additional coverages.

[DA07809]

additional coverage covers the cost of removing debris of covered property resulting from a covered cause of loss during the policy period. It would not, for example, pay to remove the debris resulting from a flood if flood is not a covered cause of loss or to remove the debris of the insured's licensed automobiles, because they are not covered property.

In some cases, the cost to remove debris of property that is not covered property is also covered. For example, the cost to remove debris of a neighboring building that a windstorm blew onto the insured's premises would be covered.

The Debris Removal additional coverage includes the cost to clean up pollution at the insured's premises caused by an insured peril. For example, if a building is shown as covered property, the cost to clean up debris from a fire that causes the release of toxic chemicals onto the floor of the insured's building would be covered. However, the Debris Removal provision does not apply to costs for cleanup or removal of pollutants from land or water. Limited coverage for these costs is available under the provisions of another additional coverage. No coverage is provided for cleanup of off-premises pollution even when it results from a covered loss.

Preservation of Property

It is sometimes necessary to move covered property to another location to protect it. The Preservation of Property additional coverage extends the policy to protect covered property while it is being moved and for up to thirty days at the new location. This coverage is broader than the normal coverage under the policy. It protects against "any direct physical loss or damage" and is not limited to either the covered causes of loss or locations stipulated in the coverage form. The protection provided under this additional coverage is subject to the limits of insurance stated in the declarations. Consequently, the additional coverage provides no protection if the applicable limit of insurance is exhausted by payment for the physical loss.

Fire Department Service Charge

In some localities, the fire department may make a charge for its services in controlling or extinguishing a fire. The Fire Department Service Charge additional coverage pays fire department charges up to the specified limit at each location if they are required by local ordinance or are assumed by contract before the loss occurs.

Pollutant Cleanup and Removal

The Pollutant Cleanup and Removal additional coverage provides limited coverage for the cleanup and removal of pollutants from land or water at the described premises. This additional coverage pays the insured's expenses to extract pollutants from land or water at the described premises if the release, discharge, dispersal, seepage, migration, or escape of the pollutants is the result of a covered cause of loss that occurs during the policy period.

Increased Cost of Construction

The Ordinance or Law exclusion contained in the causes of loss forms that can be attached to the BPP excludes the increased cost to comply with ordinances or laws regulating the repair, rebuilding, or replacement of covered buildings. The Increased Cost of Construction additional coverage provides a small amount of insurance to cover this loss exposure. The amount of insurance is equal to 5 percent of the amount of insurance or $10,000, whichever is less. It is paid in addition to the policy limit. This additional coverage applies only if the Replacement Cost optional coverage has been selected.

The Increased Cost of Construction additional coverage provides no coverage for these items:

- Loss to any undamaged portion of the building that an ordinance or law does not permit to remain in use
- The cost to demolish the undamaged portion of the structure and remove its debris

Electronic Data

Because of businesses' growing dependence on electronic data and the widespread belief that the exposure could better be treated by other forms of insurance, the BPP excludes electronic data in most instances except as provided by the Electronic Data additional coverage. This additional coverage is subject to a limit that is too low to provide meaningful coverage for most businesses and is the most that the insurer will pay per policy year, regardless of the number of occurrences or locations covered. All electronic data damage is deemed to have been sustained in the policy year that an occurrence began, even if the damage continues or results in additional loss or damage in a subsequent policy year.

Coverage Extensions

The BPP coverage extensions apply only if at least 80 percent coinsurance or a value reporting period symbol is shown in the declarations. The amounts payable under the coverage extensions are payable in addition to the overall limits of insurance stated in the declarations, subject to the special limits that apply to the coverage extensions. These are the six BPP coverage extensions:

- Newly Acquired or Constructed Property
- Personal Effects and Property of Others
- Valuable Papers and Records (Other Than Electronic Data)
- Property Off-Premises
- Outdoor Property
- Non-Owned Detached Trailers
- Business Personal Property Temporarily in Portable Storage Units

Newly Acquired or Constructed Property

If the policy covers a building, the Newly Acquired or Constructed Property extension provides automatic coverage for a new building being constructed at the premises described in the declarations. Automatic coverage is also provided for newly acquired buildings at other locations, provided the purpose of the newly acquired building is similar to the use of the building described in the declarations or the newly acquired building will be used as a warehouse. The coverage extension states a maximum amount of coverage that applies to each building.

If the policy covers business personal property, the extension also provides automatic coverage for these types of property:

- Business personal property at any newly acquired location other than fairs, trade shows, or exhibitions
- Business personal property located at newly constructed or acquired buildings at the location described in the declarations

A stated amount of coverage applies to loss of business personal property at each building.

The coverage for buildings and business personal property provided by this extension is temporary. It terminates automatically at the earliest of three dates:

- The expiration date of the policy
- Thirty days after the acquisition of the new location or the start of construction of the new building
- The date the insured notifies the insurer of the new location or new building

Personal Effects and Property of Others

The Personal Effects and Property of Others extension provides a limited amount of coverage for personal effects (such as a coat or jewelry) owned by an individual insured or a partner, a member, an officer, a manager, or an employee of the insured while on the premises described in the declarations. Personal effects are not covered for loss by theft. The extension also covers property of others in the care, custody, or control of the insured.

Valuable Papers and Records (Other Than Electronic Data)

Valuable papers and records (such as records of accounts receivable, mailing lists, legal documents, medical records, specifications, and drawings) are covered as business personal property, but only for the cost of blank records plus the labor to transcribe or copy duplicate information. This extension does not apply to electronic data; previous versions of the BPP did cover the cost of reconstructing electronic data.

Property Off-Premises

The Property Off-Premises extension provides coverage for covered property while it is away from the described premises. In addition to property temporarily at locations that the insured does not own, lease, or operate, the extension also covers property in storage at a location leased after the inception of the current policy and property at any fair, trade show, or exhibition. This extension does not apply to property in or on a vehicle or in the custody of the insured's salespersons unless the property in custody is at a fair, trade show, or exhibition.

Outdoor Property

The Outdoor Property extension covers loss to outdoor fences; radio and television antennas (including satellite dishes); and trees, shrubs, and plants in most instances. Unlike the other coverage extensions, the Outdoor Property extension has its own list of covered causes of loss. It covers only loss by fire, lightning, explosion, riot or civil commotion, and aircraft. Some of the more likely causes of loss to outdoor property—windstorm, vehicles, and vandalism—are not covered.

Non-Owned Detached Trailers

Insureds frequently lease trailers to expand office space or to provide additional storage or work areas at their own premises. The Non-Owned Detached Trailers extension permits the insured to extend Your Business Personal Property to include such trailers. The trailer must be used in the insured's business and be in the insured's care, custody, or control at the described premises. Moreover, the insured must have a contractual responsibility to pay for loss or damage to the trailer.

The coverage does not apply while the trailer is attached to any motor vehicle or motorized conveyance, whether or not it is in motion. Nor does it apply during hitching or unhitching operations or when a trailer becomes accidentally unhitched from a motor vehicle or conveyance.

Business Personal Property Temporarily in Portable Storage Units

This coverage extension provides temporary insurance for business personal property while stored in a portable storage unit, which could include either a unit specifically designed for this purpose or a detached trailer or semitrailer. For the contents of the unit to be covered, the unit must be located within 100 feet of the building or structure described in the declarations or within 100 feet of the described premises, whichever distance is greater.

The coverage is truly limited to temporary storage: coverage ends ninety days after the property is placed in the unit. Moreover, the coverage does not apply if the unit has been in use at the described premises for more than ninety days. Unless a higher limit is shown in the declarations, $10,000 is the most that the insurer will pay for business personal property under this extension, regardless of the number of units in use.

Apply Your Knowledge

A business insures its building under a BPP that has 80 percent coinsurance. As the business grows, it acquires another building for use as a distribution warehouse. Two weeks after the insured acquires the building, a lightning strike on the warehouse premises damages the building and an outdoor security fence. At the time of the lightning strike, the insured has not reported the new building to the insurer. Identify the coverage extensions that would apply to this loss.

Feedback: The Newly Acquired or Constructed Property and the Outdoor Property coverage extensions would apply to this loss. The Newly Acquired or Constructed Property coverage extension applies because the purpose of the business's newly acquired building was for it to be used as a warehouse and because the business acquired the warehouse less than thirty days before the loss. The Outdoor Property coverage extension applies to the loss because lightning is a covered cause of loss and the outdoor fence is specifically covered.

Fire damages a business's office complex, which is covered under a BPP. The blaze destroys one of the complex's two buildings, which the business intends to rebuild. The cost of rebuilding the destroyed building will be increased because of building code changes that have taken place since it was constructed. The other building sustained only minor damage, but fire-damaged covered property will need to be hauled away before repairs can begin. Identify the additional coverages that would apply to this loss.

Feedback: The Increased Cost of Construction and the Debris Removal additional coverages would apply to this loss. The Increased Cost of Construction additional coverage applies because it provides coverage for the increased cost to comply with ordinances or laws regulating the repair, rebuilding, or replacement of covered buildings. The Debris Removal additional coverage applies because it covers the cost of removing debris of covered property resulting from a covered cause of loss during the policy period.

CAUSES OF LOSS—BASIC FORM AND BROAD FORM

The perils covered in an Insurance Services Office, Inc. (ISO) commercial property policy are specified in any of three causes of loss forms.

The Causes of Loss—Basic Form (CP 10 10) and the Causes of Loss—Broad Form (CP 10 20), two of the three causes of loss forms available for use in the ISO commercial property coverage part, are nearly identical. The coverage provided by the third causes of loss form, the Causes of Loss—Special Form (CP 10 30), differs from the other two forms. This discussion focuses on three sections of the Basic Form and the Broad Form, noting instances where the two forms diverge:

- Covered Causes of Loss
- Exclusions
- Additional Coverages

Covered Causes of Loss

The Basic Form and the Broad Form both explicitly name the policy's covered causes of loss. This is known as a "named perils" approach. The Broad Form covers all of the perils covered in the Basic Form but also includes three additional perils that the Basic Form does not cover. Although the Broad Form is slightly more expensive than the Basic Form, most insureds choose it over the

Basic Form. See the exhibit "Covered Causes of Loss in the Basic Form and Broad Form."

Exclusions

Both forms contain several exclusions that further define or limit the covered causes of loss. See the exhibit "Anti-Concurrent Causation Wording."

Ordinance or Law

To promote public welfare and safety, municipalities enact and regularly upgrade the building codes that set the standards for new construction or significant remodeling. For example, a building code might require that new buildings in a certain area be fire resistive. If an existing building in that area does not comply with the code and sustains damage by fire or another peril, the building code may require that its restoration meet the standards for new buildings. In some cases, a building ordinance or law may require that a partially damaged building be totally demolished, changing what would have been a partial loss to a total loss. The Ordinance or Law exclusion eliminates coverage for consequential losses that result from the enforcement of building ordinances or laws. Some coverage for this exposure is provided by the Increased Cost of Construction additional coverage. Broader coverage for the excluded losses can be provided by an endorsement for an additional premium.

Earth Movement

Coverage is not provided for damage caused by earth movement other than sinkhole collapse. Earth movement includes earthquake, landslide, mine subsidence, and similar movements. The exclusion does not apply to damage by fire or explosion caused by earth movement. Earthquake coverage can be added for an additional premium.

Governmental Action

Seizure or destruction of property by governmental action is not covered. This exclusion does not apply to the destruction of property by governmental order to stop the spread of a covered fire.

Nuclear Hazard

Loss caused by nuclear reaction, radiation, or radioactive contamination is excluded. However, the exclusion does not apply to loss by fire resulting from these causes.

Covered Causes of Loss in the Basic Form and Broad Form

Covered Cause of Loss	Description
Fire	For most insureds, fire is the peril that poses the greatest risk of a large or total property loss.
Lightning	Lightning is a naturally occurring electrical discharge between clouds or between a cloud and the earth.
Explosion	The explosion peril includes the explosion of gases or fuel in a furnace or flue (called "combustion explosion" or "furnace explosion").
Windstorm or hail	Hurricanes and tornadoes are both examples of windstorms, although less severe windstorms can cause property damage and also fall within the coverage. Damage by rain, snow, sand, or dust to the interior of a building or to property inside the building is not covered unless the building first sustains exterior damage by wind, and the rain, snow, sand, or dust enters through the damaged part of the building. Does not include hail damage to lawns, trees, shrubs, or plants that are part of a vegetated roof.
Smoke	For smoke damage to be covered, it must be sudden and accidental. No coverage exists for damage by smoke from industrial operations or agricultural smudging (the intentional production of smoke to protect crops from frost damage).
Aircraft or vehicles	Damage caused by aircraft must result from actual physical contact with the aircraft or objects falling from it. Vehicle damage must result from accidental physical contact with a vehicle or an object thrown by the vehicle (such as a pebble propelled by a truck's tire). There is no coverage for damage caused by vehicles owned by the insured or operated in the insured's business.
Riot or civil commotion	In most states, a riot is defined by law as a violent public disturbance by three or more persons. However, the riot or civil commotion peril includes acts by striking workers while occupying the insured premises as well as looting occurring at the time and place of a riot or civil commotion.
Vandalism	Vandalism means the willful and malicious damage to or destruction of property. Although the vandalism peril does not cover loss by theft, it does cover damage to the building caused by the entry or exit of burglars.
Sprinkler leakage	Sprinkler leakage means the escape of any substance (water, carbon dioxide, or any other extinguishing agent) from an automatic fire protection or extinguishing system. The collapse of a tank constituting a part of such a system is covered, as is the cost of repairing damage to the system if the damage results in the sprinkler leakage or if the damage is caused by freezing. The cost to tear out and replace any part of the building or structure to repair damage to the automatic sprinkler system is also covered.
Sinkhole collapse	Sinkholes result from underground water dissolving limestone or dolomite and creating an empty space or cavern under the ground. When the roof of the cavern gets too close to the ground surface, the surface collapses, causing damage to buildings or other property located over or near the resulting sinkhole. This peril insures resulting damage to covered property (buildings or business personal property), but not the cost of filling the sinkhole. Loss caused by the collapse of land into man-made underground cavities, such as mineshafts, is not covered by this peril.
Volcanic action	The volcanic action peril covers damage caused by lava flow, ash, dust, particulate matter, airborne volcanic blast, or airborne shock waves resulting from a volcanic eruption. The earthquake damage that often accompanies a volcanic eruption is excluded by one of the exclusions discussed subsequently. Because such losses may occur over a relatively long period of time, both forms stipulate that all eruptions that occur within any 168-hour period are considered a single occurrence and are thus subject to only one deductible and policy limit.
Falling objects (Broad Form only)	The coverage for falling objects does not include damage to personal property in the open or to damage inside a building unless the roof or an outside wall is first damaged by the falling object.
Weight of ice, snow, or sleet (Broad Form only)	Does not cover damage to personal property in the open, or to lawns, trees, shrubs, or plants that are part of a vegetated roof.
Water damage (Broad Form only)	Despite its name, the water damage peril is not intended to cover flooding, rainfall, sewer backup, and similar causes of water damage. Instead, it is limited to covering loss caused by water or steam leakage resulting from the breaking apart or cracking of a plumbing, heating, air conditioning, or other system or appliance that is located on the described premises. If the building is covered property, the form also covers the cost to tear out and replace any part of the building to repair damage to the appliance or system that leaked. The water damage peril is subject to several exclusions, including the cost to repair any defect that caused the loss or damage and the cost to repair any gradual damage that occurs over a period of fourteen days or more.

[DA07824]

Anti-Concurrent Causation Wording

The introductory language to the first group of eight exclusions provides that losses caused directly or indirectly by any of those perils are not covered, even if another covered cause contributed to the loss, regardless of the sequence in which the causes of events occur, unless the exclusion specifically provides otherwise. This wording was developed to eliminate claims based on the concurrent causation doctrine and is therefore referred to as "anti-concurrent causation wording." The concurrent causation doctrine holds that a loss is covered when caused by two or more independent, concurrent perils if only one of the perils is covered—even if the other peril or perils are clearly excluded.

[DA07825]

Utility Services

Loss caused by power failure or failure of another utility service is excluded if the failure originates away from the described premises. For example, if electrical power to the described premises is interrupted because of lightning damage to an overhead power line situated away from the described premises, the exclusion will eliminate coverage for any loss caused by the resulting power failure.

The exclusion also applies if the utility failure originates at the described premises, but only if the failure involves equipment that supplies utility service to the described premises from a source away from the described premises. For example, if lightning takes out an overhead power line on the described premises, the exclusion will apply to any loss caused by the resulting power failure.

The exclusion does not apply to loss from a covered peril resulting from power failure. If, for example, loss of electrical power causes a natural gas leak that results in an explosion (a covered cause of loss), the Utility Services exclusion would not apply to the damage caused by the explosion.

War and Military Action

The War and Military Action exclusion eliminates coverage for loss caused by war, revolution, insurrection, or similar actions. The current insurance industry consensus is that the War and Military Action exclusion does not apply to acts of terrorism, such as the terrorist attacks of September 11, 2001. Instead, insurers attach separate terrorism exclusion endorsements unless the insured purchases terrorism coverage.

Water

Flood-related loss is difficult to insure because of the potential for a large and concentrated loss. Insurers therefore exclude flood losses from commercial property forms.

The Water exclusion eliminates coverage for damage caused by these:

- Flood, surface water, tides, waves (including tidal wave and tsunami), tides, tidal water, overflow of a body of water, or spray from any of these
- Mudslide or mudflow
- Backing up of sewers, drains, or sumps
- Underground water pressing on or flowing or seeping through foundations, walls, floors, basements, doors, windows, or other openings

The exclusion does not apply to damage by fire, explosion, or sprinkler leakage caused by any of the foregoing. The Water exclusion applies regardless of whether the loss event results in widespread damage or affects a substantial area.

"Fungus," Wet Rot, Dry Rot, and Bacteria

In recent years, mold claims have disrupted the homeowners insurance markets in some states and posed a similar problem for commercial property insurance. To mitigate this problem, ISO added a "Fungus," Wet Rot, Dry Rot, and Bacteria exclusion to the commercial property causes of loss forms. Fungus is defined to include mold or mildew and any mycotoxins, spores, scents, or by-products produced or released by fungi.

The exclusion does not apply when the fungus, wet rot, dry rot, and bacteria result from fire or lightning, but it is one of the exclusions subject to the anti-concurrent causation wording.

In addition to the foregoing exclusion, each of the causes of loss forms contains an additional coverage titled Limited Coverage for "Fungus," Wet Rot, Dry Rot, and Bacteria, which provides a modest amount of insurance for such losses.

Other Exclusions

The Basic Form and the Broad Form also contain a set of exclusions that are not subject to the anti-concurrent causation wording. These exclusions eliminate coverage for loss or damage caused by any of these:

- Electrical, magnetic, or electromagnetic energy that damages or otherwise interferes with any electrical or electronic wires or devices, including devices, appliances, systems, or networks using cellular or satellite technology. However, if a fire results, the resulting fire damage is covered.
- Rupture or bursting of water pipes, unless caused by a covered cause of loss. This exclusion does not apply to sprinkler leakage and is included only in the Basic Form.
- Leakage of water or steam from any part of an appliance or system containing water or steam (other than an automatic sprinkler system), unless caused by a covered cause of loss.

- Explosion of steam boilers, steam pipes, steam turbines, or steam engines owned by, leased to, or operated by the insured. However, if such an explosion causes a fire or a combustion explosion, the damage caused by fire or combustion explosion is covered.
- Mechanical breakdown, including rupture or bursting caused by centrifugal force.
- Loss resulting from the neglect of the insured to use all reasonable means to save and preserve property at and after the time of loss. This exclusion reinforces the insured's duty to protect covered property after a loss.

Finally, several additional exclusions apply only to certain commercial property coverage forms, such as ones that provide business income and extra expense coverage. These exclusions do not apply to the Building and Personal Property Coverage Form, also referred to as the BPP.

Additional Coverages

The Basic Form and the Broad Form both provide an additional coverage titled Limited Coverage for "Fungus," Wet Rot, Dry Rot, and Bacteria. The additional coverage is limited in dollar amount ($15,000 in the aggregate for any one twelve-month policy period) and scope of coverage.

The Broad Form also provides an additional coverage for collapse. Under this additional coverage, the insurer agrees to pay for loss resulting from collapse of a building or any part of a building if the collapse is caused by one or more of these:

- Any of the covered causes of loss.
- Hidden decay, unless such decay is known to an insured before the collapse occurs.
- Hidden insect or vermin damage, unless such damage is known to an insured before the collapse occurs.
- Weight of people or personal property.
- Weight of rain that collects on a roof.
- Use of defective materials or construction methods if the abrupt collapse occurs during the course of construction. (Collapse of a completed building caused by defective materials or construction is covered only if it is caused in part by any of the causes of loss listed here.)

Collapse is specifically and narrowly defined. It means an abrupt falling down or caving in of a building or part of a building that, as a result, can no longer be occupied for its intended purpose. It does not include a building that is in danger of falling down or caving in, nor one that is standing but shows evidence of cracking, bulging, sagging, bending, leaning, settling, shrinking, or expanding. A part of a building that is standing is not considered to be in a state of collapse even if it has separated from another part of the building.

The additional coverage for collapse also covers loss to property caused by the collapse of personal property inside a building (such as storage racks in a warehouse) if the collapse is a result of one of the causes listed previously.

Apply Your Knowledge

Assuming that each of these losses involved covered property, indicate whether each loss would be covered by the Broad Form:

Leaking natural gas accumulated in the insured's storage room and exploded.

Feedback: This loss would be covered under the Broad Form's explosion peril.

Vandals break several windows in the insured building.

Feedback: This loss would be covered under the Broad Form's vandalism peril.

A tree branch falls and damages the roof of the insured's store.

Feedback: This loss would be covered under the Broad Form's falling objects peril.

An earthquake damages an insured building.

Feedback: The loss would not be covered under the Broad Form, because earthquake is not a covered cause of loss (and is excluded by the Earth Movement exclusion).

CAUSES OF LOSS—SPECIAL FORM

Because it is the broadest option for covered causes of loss, the Insurance Services Office, Inc. (ISO) commercial property policy's Causes of Loss—Special Form is the most frequently selected of the three causes of loss forms.

The Causes of Loss—Special Form (CP 10 30) states that it covers "direct physical loss unless the loss is excluded or limited in this policy," instead of listing the perils covered. Moreover, the loss or damage must be accidental and unforeseen by the insured in order to be covered. The Special Form is designed to cover any loss that would be covered by the Basic and Broad Forms. In addition, the Special Form covers perils that are not specified in the Basic and Broad Forms.

The Special Form offers these advantages to the insured:

- Certain causes of loss that are omitted or excluded under the Broad Form are not excluded—and are therefore covered—under the Special Form. Most significantly, the Special Form covers theft of covered property under a wide variety of circumstances, subject to some exclusions and limitations. The Basic and Broad Forms cover theft by looting at the time of a riot or civil commotion, but in no other circumstances.

- By covering direct physical losses other than those that are specifically excluded, the Special Form covers losses that the insured might not have anticipated.
- The Special Form shifts the "burden of proof" from the insured to the insurer. Under a named perils form, such as the Basic or Broad Form, the insured must prove that the loss was caused by a covered cause. Under the Special Form, an accidental loss to covered property is presumed to be covered unless the insurer can prove that it was caused by an excluded peril.

Exclusions and Limitations

The Special Form contains most of the exclusions of the Basic and Broad Forms, including many (but not all) of the limitations expressed in the descriptions of the basic and broad covered causes of loss. In those instances in which the Special Form does not contain an exclusion or a limitation equivalent to any of those contained in the Basic and Broad Forms, it provides broader coverage, as in these examples:

- The vehicle peril in both the Basic and Broad Forms excludes loss or damage caused by or resulting from vehicles owned by the named insured or operated in the course of the named insured's business. The Special Form, in contrast, does not contain such an exclusion. For example, the Special Form covers loss or damage to an insured building when an employee accidentally drives a truck owned by the insured into the building's garage wall.
- The windstorm peril in the Basic and Broad Forms excludes damage to the interior of a building by rain, snow, sleet, ice, sand, or dust, unless the roof or walls of the building are first damaged by a Covered Cause of Loss. The Special Form contains the same exclusion, but with an additional exception—the Special Form exclusion does not apply if loss results from the melting of ice, sleet, or snow on the building or structure. Therefore, unlike the Basic and Broad Forms, the Special Form covers water damage that occurs when water backs up under roof shingles because roof gutters are clogged with ice, a phenomenon known as ice damming.

Exclusions and Limitations Unique to the Special Form

Because the Special Form covers more causes of loss than the Broad Form, it contains some exclusions and limitations that are not needed in the Broad Form. The Special Form covers any risks of loss other than those that are specifically excluded. Thus, many difficult-to-insure perils that are not covered under the Basic and Broad Forms (because they are not named as covered causes of loss in those forms) must be specifically excluded in the Special Form. Examples of perils that the Special Form specifically excludes are these:

- Wear and tear
- Rust, corrosion, decay, deterioration, or hidden or latent defect
- Smog
- Settling, cracking, shrinking, or expansion
- Infestations and waste products of insects, birds, rodents, or other animals
- Mechanical breakdown
- Dampness or dryness of atmosphere, changes or extremes in temperatures, or marring or scratching (applicable to personal property only)

However, the insurer will pay losses caused by a "specified cause of loss" that results from the excluded peril. The Special Form defines "specified causes of loss" to include all of the causes of loss insured under the Broad Form. However, if one of these excluded causes of loss results in a"specified cause of loss," the insurer will pay for the loss caused by the resulting "specified cause of loss."

The Special Form also excludes loss caused by these:

- Weather conditions that contribute to other excluded causes of loss. If, for example, covered property is damaged by flood waters that were driven in part by high winds, the flood damage will not be covered even though windstorm is not otherwise excluded.
- Acts or decisions, including the failure to act or decide, of any person, group, organization, or governmental body. Thus, for example, if flooding occurs because municipal authorities fail to take proper flood control measures, the flood exclusion cannot be overcome by the insured's claim that the municipality's failure to act was the cause of the loss.
- Faulty or inadequate planning, zoning, surveying, siting, design, specifications, workmanship, repair, construction, renovation, remodeling, grading, compaction, materials, or maintenance.

If one of these excluded causes of loss results in a Covered Cause of Loss, the insurer will pay the loss resulting from the covered cause. For example, the failure of a city's fire department to take necessary measures might allow a fire to spread and burn down several row houses adjoining the insured's building. Even though the fire department's failure to act contributed to the destruction of the adjoining row houses, they were destroyed by fire, a Covered Cause of Loss. Thus, fire damage to the insured's building would be covered.

The Loss or Damage to Products exclusion eliminates coverage for damage to merchandise, goods, or other products resulting from production errors, such as adding wrong ingredients or measuring ingredients incorrectly. Many insurers believe that damage to products resulting from errors in the production process is a business risk that should not be insurable under commercial property policies. However, the exclusion specifically does not apply to loss or damage caused by a Covered Cause of Loss that results from an error or omission in the production process. If, for example, an error in the production process results in an explosion, the explosion damage will be covered.

Another noteworthy exclusion that is unique to the Special Form eliminates coverage for the release, discharge, or dispersal of pollutants. However, the exclusion does not apply to any release of pollutants caused by any of the specified causes of loss, nor does it apply to glass damaged by chemicals applied to the glass.

Loss to these kinds of property is covered only if it is caused by specified causes of loss:

- Valuable papers and records
- Animals, and then only in the event of their death
- Fragile articles if broken, such as glassware, statuary, marble, chinaware, and porcelain (but not including building glass and containers of property held for sale)
- Builders' machinery and equipment owned or held by the insured unless on or within 100 feet of the described premises

Another exclusion unique to the Special Form concerns trees, shrubs, plants, and lawns that are part of a vegetated roof. Covered property under the Building and Personal Property Coverage Form (BPP) includes trees, shrubs, plants, and lawns that are part of a vegetated roof.

Consequently, the BPP covers such items without application of the per item and per occurrence limits and the restricted specified perils that apply to other trees, shrubs, and plants under the BPP's Outdoor Property coverage extension. However, the Special Form excludes these causes of loss to trees, shrubs, plants, or lawns that are part of a vegetated roof:

1. Dampness or dryness of atmosphere or of soil supporting the vegetation;
2. Changes in or extremes of temperature;
3. Disease;
4. Frost or hail; or
5. Rain, snow, ice or sleet [1]

The excluded perils are either commercially uninsurable or would require a significant additional premium to insure. It is noteworthy that the Special Form covers trees, shrubs, plants, and lawns that are part of a vegetated roof against loss by windstorm as well as any other causes of loss that are not specifically excluded.

Theft-Related Exclusions and Limitations

The Special Form does not contain an absolute exclusion of theft, and thus it covers any theft of covered property that is not specifically excluded. Several theft-related exclusions and limitations define the scope of theft coverage under the Special Form.

The Special Form excludes dishonest or criminal acts (including theft) of the insured or of partners, members, officers, managers, directors, or employees of the insured, but the exclusion does not apply to acts of destruction by employees. For example, if Fred vandalizes his employer's property in response to being demoted, the vandalism damage is covered. If, however, Fred steals money from his employer, this dishonest act is subject to the exclusion. Losses resulting from the excluded types of dishonest acts can be covered under separate crime coverage forms.

The Special Form also excludes the voluntary surrendering of property as the result of a fraudulent scheme or trickery. If, for example, a thief posing as an honest customer tricks the insured's salesperson into voluntarily allowing the thief to remove merchandise from the insured's store, the resulting theft loss will not be covered. Similarly, the Special Form excludes loss of property transferred outside the described premises on the basis of unauthorized instructions.

Loss by theft of construction materials not attached as part of the building is excluded unless the materials are held for sale by the named insured. Moreover, the Special Form excludes loss of property that is simply missing without explanation or that is evidenced only by an inventory shortage.

The Special Form imposes special limits on theft loss of certain kinds of property that are especially attractive to thieves, such as furs, jewelry, precious metals, and tickets. Such property can be insured for higher limits under separate crime or inland marine forms.

A theft exclusion endorsement can be attached to the policy to eliminate theft coverage entirely when the underwriter feels that the risk is unacceptable or when the insured wants to reduce the policy premium.

Additional Coverages and Coverage Extensions

The Special Form includes the same additional coverages for collapse and fungus as the Broad Form. It also contains three coverage extensions that insure certain losses not otherwise covered.

The Property in Transit extension provides up to $5,000 of additional protection for loss to the insured's property in transit. The property must be in or on a motor vehicle owned, leased, or operated by the insured and cannot be in the custody of the insured's sales personnel. It covers only those losses that occur within the coverage territory.

The transit extension does not provide special form coverage. The perils insured against are fire, lightning, explosion, windstorm, hail, riot, civil commotion, vandalism, upset or overturn of the conveying vehicle, collision of the conveying vehicle with another vehicle or an object other than the roadbed, and theft. The coverage for theft is limited to theft of an entire bale, case, or package by forced entry into a securely locked body or compartment of the vehicle, evidenced by marks of the forced entry.

Because the transit extension has a low coverage limit and restricted covered perils, insureds who have property in transit should consider covering such property under an inland marine or ocean marine policy.

The Water Damage, Other Liquids, Powder or Molten Material Damage extension covers the cost to tear out and replace any part of a building necessary to repair an appliance or a system from which water or another liquid—or even powder fire-extinguishing agents or molten materials—has escaped. The extension does not pay for the repair of any defect that resulted in the leakage. It does pay for repairs to fire extinguishing equipment if the damage results in the discharge of any substance from an automatic fire protection system or is directly caused by freezing.

The Glass extension covers the expenses of installing temporary glass plates or boarding up openings when repair or replacement of damaged glass has been delayed. The insurer will also pay for the cost to clear obstructions (but not window displays) that prevent replacement of the glass. While the Basic, Broad, and Special Forms all insure glass breakage by a Covered Cause of Loss, only the Special Form includes this Glass coverage extension.

Apply Your Knowledge

A soft-drink producer is insured under the Building and Personal Property Coverage Form, also referred to as the BPP, with Special Form coverage. A mistake during the production process for one of its diet sodas causes too much artificial sweetener to be added to a large quantity of the beverage, forcing the soft drink producer to dispose of the entire batch. Would the cause of this loss be covered under the soft-drink producer's Special Form?

Feedback: No, the cause of the loss would not be covered under the soft-drink producer's Special Form, because the Loss or Damage to Products exclusion eliminates coverage for damage to merchandise, goods, or other products resulting from production errors, such as adding wrong ingredients or measuring ingredients incorrectly.

An office building is insured under the BPP with Special Form coverage. Firefighters' efforts to extinguish a fire caused extensive water damage to the insured building. In addition, several windows were broken by the intense heat of the fire. Would the cause of these losses be covered under the Special Form? Additionally, would the Special Form cover the cost of boarding up the windows?

Feedback: Yes, the Special Form would cover the cause of this loss, which was fire, because the Special Form does not exclude fire or any of the consequences of the fire.

BPP LIMITS OF INSURANCE AND DEDUCTIBLE

The dollar amount that the insurer is obligated to pay for a loss covered under the Building and Personal Property Coverage Form, also referred to as the BPP, is largely determined by the Limits of Insurance and Deductible provisions of the BPP.

The BPP's Limits of Insurance section contains provisions explaining how the insurer will apply the limit(s) of insurance to covered losses. The amount that the insurer will pay for a covered loss is also affected by the BPP's Deductible provision, which provides the rules for applying the deductible shown in the declarations.

Limits of Insurance

The Insurance Services Office, Inc. (ISO) BPP's Limits of Insurance section states that the most the insurer is obligated to pay for a loss in any one occurrence is the applicable limit of insurance shown in the declarations. Total commercial property losses are rare, and the forms contain other limitations that reduce the amount the insurer pays. Therefore, the amount that the insurer pays for a loss covered under the BPP is generally less than the applicable limit of insurance. However, payments under all of the BPP's coverage extensions and under most of the additional coverages are paid in addition to the limit of insurance, which makes it possible for the total payment for one loss to exceed the limit of insurance.

A BPP can be subject to one or more limits, which can be either specific or blanket limits. When specific limits are used, the declarations show separate limits of insurance for each covered building and for personal property at each location. For example, a BPP's declarations could show these limits for the insured location:

- $1,000,000 for a Building
- $800,000 for Your Business Personal Property
- $50,000 for Personal Property of Others

A blanket limit is the alternative to specific limits. A blanket limit can apply one amount of insurance to all property covered by the policy. If the property described in the previous example was insured on a blanket basis, then the declarations would state that $1,850,000 blanket coverage is available on the Building, Your Business Personal Property, and Personal Property of Others at the address.

Property at different locations can also be covered on a blanket basis, in which case one limit of insurance can apply to all covered property at all locations. Alternatively, one blanket limit could apply to all of the insured's buildings (at one or more locations) and another blanket limit could apply to all the insured's business personal property (at one or more locations).

Deductible

An insurer is not obligated to pay anything to the insured unless the loss exceeds the deductible shown in the policy declarations. The limit of insurance then applies to the loss in excess of the deductible. That is, the deductible is subtracted from the loss, not from the limit of insurance. For example, under a policy that has a $100,000 limit on a building and a $1,000 deductible, an insurer's payment would be calculated as shown:

Amount of Loss	Insurer's Payment
$500	No payment (loss is less than deductible)
$100,000	$99,000 ($100,000 – $1,000 deductible)
$110,000	$100,000 ($110,000 – $1,000 deductible exceeds limit of insurance)

Unless a BPP is written for a single blanket limit, it typically covers two or more categories of property (such as two buildings, or a building and business personal property) with a separate limit applying to each category. How the deductible applies in such situations is determined by this passage in the Deductible provision:

> When the occurrence involves loss to more than one item of Covered Property and separate Limits of Insurance apply, the losses will not be combined in determining application of the Deductible. But the deductible will be applied only once per occurrence.

For example, a BPP covers five buildings at one location, each building is insured for a separate limit, and a $5,000 deductible applies. A windstorm (one occurrence) causes less than $5,000 damage to each of the buildings, but the combined total is $10,000 of damage. As stated in the Deductible provision, the losses will not be combined for purposes of applying the deductible. Therefore, because the insurer is not obligated to pay anything to the insured unless the loss on at least one building exceeds the deductible, the insurer will pay nothing for this loss.

If, instead, the amount of loss on one of the buildings is $6,000, the insurer will pay the $1,000 amount of loss on this building that exceeds the $5,000 deductible. And, because the deductible has now been applied (and "the deductible will be applied only once per occurrence"), the insurer will also pay the amount of loss on each of the other buildings even if it does not exceed the deductible amount.

If the Coinsurance condition or the Agreed Value optional coverage applies, the amount of the loss is first reduced by any penalty imposed by those provisions before applying the deductible.

Under ISO *Commercial Lines Manual* (CLM) rules, the standard deductible is $500. This may be reduced to $250 for an additional premium or increased to a higher amount that reduces the premium. A $1,000 or $5,000 deductible is common for middle-market insureds. The savings for higher deductibles are seldom attractive to smaller firms, but underwriters tend to prefer higher deductibles because they save the insurer the expense of handling small claims. In some cases, an underwriter may require a higher deductible before agreeing to provide coverage for an insured with frequent small losses.

Apply Your Knowledge

The owners of a restaurant are insured under a BPP coverage form that covers their building for a $400,000 limit and their business personal property for a $200,000 limit. The policy has a $1,000 deductible. A covered cause of loss results in $100,000 worth of damage to the building and a $50,000 loss of business personal property. Assuming that no coinsurance penalty applies, apply the policy's limits and deductible to this loss to determine the amount payable.

Feedback: In accordance with the Deductible provision, the $1,000 deductible is subtracted from the building loss before applying the building limit: $100,000 – $1,000 = $99,000. Because this amount is less than the $400,000 building limit, the insurer will pay $99,000 for the building loss. Because the deductible applies only once per occurrence and has already been applied to the building loss, it does not apply to the business personal property loss. Moreover, the business personal property loss does not exceed the applicable $200,000 limit. Therefore, the insurer will pay the $50,000 business personal property loss in full. The insurer's total payment will be calculated as $99,000 + $50,000 = $149,000.

A business office is insured under a BPP coverage form that specifies a $2 million limit of insurance on the office building and a $900,000 limit of insurance on business personal property at the building's address. The policy has a $5,000 deductible. A covered cause of loss results in $2.2 million worth of damage to the building and a $300,000 loss of business personal property. Two shrubs are destroyed, resulting in a $500 loss fully covered by the BPP coverage form's Outdoor Property coverage extension. Assuming that no coinsurance penalty applies, apply the policy's limits and deductible to this loss to determine the amount payable.

Feedback: The $5,000 deductible is subtracted from the amount of the building loss before applying the building limit: $2,200,000 – $5,000 = $2,195,000. Because this amount exceeds the applicable limit of insurance, the insurer will pay the full $2 million limit of insurance for the building loss. The deductible applies only once per occurrence and has already been applied to the building loss; therefore, it does not apply to the business personal property loss. Moreover, because the business personal property loss does not exceed the applicable $900,000 limit of insurance, the insurer will pay the $300,000 business personal property loss in full. Finally, the $500 payment for the shrubs under the Outdoor Property coverage extension is payable in addition to the limits of insurance. Therefore, the insurer will pay a total of $2,300,500, calculated as $2,000,000 + $300,000 + $500.

SUMMARY

Three important aspects of commercial property loss exposures are the types of property that might be exposed to loss, damage, or destruction; the causes of loss that might result in property being lost, damaged, or destroyed; and the financial consequences of a property loss. Many of the basic property coverages an organization needs are commonly provided under a commercial property coverage part, which consists of commercial property declarations, one or more commercial property coverage forms, one or more causes of loss forms, Commercial Property Conditions, and any applicable endorsements.

The BPP can be used to insure buildings; business personal property of the named insured; and personal property of others in the named insured's care, custody, or control. With only minor exceptions, property is covered only while located on or within 100 feet of the building or structure or within 100 feet of the described premises, whichever distance is greater. The Property Not Covered section lists the various types of property that are not covered by the BPP. However, most types of property not covered can be insured by adding optional coverage endorsements to the BPP.

The BPP's additional coverages and coverage extensions cover loss exposures that would not otherwise be covered by the BPP's basic coverages. However, in some cases, the special limits that apply to these supplemental coverages are inadequate for many businesses. The limits stated in the form can often be increased by showing a higher limit in the declarations, adding an appropriate coverage endorsement, or buying another type of policy to supplement the BPP.

The perils covered in an ISO commercial property coverage part are specified in any of three causes of loss forms. The Causes of Loss—Basic Form and the Causes of Loss—Broad Form include nearly all of the same covered perils, but the Broad Form covers three additional perils, including collapse. This additional coverage makes the Broad Form the choice of most insureds over the Basic Form.

The most frequently selected of the three causes of loss forms, the Causes of Loss—Special Form is designed to cover any loss that would be covered by the Basic and Broad Forms. In addition, the Special Form provides coverages not found in the Basic and Broad Forms.

The Special Form offers several advantages to the insured, including coverage for certain causes of loss that are omitted or excluded under the Broad Form, coverage for losses the insured might not have anticipated, and the placement of the "burden of proof" on the insurer as opposed to the insured.

Under the ISO BPP, the most the insurer is obligated to pay for loss in any one occurrence is the applicable limit of insurance shown in the declarations. The insurer is not obligated to pay anything to the insured unless the loss exceeds the deductible; the limit of insurance then applies to the loss in excess of the deductible.

ASSIGNMENT NOTE

1. Includes copyrighted material of Insurance Services Office, Inc. with its permission. Copyright, Insurance Services Office, Inc., 2011.

Direct Your Learning

4

Commercial Property Insurance, Part II

Educational Objectives

After learning the content of this assignment, you should be able to:

- Explain how each of the Loss Conditions and Additional Conditions affects coverage under the Building and Personal Property Coverage Form.
- Explain how each of the following optional coverages described in the BPP modifies the basic coverage of the BPP:
    - Agreed Value
    - Inflation Guard
    - Replacement Cost
    - Extension of Replacement Cost to Personal Property of Others
- Summarize each of the Commercial Property Conditions.
- Explain how each of the conditions contained in the Common Policy Conditions affects coverage under a commercial property coverage part.
- Explain how each of these documents modifies the Building and Personal Property Coverage Form:
    - Ordinance or Law Coverage endorsement
    - Spoilage Coverage endorsement
    - Flood Coverage endorsement
    - Earthquake and Volcanic Eruption Coverage endorsement
    - Peak Season Limit of Insurance endorsement
    - Value Reporting Form
- Explain how and why each of the following coverage forms differs from the Building and Personal Property Coverage Form (BPP):
    - Builders Risk Coverage Form
    - Condominium Association Coverage Form

Outline

4

Educational Objectives, continued

- Condominium Commercial Unit-Owners Coverage Form

- Given a case, determine whether, and for what amount, a described loss would be covered by a commercial property coverage part that includes the Building and Personal Property Coverage Form and any of the three causes of loss forms.

Commercial Property Insurance, Part II

4

BPP LOSS CONDITIONS AND ADDITIONAL CONDITIONS

The Building and Personal Property Coverage Form, also referred to as the BPP, requires both the insurer and the insured to perform certain duties and follow certain procedures in connection with any claim made under the BPP.

The Loss Conditions section of the BPP stipulates the duties of the insured and the insurer after a loss has occurred and establishes procedures for adjusting claims. It also includes an explanation of methods for establishing the value of damaged property. The BPP's Additional Conditions deal with coinsurance and the interests of a mortgageholder (mortgagee).

Abandonment

The Abandonment condition prohibits the insured from abandoning damaged property to the insurer for repair or disposal. Although the Loss Payment condition permits the insurer, at its option, to take all or any part of damaged property at an agreed or appraised value, the Abandonment condition clarifies that making arrangements for the repair or disposal of covered property is the insured's responsibility, unless the insurer chooses to exercise its option under the Loss Payment condition.

Appraisal

The Appraisal condition establishes a method for the insurer and the insured to resolve disputes about the insured property's value or amount of loss. It does not apply to policy coverage disputes. If the insured and the insurer cannot agree on the value of the property or the amount of loss, either party may issue a written demand for an appraisal. When either party demands an appraisal, the appraisal process described in the BPP must be followed.

Duties in the Event of Loss or Damage

The BPP imposes several duties on the insured when a loss occurs. If the insured fails to perform any of them, the insurer may not have to pay for the loss. When a loss occurs, the insured must take several actions:

- Notify the police if the loss appears to have resulted from a violation of law, such as vandalism, arson, or theft.
- Give the insurer prompt notice of the loss, including a description of the property damaged. Prompt notice is generally held to mean as soon as feasible under the circumstances.
- Provide information as to how, when, and where the loss occurred.
- Take all reasonable steps to protect the property from further loss.
- At the insurer's request, furnish the insurer with inventories of the damaged and undamaged property and permit the insurer to inspect the property and records.
- Submit to examination under oath regarding any matter related to the loss.
- Cooperate with the insurer in the adjustment of the loss.
- Send a signed, sworn **proof of loss** to the insurer within sixty days after the insurer's request for one.

Proof of loss

A statement of facts about a loss for which the insured is making a claim.

Loss Payment

If loss or damage is covered, the insurer has four loss payment options:

- Pay the amount of the loss or damage
- Pay the cost of repairing or replacing the damaged property (does not include any increased cost attributable to enforcement of ordinances or laws regulating the construction, use, or repair of the property)
- Take over all or any part of the property and pay its agreed or appraised value
- Repair, rebuild, or replace the damaged property with other property of like kind and quality

Insurers seldom exercise the last option because it may cause the insurer to become a guarantor of the repaired or replaced property. If the repaired or replaced property proves to be unsatisfactory, the insurer might be required to make it satisfactory, even if the cost of doing so exceeds the applicable limit of insurance.

The Loss Payment clause also states that regardless of the value of the loss, the insurer will pay no more than the insured's financial interest in the covered property.

The insurer is required to notify the insured of its intent either to pay the claim or to deny payment within thirty days after receipt of a satisfactory proof of loss. The insurer may, for example, deny payment because of lack of coverage under the policy or failure of the insured to comply with one or more of the policy conditions. Actual payment is due within thirty days after the parties have agreed on the amount of loss or an appraisal has been completed.

Recovered Property

If either the insurer or the insured recovers property, such as stolen merchandise, for which the insurer has paid a loss, the party that makes the recovery is obligated to promptly notify the other party. The insured has the option of taking the recovered property and refunding the loss payment to the insurer. The insurer would then pay the cost of recovering the property and the cost, if any, of repairing it. If the insured elects not to take the recovered property, the insurer may dispose of the property as it sees fit.

Vacancy

If the building where a loss occurs has been vacant for more than sixty consecutive days before the loss occurs, the insurer will not pay if the loss is caused by vandalism, sprinkler leakage (unless the sprinkler system was protected against freezing), breakage of building glass, water damage, theft, or attempted theft. If any other covered peril causes the loss, loss payment will be reduced by 15 percent.

The vacancy conditions apply differently for a building's tenant than for its owner or general lessee. A general lessee is an entity that leases the entire building and subleases portions of the building to others. In the case of a tenant, a vacant "building" means the unit or suite rented or leased to the tenant. A building is vacant when it does not contain enough business personal property to conduct customary operations.

If the policy covers a building owner or general lessee, "building" means the entire building, and it is considered vacant unless at least 31 percent of its total square footage is rented to a lessee or sublessee and is used by that party to conduct its customary operations or by the building owner to conduct its customary operations. Buildings under construction or renovation are not considered to be vacant.

Because of the differing definitions for tenants and building owners, when the building does not meet the 31 percent standard, the loss payment to the building owner may be reduced or eliminated, but a tenant may be able to collect in full. Similarly, if the building meets the 31 percent standard, the building owner may have full coverage, but a tenant may be penalized when its premises do not contain enough business personal property to conduct the tenant's customary operations.

Valuation

Actual cash value (ACV)
Cost to replace property with new property of like kind and quality less depreciation.

The Valuation condition sets forth rules for establishing the value of insured property. Subject to the exceptions summarized in the exhibit, the insured property is valued at its **actual cash value (ACV)**. ACV valuation can be changed to replacement cost valuation by activating the BPP's optional coverages for replacement cost, which are printed in the BPP. See the exhibit "BPP Valuation Provisions."

BPP Valuation Provisions

Property Type	Valuation Basis
Property other than that specifically listed	Actual cash value
Building damage of $2,500 or less	Replacement cost except for awnings, floor coverings, appliances, and outdoor equipment or furniture
Stock sold but not delivered	Selling price less discounts and unincurred costs
Glass	Replacement cost for safety glazing if required by law
Improvements and betterments:	
(a) replaced by other than the insured	Not covered
(b) replaced by insured	Actual cash value
(c) not replaced	Percentage of cost based on remaining life of lease
Valuable papers and records (excluding electronic data)	Cost of blank media and cost of transcription or copying ($2,500 coverage extension to replace or restore lost information)
Electronic data	(Covered only under additional coverage with a $2,500 annual aggregate limit)
If replaced	Cost to replace or restore electronic data that have been destroyed or corrupted by a covered cause of loss
If not replaced	Cost to replace the media with blank media of substantially identical type

[DA02466]

Coinsurance

The Coinsurance condition requires the insured to carry insurance equal to at least a specified percentage of the covered property's ACV (or replacement cost, if that optional valuation approach is in effect). The coinsurance percentage is shown in the declarations. If the amount of insurance carried is equal to or greater than the required percentage, the insurer will pay covered losses in full (subject to any applicable deductible) up to the limit of insurance. If the amount of insurance carried is less than the required percentage, loss payments are reduced proportionately.

If the amount of insurance carried does not meet the coinsurance requirement, the amount the insurer will pay (subject always to the limit of insurance) is calculated by this formula:

$$\text{Loss payment} = \left(\frac{\text{Amount of insurance carried}}{\text{Amount of insurance required}} \times \text{Loss}\right) - \text{Deductible}$$

The amount of insurance required is the property's ACV (or replacement cost, if that option has been chosen) immediately before the loss occurred multiplied by the coinsurance percentage. The deductible is subtracted after the coinsurance penalty has been calculated. The example in the exhibit illustrates this calculation. See the exhibit "Coinsurance Example."

Coinsurance Example

ACV of covered building at time of loss	$200,000
Limit of insurance	$140,000
Coinsurance percentage	80%
Amount of loss	$40,000
Deductible	$500

Amount of insurance required = 0.80 × $200,000 = $160,000

$$\text{Loss payment} = \left(\frac{140{,}000}{160{,}000} \times \$40{,}000\right)$$

$$= (0.875 \times 40{,}000) - 500$$

$$= 35{,}000 - 500$$

$$= 34{,}500$$

If the amount of insurance carried had been $160,000 or more, the insurer would have paid $39,500, the amount of loss less the deductible.

[DA02468]

Mortgageholder

If a mortgageholder (such as a bank that has made a mortgage loan to the named insured) is shown in the declarations, the insurer is obligated to include the mortgageholder in any payment for loss to the mortgaged property. In practice, the loss payment check or draft is usually made payable jointly to the insured and all mortgageholders so that they can agree on the division of the payment. In most cases, the loss payment is used to repair or rebuild the mortgaged property, and the mortgages continue in force as before.

Any act or default of the insured does not impair the rights of the mortgageholder, provided the mortgageholder pays any premium due that the insured has not paid, submits a proof of loss if requested, and has notified the insurer of any change in ownership, occupancy, or substantial increase in risk of which the mortgageholder is aware. Consequently, the insurer is sometimes obligated to make a loss payment to the mortgageholder even though it has denied coverage, for example, to an insured who has committed arson. In such cases, the insurer, at its option, can take either of these actions:

- Take over the rights of the mortgageholder to the extent of such payment and collect the amount of payment from the insured
- Pay off the outstanding balance of the mortgage and take over all of the rights of the mortgageholder

If the insurer cancels the policy because the insured failed to pay the premium or if the insurer does not renew the policy for any reason, it must notify the mortgageholder ten days before the termination of coverage. If the insurer cancels the policy for any reason other than nonpayment of premium, it must give thirty days' advance notice to the mortgageholder. If the insurer fails to give the required notice to the mortgageholder, the policy remains in force for the protection of the mortgageholder even though it may not provide any protection for the insured.

BPP: OPTIONAL COVERAGES

The Optional Coverages section of the BPP contains provisions for four optional coverages:

- Agreed Value
- Inflation Guard
- Replacement Cost
- Extension of Replacement Cost to Personal Property of Others

The optional coverages apply only when an appropriate notation is made on the declarations page. Agreed Value, Inflation Guard, and Replacement Cost may be used for buildings only, personal property only, or both buildings and personal property.

Agreed Value

Agreed Value optional coverage
Optional coverage that suspends the Coinsurance condition if the insured carries the amount of insurance agreed to by the insurer and insured.

To activate the **Agreed Value optional coverage**, an amount is entered under the Agreed Value heading in the declarations for each category of property (building, personal property, or both) to which the option applies. This option enables the insured to remove the uncertainty as to whether the amount of insurance carried complies with the Coinsurance condition. With the option in force, the insurer and the insured have agreed in advance that the amount stated in the declarations—the agreed value—is adequate for coinsurance purposes. Because most losses are partial, insureds are often tempted to underinsure, knowing they will not suffer a coinsurance penalty when the agreed value option is in effect. Therefore, insurers underwrite agreed value carefully, requiring proof of value before providing agreed value coverage. At the very least, the insured ordinarily must submit a signed statement of values. Insurance Services Office, Inc. (ISO) Form CP 16 15, Statement of Values, can be used for this purpose.

The BPP Coinsurance condition does not apply to property insured under the agreed value option. However, it is replaced by a provision that, while not called coinsurance, is the practical equivalent of 100 percent coinsurance based on the agreed value. The agreed value option provides that if the limit of insurance equals or exceeds the agreed value stated in the declarations, losses will be paid in full up to the limit of insurance. If the limit of insurance is less than the agreed value, the amount of loss payment is calculated by this equation:

$$\text{Loss payment} = \left(\frac{\text{Limit of insurance}}{\text{Agreed value}} \times \text{Loss}\right) - \text{Deductible}$$

Coverage under this option extends until the agreed value expiration date shown on the declarations or the expiration date of the policy, whichever occurs first. If the coverage option is not renewed, the Coinsurance condition is reinstated.

Inflation Guard

Inflation Guard optional coverage is coverage for the effects of inflation that automatically increases the limit of insurance by the percentage of annual increase shown in the declarations. This percentage is applied on a pro rata basis, from the date the limit of insurance became effective to the date of the loss, before the loss payment is computed. The percentage of annual increase is shown separately for buildings and personal property.

Inflation Guard optional coverage

Coverage for the effects of inflation that automatically increases the limit of insurance by the percentage of annual increase shown in the declarations.

Replacement Cost

The **Replacement Cost optional coverage** replaces the phrase "actual cash value" with "replacement cost" in the BPP Valuation condition. As a result, the insurer is obligated to pay the cost to replace the damaged or destroyed property with new property of like kind and quality without any deduction for depreciation or obsolescence.

Replacement Cost optional coverage

Coverage for losses to most types of property on a replacement cost basis (with no deduction for depreciation or obsolescence) instead of on an actual cash value basis.

The insurer is not obligated to pay replacement cost until the property has been repaired or replaced, and then only if such repair or replacement is completed in a reasonable time. If repair or replacement is not completed in a reasonable time, the loss payment is based on the actual cash value (ACV) at the time of loss.

The insured may make a claim on the basis of ACV, with the difference between ACV and replacement cost to be paid upon completion of repair or reconstruction. The insurer must be notified within 180 days after the occurrence of loss that a claim will be made for replacement cost.

If the replacement cost option is activated, the Coinsurance condition continues to apply, but with one important difference. The amount of insurance required by the Coinsurance condition is calculated by multiplying replacement cost by the coinsurance percentage if the claim is made on a replacement cost basis. If the insured makes a claim on an ACV basis, coinsurance is also calculated on an ACV basis.

If the replacement cost option is selected, tenants' improvements and betterments are also valued at replacement cost if the tenant actually repairs or replaces them, at its own cost, as soon as reasonably possible after the loss.

The replacement cost option does not apply to property of others; contents of a residence; manuscripts; or works of art, antiques, or rare articles. It also does not apply to "stock" unless the declarations indicate that the replacement cost option includes stock. The BPP defines stock to mean merchandise, raw materials, goods in process, and finished goods.

Extension of Replacement Cost to Personal Property of Others

Insureds frequently lease photocopiers, computers, phone systems, and other equipment. These leases or agreements may make the insured responsible for the replacement cost of these items in the event they are damaged. To cover this loss exposure, insureds who have selected the replacement cost option may also elect to have the personal property of others valued at replacement cost. In such cases, the amount of the loss is calculated according to the written agreement between the insured and the owner of the property, but it cannot exceed the replacement cost of the property or the applicable limit of insurance.

COMMERCIAL PROPERTY CONDITIONS

Even if an insurance policy would otherwise cover an insured's loss, an insurer may deny coverage if the policy's conditions have not been met.

The Building and Personal Property Coverage Form and the other coverage forms that can be included in a commercial property coverage part each contain several conditions specific to those forms. In addition, the Commercial Property Conditions Form contains nine conditions that apply to any of the Commercial Property Coverage Forms to which they are attached. These nine conditions are titled as shown:

- Concealment, Misrepresentation, or Fraud
- Control of Property
- Insurance Under Two or More Coverages
- Legal Action Against Us
- Liberalization
- Transfer of Rights of Recovery Against Others to Us
- No Benefit to Bailee
- Other Insurance
- Policy Period, Coverage Territory

Concealment, Misrepresentation, or Fraud

The commercial property coverage part is void if the insured commits any fraudulent act related to the coverage or conceals or misrepresents any material fact pertaining to the coverage part, the covered property, or the insured's interest in the covered property. Concealment and misrepresentation are related but distinct acts:

- A misrepresentation is an active, deliberate misstatement of fact. For example, assume that John Doe, who has previously been convicted of arson, applies for fire insurance. If the application asks whether the applicant has ever been convicted of arson, and Doe responds that he has not, his answer is a misrepresentation.
- Concealment does not involve a misstatement of fact, but instead is an intentional failure to disclose a material fact. In the John Doe example, if the application does not ask about past convictions for arson, and Doe does not offer information about his conviction, some courts might consider Doe's action to be concealment.

Misrepresentation or concealment does not always void coverage: Only material misrepresentation or concealment voids coverage. A fact is material if knowledge of it would cause the insurer to charge a higher premium or decline to write the coverage. For example, an insured might state that his or her building is painted red when in fact it is painted yellow. This misstatement would have no bearing on the insurance and is therefore not material.

Control of Property

The Control of Property condition consists of two parts. The first part states that coverage under the policy will not be affected by acts or omissions of persons other than the insured if those persons are not acting under the direction or control of the insured. The second part of the condition states that violation of a policy condition at one location will not affect coverage at any other location.

To illustrate how this clause might apply, assume that a liquor store's policy is endorsed, requiring the store's burglar alarm system to be maintained in working order at all insured locations. Assume also that the insured leases these locations from other parties. The first part of the clause would protect the insured if the alarm system was disconnected by a building owner, provided that the owner was not under the insured's control.

The second part of the Control of Property condition would be important in this example if the liquor store's policy provides coverage at more than one location. In the absence of this part of the condition, the insured's failure to maintain the alarm system at one location might suspend coverage at all locations, even if the alarm systems are properly maintained at the other locations. Under the second part of the condition, only coverage at the location with the deficient alarm system would be affected.

Insurance Under Two or More Coverages

This policy condition is necessary because some property might be covered under two or more coverage parts that can be included in a single commercial package policy (such as commercial property and commercial inland marine). The Insurance Under Two or More Coverages condition prevents double recovery by the insured in such instances. The total payment under all applicable coverage parts is limited to the actual amount of the loss. Duplication, or "stacking," of the limits is avoided.

Legal Action Against Us

This condition spells out two requirements the insured must meet before legal action can be brought against the insurer ("Us") to enforce the policy. First, the insured must have complied with all conditions of the policy, including those in the coverage part and the Common Policy Conditions, as well as the applicable Loss Conditions. Second, the action must be brought within two years after the date on which the direct physical loss occurred.

Liberalization

If the insurer adopts any revision that would broaden coverage under the commercial property coverage part and for which there is no additional premium charge, the broader coverage is extended automatically to policies already in effect. This automatic coverage applies only if the broadening amendment is adopted during the policy term or within forty-five days before the effective date of the policy. Liberalization applies only to amendments that broaden coverage, not to those that restrict coverage.

Transfer of Rights of Recovery Against Others to Us

Subrogation is a term commonly used by insurance practitioners but not used in Insurance Services Office, Inc. (ISO) commercial property forms. If the insured takes any action that eliminates the insurer's right of recovery (other than one specifically authorized by this condition), the insurer may not be required to pay the loss. This condition specifically permits the insured to waive the right of recovery against any other party, provided the waiver is made in writing and before the loss occurs. A waiver of recovery may be given by the insured after loss only to another party insured under the same policy, a parent or subsidiary company, or a tenant of the insured property. Any other waiver given by the insured after loss has occurred may impair the insured's right to collect from the insurer for the loss.

Subrogation

The process by which an insurer can, after it has paid a loss under the policy, recover the amount paid from any party (other than the insured) who caused the loss or is otherwise legally liable for the loss.

Reality Check

Subrogation

The importance of subrogation to insurers and their insureds can be illustrated by this hypothetical case. The insured's building and its contents, valued at $600,000, were destroyed by a fire that was covered under the insured's commercial property insurance. While investigating the claim, the insurer's claims representative discovered that the fire was caused by faulty electrical wiring that had been installed in the building only a few months before the loss. After paying its insured's loss in full, minus the policy's $1,000 deductible, the insurer exercised its subrogation rights against the contractor that did the faulty work and was legally liable for the resulting damage. The contractor's liability insurer paid the entire $600,000 loss to the commercial property insurer. Out of this subrogation recovery, the commercial property insurer reimbursed its insured for the $1,000 deductible and recovered the entire amount that the insurer had paid its insured for the loss.

[DA07822]

No Benefit to Bailee

A bailee is a person or business organization that has temporary custody of the property of another. Examples are dry cleaners, television repair shops, laundries, and fur-storage firms. Bailees may become legally liable to bailors (the owners of the property) for damage to the property they hold. Bailees sometimes try to limit their liability with contractual provisions stating that the bailee is not liable for damage if the damage is recoverable under insurance carried by the bailor. The No Benefit to Bailee condition is intended to defeat such provisions in the bailment contract and to reinforce the insurer's right of subrogation against the bailee.

Other Insurance

An insured may have more than one policy covering a given loss. In keeping with the principle of indemnity, the Other Insurance condition limits the total recovery from all applicable insurance to an amount not in excess of the actual loss sustained.

If the other insurance is provided by an additional policy subject to the same plan, terms, and conditions, then each policy pays in relation to all applicable policies. If the other insurance is not subject to all of the conditions of the commercial property coverage part, then the policy subject to the commercial property coverage part is considered excess coverage and pays only the covered loss amount that exceeds what is due from the other policy.

Policy Period, Coverage Territory

This condition states that coverage begins on the effective date and ends on the expiration date shown in the declarations. The declarations state that the beginning and ending time is 12:01 a.m., determined by standard time at the insured's mailing address as shown in the declarations, even though some or all of the insured property may be located in a different time zone. The insured property is covered only while it is located within the United States (including its territories and possessions), Puerto Rico, or Canada.

COMMON POLICY CONDITIONS

The Insurance Services Office, Inc. (ISO) *Commercial Lines Manual (CLM)* requires that a common policy conditions form be attached to every Commercial Package Policy (CPP) or monoline policy. The Common Policy Conditions (IL 00 17) form contains six conditions, which apply to all coverage parts in the policy unless a particular coverage part states otherwise. This approach avoids the need to repeat these common conditions in each coverage part. These are the six conditions contained in the form:

- Cancellation
- Changes
- Examination of Books and Records
- Inspections and Surveys
- Premiums
- Transfer of Rights and Duties Under This Policy

Cancellation

The insured may cancel the policy at any time by mailing or delivering written notice of cancellation to the insurer. If two or more insureds are listed in the declarations, only the one listed first (called the first named insured) can request cancellation.

The insurer can cancel the policy by mailing or delivering written notice of cancellation to the first named insured. To provide time for the insured to obtain other insurance, the insurer is required to give advance notice of cancellation. The notice must be mailed or delivered to the insured at least ten days before the date of cancellation if the cancellation is for nonpayment of premium. The notice must be mailed at least thirty days before the date of cancellation for any other reason. If the cancellation results in a return premium, the insurer will send the refund to the first named insured.

In almost every state, the Cancellation condition is superseded by state law and an endorsement is added to the policy. The endorsement modifies the cancellation provisions to conform with the applicable law.

The state laws commonly address permissible reasons for cancellation and a longer advance notification period if the cancellation occurs for a reason other than nonpayment of premium.

Changes

The Changes condition states that the policy constitutes the entire contract between the insurer and the named insured, and that the policy can be changed only by a written endorsement issued by the insurer.

In practice, changes are often first made by verbal communication and confirmed afterwards in writing. In most states, such verbal changes are binding because an authorized agent of the insurer is viewed as having the power to waive the written endorsement requirement. Such changes may be made, with the insurer's consent, upon the request of the first named insured.

Only the first named insured has the authority to request policy changes, and the insurer is authorized to make changes upon the request of the first named insured without specific permission of any other insured.

Examination of Books and Records

The insurer reserves the right to examine and audit the insured's books and records related to the policy at any time during the policy period and for up to three years after the policy's termination. This provision is included because many commercial insurance policies are issued with estimated premiums. The final premium is determined after the policy expires, based on reported values of the insured property, the amount of the insured's sales or payroll, or some other variable premium base. The insured is required to report the final figures to the insurer, and the insurer may accept the insured's reports without verification.

However, if the insurer prefers to verify the reports by making an on-site inspection of the insured's books and records, the condition permits the insurer to do that. An insurer may also choose to exercise its rights under this condition in the process of investigating a claimed loss.

Inspections and Surveys

The insurer has the right, but not the obligation, to inspect the insured's premises and operations at any reasonable time during the policy period.

The inspections may be made by the insurer's own personnel or by another organization acting on the insurer's behalf. Such inspections are important in determining the insurability of the insured's property and operations, in setting proper insurance rates, and in making risk control recommendations.

The insurer may inform the insured of the results of such inspections and may recommend changes. However, it does not have a duty to do either. The condition makes it clear that the insurer does not make safety inspections, does not guarantee that conditions are safe or healthful, and does not guarantee that the insured is in compliance with safety or health regulations.

These disclaimer clauses have been included in the policy to protect the insurer against suits made by persons who allege that their injuries would not have occurred but for the insurer's failure to detect a hazardous condition or a violation of laws or regulations, and that the insurer is therefore responsible for the resulting damages, fines, or penalties assessed against the insured.

Premiums

The first named insured is responsible for paying the policy premium. If the insurer owes a return premium, it will make payment only to the first named insured.

Transfer of Rights and Duties Under This Policy

The insured cannot transfer any rights or duties under the policy to any other person or organization without the insurer's written consent. For example, if the insured sells a building covered by the policy, the insurance cannot be transferred to the new owner of the property without the insurer's written consent.

Such a transfer of insurance is generally referred to as assignment of the policy. The condition also provides specifically for the automatic transfer of coverage if an individual named insured dies. (An individual named insured is a person whose name is listed on the "Named Insured" line in the policy declarations.) In that case, the insured's rights and duties under the policy are automatically transferred to the insured's legal representatives or, if the insured's legal representatives have not yet been appointed, to any person having proper temporary custody of the insured property.

COMMERCIAL PROPERTY ENDORSEMENTS

The Building and Personal Property Coverage Form, also referred to as the BPP, can be modified by a variety of endorsements.

The BPP's endorsements are useful for these tasks:

- Providing coverage enhancements that some insureds may want but that others either do not believe they need or cannot afford
- Eliminating coverage for certain exposures, enabling underwriters to accept applications that they would otherwise decline
- Changing policy provisions to match the specific characteristics of certain industries or insureds
- Amending the policy to comply with state insurance regulations

The Insurance Services Office, Inc. (ISO) portfolio of commercial property forms contains more than 100 multistate forms and endorsements and an even greater number of state-specific endorsements. In addition, many insurers use independently developed endorsements or draft manuscript endorsements to accommodate special requirements. This selection of endorsements illustrates their diversity:

- Ordinance or Law Coverage Endorsement
- Spoilage Coverage Endorsement
- Flood Coverage Endorsement
- Earthquake and Volcanic Eruption Coverage Endorsement
- Peak Season Limit of Insurance Endorsement
- Value Reporting Form

Ordinance or Law Coverage

The Ordinance or Law Coverage endorsement provides three coverages for losses resulting from the enforcement of building ordinances or laws:

- Coverage A covers the value of the undamaged portion of a building that must be demolished. For example, an entire structure may have to be totally demolished if it is a frame building in an area where only fire-resistive construction is currently permitted. Demolishing the undamaged parts of the building changes what would have been a partial loss to a total loss.

- Coverage B covers the cost to demolish the undamaged portion of a building and remove its debris when demolition is required by the building code.
- Coverage C covers the increased cost to repair or rebuild the property resulting from the enforcement of a building, zoning, or land use law. Building codes may require that reconstruction of damaged property meet higher standards, such as heavier electrical service, elevators to upper floors, and fire-resistive stairwells. Coverage C pays the added expense for these improvements.

Coverages B and C can be provided under one blanket limit. The unendorsed commercial property coverage forms exclude these losses except for the additional coverage for increased cost of construction, which adds a small amount of coverage for the types of loss insured by Coverage C of the endorsement.

Spoilage Coverage

The Spoilage Coverage endorsement covers damage to perishable stock resulting from power outages; on-premises breakdown; or contamination of the insured's refrigerating, cooling, or humidity control equipment. The power outage must be caused by conditions beyond the insured's control. The coverage is not subject to coinsurance and cannot be provided under a blanket limit.

Flood Coverage

In the United States, losses from flooding accompany hurricanes, heavy rains, and melting snow. Collapsing dams can also cause floods. Any of these events can cause catastrophic losses. Because of the movable nature of the property they insure, auto physical damage insurance and many inland marine forms include flood as an insured peril. However, insurers are reluctant to write flood insurance on property at fixed locations, such as buildings and their contents. Therefore, all three of the causes of loss forms exclude flood.

Flood insurance for buildings and their contents is available, though, in two ways.

The National Flood Insurance Program (NFIP) is a federal government resource that provides insurance for properties located in eligible communities. The NFIP is administered by the Federal Insurance Administration, part of the Federal Emergency Management Agency (FEMA). For commercial properties, the maximum NFIP limit is $500,000 per building and $500,000 for the contents of a building. Although the demand for flood insurance is greatest from insureds in the most hazardous flood zones, NFIP provides coverage in all areas of eligible communities. National flood insurance is sold through private insurers and agents and is backed by the U.S. government.

The other source for flood insurance on buildings and contents is private insurers without federal participation. Most private insurers are unwilling to provide flood coverage for commercial properties located in zones that have more than a once-in-100-years flooding probability risk (shown in NFIP flood maps as Zone A). For properties located outside the high-hazard flood zones, private insurers often write flood coverage by endorsement to the insured's commercial property policy, subject to a substantial deductible (often $25,000 or more). The ISO commercial property program includes a Flood Coverage endorsement for use with the ISO commercial property coverage forms. In some cases, insurers will provide only excess flood coverage that applies in addition to the maximum limit available from NFIP.

Earthquake and Volcanic Eruption Coverage

Earthquake and volcanic eruption, like flooding, present potentially catastrophic loss exposures. Consequently, earthquake insurance is expensive and limited in availability in areas with a high probability of severe earthquake damage, principally in parts of California and locations near the New Madrid Fault, which extends into portions of Arkansas, Illinois, Indiana, Kentucky, Mississippi, Missouri, and Tennessee.

In other areas, earthquake insurance is generally available but is often overlooked. Overlooking the earthquake exposure can be a costly mistake. In the past 100 years, earthquakes have occurred in thirty-nine of the fifty states.[1] One of the most severe earthquakes in U.S. history was centered in Charleston, South Carolina.

Insurers can use either of two ISO endorsements to add earthquake and volcanic eruption as covered perils under a commercial property coverage part. Independently filed earthquake endorsements are also available from some insurers. The two ISO endorsements are these:

- Earthquake and Volcanic Eruption Endorsement
- Earthquake and Volcanic Eruption Endorsement (Sub-Limit Form)

Both endorsements extend commercial property coverage to include earthquake and volcanic eruption. The first endorsement includes coverage for the full policy limit and contains a coinsurance condition. The second endorsement includes earthquake and volcanic eruption coverage subject to a sublimit that is lower than the regular policy limit, and it does not contain a coinsurance condition.

Peak Season Limit of Insurance Endorsement

Many organizations experience wide fluctuations (increases and decreases) in personal property values, especially the value of goods held for sale. The BPP does not provide a totally satisfactory method to cover fluctuating values. If the insured organization carries high enough limits to cover the maximum value, it is overinsured for much of the year and pays too much in premiums. If it carries less than the maximum value, it is underinsured during its peak inventory period. Continually amending the amount of insurance to correspond to changes in value would be an administrative burden on the insured and the insurer.

The Peak Season Limit of Insurance endorsement covers the fluctuating values of business personal property by providing differing amounts of insurance for certain time frames during the policy period. For example, a toy store may have a policy providing $100,000 of coverage on personal property with a peak season endorsement increasing coverage to $200,000 from October 1 to December 31, when the store expects to have higher inventory values.

Using this endorsement would have exactly the same effect as endorsing the policy on October 1 to increase the coverage and endorsing it again on December 31 to reduce the coverage. The peak season endorsement eliminates the need for these extra transactions and the possibility that they may be overlooked.

The peak season endorsement is usually attached when the policy is issued (although it may be added midterm), and a pro rata premium is charged for the period during which the limit is increased.

Value Reporting Form

Unlike the peak season endorsement, which actually modifies the limit of insurance, the Value Reporting Form covers the fluctuating values of business personal property by providing insurance for the insured's maximum expected values and requiring the insured to periodically report property values to the insurer. The insurer calculates the final policy premium based on the reported values instead of the limit of insurance. In this way, the insured has an adequate limit to cover maximum personal property values but pays a premium based on the reported property values.

Under the Value Reporting Form, the insured is required to report the value of the insured business personal property to the insurer periodically during the policy period. The frequency of reporting is indicated by a symbol entered in the declarations. For example, MR, the most common choice, calls for reporting values on hand on the last day of the month, with the report due within thirty days after the end of the month. Daily, weekly, quarterly, and annual periods can also be selected as a basis for reports by entering other codes in the declarations.

As long as the insured reports values accurately and on time, the insurer will pay the full amount of any loss that occurs (but not more than the policy limit), even if the values on hand at the time of the loss are greater than those last reported to the insurer.

To encourage accurate and timely reports, the Value Reporting Form specifies penalties for failure to comply with its reporting requirements. Separate rules

Reality Check

Value Reporting Form

A wholesaler insures its business personal property under a Value Reporting Form subject to a limit of $1 million for its single warehouse location. Its last monthly report of values was made on time and accurately showed the full value of business personal property—$800,000—as of the date of the report. Three weeks later, a fire destroyed the warehouse and its contents. Even though the value of covered personal property had increased to $900,000 since the last report, the loss is covered in full (minus the deductible).

[DA07816]

apply when no report is made (loss payment is reduced to 75 percent of the otherwise collectible loss), one or more reports are past due after the initial report (loss payment is limited to the last reported values), and reports are inaccurate (the loss is reduced by the proportion that the value reported bears to the correct value).

The insured pays an advance premium at the inception of the policy. The advance premium is based on 75 percent of the limit of insurance. The final premium is determined after the policy anniversary, based on the reported values. The premium is based on the values reported, even if the values reported exceed the policy limit. However, the insurer is not obligated to pay more than the policy limit in the event of loss, even if the reported values are higher. Thus, care should be taken to set the limit high enough to cover any possible increase in value.

Although the Value Reporting Form can more effectively match coverage to exposures than the Peak Season Limit of Insurance endorsement, many smaller firms do not have accounting systems of sufficient sophistication to generate the required reports accurately and on time. Furthermore, many insurers would decline to issue a Value Reporting Form for a smaller insured because the premium may not be large enough to warrant the added expense of processing the reports and calculating the final premium.

DIFFERENCES BETWEEN THE BPP AND OTHER COMMERCIAL PROPERTY COVERAGE FORMS

In addition to the Building and Personal Property Coverage Form (BPP), several other commercial property forms are available for insuring special exposures. Commercial property coverage forms can be any of several commercial property forms containing an insuring agreement and related provisions.

The BPP is intended to meet the needs of most organizations that wish to insure their buildings and/or business personal property. More specialized commercial property coverage forms for insuring buildings and/or business personal property are available for those that need them. Three such Insurance Services Office, Inc. (ISO) forms are the Builders Risk Coverage Form, the Condominium Association Coverage Form, and the Condominium Commercial Unit-Owners Coverage Form.

Builders Risk Coverage Form

The BPP provides some protection for new buildings while they are under construction. However, that coverage is limited and is intended only as incidental protection. Buildings under construction are insured more appropriately under the **Builders Risk Coverage Form**. This section describes the ISO Builders Risk Coverage Form in terms of its notable differences from the BPP. Builders risk coverage is also available in inland marine forms.

Builders Risk Coverage Form

A form that covers buildings in the course of construction, including additions or alterations to existing buildings.

Eligible Property and Insureds

The builders risk form may be used to insure any building in the course of construction, including buildings (such as farm buildings and dwellings) that will not be eligible for coverage under the BPP when construction is completed. By using special endorsements, the builders risk form can also be adapted for covering additions or alterations to existing buildings. The parties that can be insured by a builders risk policy include the building owner and the building contractor.

Covered Property

The property covered by the builders risk form is the building described in the declarations while in the course of construction, including these:

- Foundations
- Fixtures and machinery
- Equipment that is used in servicing the building
- Temporary structures built or assembled on site such as scaffolding or concrete forms (if not covered by other insurance)
- Property intended to become part of the building—such as lumber, uninstalled windows, doors, sinks, and furnaces—while located within 100 feet of the described premises

The builders risk form does not cover land or water. Also not covered (when located outside the buildings) are lawns, trees, shrubs, plants, radio or television antennas, satellite dishes, and signs not attached to the building.

Coverage Extensions

The builders risk form contains all of the additional coverages found in the BPP except for increased cost of construction, but the builders risk form contains only two coverage extensions. The first builders risk coverage extension provides up to $5,000 at each covered location for damage to building materials or supplies owned by others, such as a plumbing or roofing subcontractor. In order to be covered, the materials must be in the insured's care, custody, or control; must be located in or on the building or within 100 feet of its premises; and must be intended to become a permanent part of the building. The $5,000 limit can be increased by showing a higher limit in the declarations.

The second extension covers loss of or damage to sod, trees, shrubs, and plants outside of buildings on the described premises, but only if the loss or damage is caused by fire, lightning, explosion, riot, civil commotion, or aircraft. The most the insurer will pay under the extension is $1,000 per occurrence, subject to a sublimit of $250 for any one tree, shrub, or plant.

The builders risk form does not contain the BPP coverage extension for nonowned detached trailers. This omission can be important because a leased trailer is frequently used as a construction office or storage facility at a job site.

Causes of Loss

Like the BPP, the builders risk form must be combined with a basic, broad, or special causes of loss form. These are some especially important points about the causes of loss forms, as they apply to builders risks:

- Collapse During Construction—The broad and special causes of loss forms cover collapse of a building caused by certain named perils, including defective materials or faulty construction, if the collapse occurs during construction. However, the builders risk form specifically excludes collapse occurring during construction. For an additional premium, collapse coverage can be added to a builders risk policy by using the Builders Risk—Collapse During Construction endorsement.
- Theft of Building Materials—Uninstalled building materials at construction sites are a target for thieves. Thus, owners and contractors usually want theft coverage, but insurers are understandably cautious in providing it.

The basic and broad causes of loss forms do not cover theft. Although the Special Form covers theft, it excludes theft of building materials and supplies not attached as part of the building or structure. Thus, even with the Special Form, the builders risk form does not cover theft of uninstalled building materials. However, the excluded exposure can be insured by adding an optional endorsement, titled Builders Risk—Theft of Building Materials, Fixtures, Machinery, Equipment. This approach allows the insurer to provide coverage for an additional premium.

Need for Adequate Insurance

Builders risk insurance is usually written on a completed-value basis, which means that the amount of insurance equals the expected value of the completed building. Because the insured value increases during construction from zero to the completed value, the regular building insurance rate is decreased, reflecting the reduced exposure during most of the policy term. To be sure that the insured is complying with the completed-value requirement, the builders risk form contains a condition titled Need for Adequate Insurance, which applies instead of the standard coinsurance condition.

The Need for Adequate Insurance condition requires the insured to carry insurance in an amount that is at least equal to the actual cash value of the building on completion. If the insured fails to carry the required amount of insurance, the insured cannot recover the full amount of the loss. The amount of loss payable is calculated by the following formula:

$$\text{Loss payment} = \left(\frac{\text{Limit of insurance}}{\text{Actual cash value of building on completion}}\right) \times \text{Loss} - \text{Deductible}$$

Builders risk insurance can also be provided on a reporting basis. When this approach is used, policy premiums are determined on the basis of periodic reports of value rather than on an estimate of the completed value. The reporting approach is seldom used because of the difficulty of making timely and accurate reports of value.

When Coverage Ceases

Coverage under the builders risk form terminates upon the earliest of these dates:

- The expiration date shown in the declarations
- The date of cancellation
- The date when the property is accepted by the purchaser
- When the insured's interest in the property ceases
- When the insured abandons construction with no intention to complete it
- Unless the insurer indicates otherwise in writing, ninety days after the construction is completed or sixty days after the building is occupied in whole or in part or is put to its intended use

Other Provisions

In addition to these provisions, the builders risk form includes provisions relating to the limits of insurance, deductible, abandonment, appraisal, duties in the event of loss or damage, loss payment, recovered property, and mortgageholders. These provisions are essentially the same as the corresponding clauses in the BPP. The Valuation condition is much briefer than that included in the BPP, merely indicating that the covered property will be valued at actual cash value at the time of loss. Little difference exists between actual cash value and replacement cost for most buildings under construction because they usually experience little, if any, depreciation before completion.

Condominium Coverage Forms

Condominiums involve the separate ownership of individual units in a multiple-unit building or buildings. In a condominium, each unit's owner owns that particular condominium unit and has an undivided interest with all other unit owners in the jointly owned "common elements" of the building. A condominium association is formed by unit owners to manage the condominium and to own the common elements.

The precise division between the condominium unit (owned by the unit owner) and the common elements (owned by the association) depends on the terms of the particular condominium association agreement, also referred to as the master deed, declarations, or bylaws. State laws can also specify the division of property ownership and insurance obligations.

Whenever insurance is arranged for a condominium unit owner or association, the pertinent documents and laws must be reviewed carefully in order to ascertain insurance needs.

The unique legal characteristics of condominiums make it necessary to use specialized forms for insuring the respective interests of condominium associations and unit owners. There are two commercial property condominium forms: one for condominium associations and another for owners of commercial condominium units.

Two other forms of community ownership, the cooperative corporation and the planned unit development (also called a "homeowners association"), are in many respects similar to condominiums. In each case there is joint ownership of some property. Insurers often use condominium forms to insure cooperative corporations and planned unit developments.

Condominium Association Coverage Form

Like the BPP, the ISO **Condominium Association Coverage Form**, which covers buildings and personal property of condominium associations, provides coverage for property in three categories:

- Building
- Business personal property of the named insured (which is the association of unit owners)
- Personal property of others

This discussion emphasizes the fundamental differences between the condominium association form and the BPP. These differences, which principally

Condominium Association Coverage Form
Form that covers buildings and business personal property of condominium associations.

concern the building and business personal property items, stem from the unique nature of condominium property ownership.

The building coverage of the condominium association form closely resembles the building coverage of the BPP. However, a significant difference relates to these types of property contained within individual units of a condominium building:

- Fixtures, improvements, and alterations
- Appliances, including (but not limited to) those used for refrigerating, ventilating, cooking, dishwashing, laundering, or housekeeping

Under both ISO and American Association of Insurance Services (AAIS) condominium forms, building coverage applies to the above items only if the condominium association agreement requires the association to insure them. Otherwise, such property items are not included in the association's building coverage. Some independently developed condominium association policies cover building additions regardless of whether the association is required to insure them. The unit owner's coverage covers what the association's coverage does not, and vice versa.

Many condominiums have community clubhouses, health clubs, and so forth. The furnishings and equipment of these facilities can be covered as business personal property. As in the case of building coverage, the condominium association form clarifies the division between personal property insured by the association and that insured by individual unit owners:

- Business personal property is covered if it is owned by the association or if it is indivisibly owned by all unit owners.
- Business personal property is not covered if it is owned only by a unit owner.

Most of the conditions of the condominium association form are the same as those of the BPP. Some of the more notable variations from the BPP are described subsequently.

The condominium association form provides primary coverage for any loss covered by both that form and the condominium commercial unit owners form. The unit owners form provides excess coverage in such situations.

The condominium association form also includes a provision waiving the insurer's right to recover from a unit owner for any loss the insurer has paid to the condominium association. For example, suppose the condominium building burned down because of a fire that resulted from a unit owner's negligence. In that case, the insurer, after paying the loss, would not be able to exercise its usual right to recover damages from the unit owner.

If the division of ownership between the association and the unit owners (as determined by the condominium association agreement or by state law) differs from the division indicated in the policy form, an endorsement can be used to adapt the policy to meet such requirements. Standard endorsements are provided by ISO to comply with most applicable state laws, but manuscript endorsements (drawn up specifically for a given policy) may be needed to comply with some condominium association agreements.

Condominium Commercial Unit-Owners Coverage Form

Commercial condominium units are used for offices, stores, and other business activities. The ISO **Condominium Commercial Unit-Owners Coverage Form** is used for insuring owners of such commercial condominium units only. Owners of residential condominium units should purchase coverage under homeowners policies designed for unit owners.

The unit-owners form covers only "your business personal property" and personal property of others. These coverages are basically the same as in the BPP. Fixtures, improvements, and alterations that are part of the building and owned by the unit owner are included in the definition of "your business personal property" in the unit-owners form.

Two optional coverages that are often needed by condominium unit owners are available in a single endorsement that can be attached to the unit-owners coverage form.

One of these optional coverages is **loss assessment coverage**. Typically, a condominium association has the right to assess all unit owners for uninsured losses that the association incurs. These uninsured losses can result, for example, from a large deductible on the association's property policy.

The other optional coverage is **miscellaneous real property coverage**. An example of property insurable under this endorsement is a storage or garage building owned by the association but used solely by the unit owner.

Insurance for Highly Protected Risks

Insurance for highly protected risks originated with New England textile manufacturers who, in the early 1830s, formed mutual insurance companies, known as factory mutuals, to obtain lower insurance rates for their mills. They believed that lower rates were justified by the heavy-timber construction of their mills and the extensive fire protection equipment that they had installed.

Highly proctected risks (HPR) coverages are broader in many respects than standard forms. HPR rates are often considerably lower than most insurers' standard commercial property rates. Not every insured can qualify for HPR insurance, and not every insurer is able to provide it. The insured must have a proactive management that is determined to control the risk of property loss. The insurer must be able to provide the specialized engineering services needed to implement a highly effective loss prevention plan for the insured's property. Most HPR insurance is written by a few large insurers.

Condominium Commercial Unit-Owners Coverage Form
Form that covers business personal property and building property exposures of commercial (nonresidential) condominium units.

Loss assessment coverage
Coverage for a commercial condominium unit-owner's share of any assessment made by the association against all unit owners because of physical loss to condominium property caused by a covered cause of loss.

Miscellaneous real property coverage
Coverage for real property (such as a storage shed or garage building) that pertains only to the named insured's condominium unit or real property that the named insured has a duty to insure according to the condominium association agreement.

Insurance for highly protected risks
Property insurance that covers large property risks with superior loss protection characteristics; has broader coverage than most commercial property policies and usually a lower premium rate.

DETERMINING WHETHER THE BPP COVERS A LOSS

Knowing how to apply the commercial property coverage provided by the Insurance Services Office, Inc. (ISO) Building and Personal Property Coverage Form, also referred to as the BPP, to the facts of a case is an important skill. This case study will help you make the transition from knowing policy language to applying policy language to losses to determine whether coverage applies. As you progress through the case study, you can check your understanding of the coverage provided by answering the Knowledge to Action questions.

Case Facts

Jim owns a building in a beach town on the New Jersey coast. During the tourist season, the building had been occupied by a surfing-supply retailer to whom Jim rented the premises. At the end of the tourist season, on September 15, 20X1, the retailer vacated the building and relocated to Florida, leaving it empty. Jim was unable to find a new tenant, so the building remained vacant.

A tropical storm struck just north of the New Jersey beach town on October 25, 20X1. The storm's precipitation did not reach Jim's area, but strong wind associated with the storm ripped shingles from the building's roof and shattered several windows with flying debris. A storm surge from the ocean caused salt water to enter Jim's building, causing extensive damage to its interior. See the exhibit "Damage Estimates."

Damage Estimates

Item	Description	Replacement Cost	Actual Cash Value
Wind damage to building	Destroyed roof shingles and broken windows	$20,000	$12,000
Water damage to building	Damage to walls, floors, and fixtures	$95,000	$76,000
Water damage to maintenance equipment	Total loss to a lawnmower, an electric hedge trimmer, and a vacuum cleaner stored on the first floor	$750	$375
Total		$115,750	$88,375

[DA07841]

Jim has a commercial package policy (CPP) that includes a BPP and a Causes of Loss—Broad Form covering the building. The CPP's Common Policy Declarations form indicates that the policy's coverage period is one year. The policy does not contain any endorsements.

Given the facts presented in the case, will the claim for damage related to the storm be covered? If so, what amount will the insurer pay for the claim? When answering the questions in this case-based activity, consider only the information provided as part of this case.

Necessary Reference Materials

To determine whether the BPP provides coverage for the losses associated with the storm, you need to consult the relevant portions of the declarations page and any policy provisions that apply to the loss.

Overview of Steps

When examining policy forms to determine whether coverage applies to a loss, you can apply the four steps of the DICE method. Next, you can determine the amount payable for the loss under the applicable policy or policies. Doing this involves applying the limit(s) of insurance and any deductibles that apply. It also involves determining whether more than one policy provides coverage for the same loss.

Determination of Coverage

Determining whether the BPP applies to this loss involves analyzing the relevant portions of the policy and determining whether any information found at each step in the DICE process precludes coverage at the time of the loss. You should also examine other categories of policy provisions, such as the insured's duties, general provisions, endorsements (if applicable), and terms defined in the policy in relation to the declarations, insuring agreement, conditions, and exclusions.

DICE Analysis Step 1: Declarations

The first DICE step is to review the declarations page. In this case, the review will determine whether Jim and the building were covered by the BPP when the storm struck. See the exhibit "Excerpt of Declarations Page."

Knowledge to Action

Action Task: Review the relevant portion of the declarations in Jim's policy.

According to your analysis of the excerpt of the declarations page, is coverage applicable for Jim and his building during the coverage period?

Feedback: The declarations page confirms Jim as the insured for the premises damaged. The loss occurred during the policy period.

Excerpt of Declarations Page

POLICY NO. SP 0001 **EFFECTIVE DATE** 07 / 01 / 20X1 ☐ **"X" If Supplemental Declarations Is Attached**

NAMED INSURED

Jim Smith

DESCRIPTION OF PREMISES

Prem. No.	Bldg. No.	Location, Construction And Occupancy
001	001	100 Beach View Blvd., Jersey Shore Town, NJ 08000 Joisted Masonry Retail Store

COVERAGES PROVIDED **Insurance At The Described Premises Applies Only For Coverages For Which A Limit Of Insurance Is Shown**

Prem. No.	Bldg. No.	Coverage	Limit Of Insurance	Covered Causes Of Loss	Coinsurance*	Rates
001	001	Building	$1,000,000	Broad	80%	

***If Extra Expense Coverage, Limits On Loss Payment**

OPTIONAL COVERAGES **Applicable Only When Entries Are Made In The Schedule Below**

Prem.	Bldg.	Agreed Value			Replacement Cost (X)		
No.	No.	Expiration Date	Cov.	Amount	Building	Pers. Prop.	Including "Stock"
001	001				X		

Inflation Guard (%)		*Monthly Limit Of Indemnity (Fraction)	Maximum Period Of Indemnity (X)	*Extended Period Of Indemnity (Days)
Bldg.	Pers. Prop.			

***Applies to Business Income Only**

MORTGAGEHOLDERS

Prem. No.	Bldg. No.	Mortgageholder Name And Mailing Address

DEDUCTIBLE

$500. Exceptions:

[DA07842]

DICE Analysis Step 2: Insuring Agreement

The second DICE step is to review the insuring agreement to determine whether it is applicable to the described loss. Specifically, it must be determined whether each item of damaged property qualifies as Covered Property under the Building description. For the purposes of this case, assume that none of the property damaged is Property Not Covered. Also assume that none of the additional coverages or coverage extensions apply.

An analysis of whether the insuring agreement is applicable to a loss requires not only determining whether the damaged property qualifies as Covered Property, but also whether the damage was caused by a Covered Cause of Loss and whether any exclusions apply to coverage. These two items will be considered in Step 4. The relevant excerpt of the BPP insuring agreement indicates the types of Building property that qualify as covered property:

> 1. Covered Property
>
> Covered Property, as used in this Coverage Part, means the type of property described in this section, A.1., and limited in A.2., Property Not Covered, if a Limit Of Insurance is shown in the Declarations for that type of property.
>
> a. Building, meaning the building or structure described in the Declarations, including:
>
> (1) Completed additions;
>
> (2) Fixtures, including outdoor fixtures;
>
> (3) Permanently installed:
>
> (a) Machinery and
>
> (b) Equipment;
>
> (4) Personal property owned by you that is used to maintain or service the building or structure or its premises, including:
>
> (a) Fire extinguishing equipment;
>
> (b) Outdoor furniture;
>
> (c) Floor coverings; and
>
> (d) Appliances used for refrigerating, ventilating, cooking, dishwashing or laundering;

Knowledge to Action

Action Task: Review the relevant portions of the BPP insuring agreement.

According to your analysis of the excerpt of the insuring agreement, does the definition of Covered Property in Jim's BPP include the damaged walls, floors, and fixtures; the destroyed roof shingles; and the broken windows?

Feedback: Yes, the definition of Covered Property in Jim's BPP includes all of these items because the walls, floors, roof shingles, and windows are parts of the building described in the declarations, and the Building description specifically includes fixtures.

According to your analysis of the excerpt of the insuring agreement, does the definition of Covered Property in Jim's BPP include the water-damaged maintenance equipment?

Feedback: Yes, the definition of Covered Property in Jim's BPP includes the water-damaged maintenance equipment because the Building definition includes "personal property owned by you that is used to maintain or service the building or structure or its premises."

DICE Analysis Step 3: Conditions

The third DICE step is to review the policy conditions to determine whether they affect coverage at the time of the loss. Jim protected the covered property from further loss by covering the damaged roof with a tarp, sent the insurer the required proof of loss, and fulfilled the other duties required of him after a loss. However, it is necessary to consider that Jim's building was vacant between September 15, 20X1, and October 25, 20X1, possibly making the Vacancy condition applicable to this loss. The Coinsurance condition also needs to be considered. If Jim does not have an amount of insurance that meets the Coinsurance requirement, a Coinsurance penalty will apply.

Knowledge to Action

Action Task: According to your analysis of the Vacancy condition, does it apply in this case? If so, how will it affect coverage?

Feedback: Part a. (Description Of Terms) of the Vacancy condition defines a building owned by the insured as being vacant "unless at least 31% of its total square footage is: (i) Rented to a lessee or sub-lessee and used by the lessee or sub-lessee to conduct its customary operations; and/or (ii) Used by the building owner to conduct customary operations." Because none of the building was being used by a lessee or sub-lessee or by Jim to conduct customary operations at the time of the loss, the building meets the definition of being vacant.

It is therefore necessary to consider Part b. (Vacancy Provisions) of the condition, which states that if "the building where loss or damage occurs has been vacant for more than 60 consecutive days before that loss or damage occurs," the insurer will not pay anything for loss caused by certain listed causes of loss and will reduce by 15 percent the amount that would otherwise be payable for loss caused by any other covered cause of loss.

Because Jim's building had been vacant for less than sixty days at the time of loss, neither the full exclusion of coverage nor the 15 percent reduction of loss payment applies. However, if another loss were to occur more than sixty days after the building became vacant, either of those consequences could apply, depending on the cause of the loss. To protect against that possibility in a future loss, Jim's insurance agent can ask the insurer to add (for an additional premium) a Vacancy Permit endorsement that suspends the Vacancy condition during a specified period while Jim's building is vacant.

Action Task: According to your analysis of the Coinsurance condition in relation to the facts in Jim's loss, does the amount of insurance carried by Jim satisfy the Coinsurance condition?

Feedback: The Coinsurance condition states that the insurer "will not pay the full amount of any loss if the value of Covered Property at the time of loss times the Coinsurance percentage shown for it in the declarations is greater than the Limit of Insurance for the property." The insurer determines that the value of Covered Property at the time of loss was $1,200,000. The declarations in Jim's policy show the Coinsurance percentage as 80 percent and the limit of insurance for the building as $1,000,000. Eighty percent of the value of the Covered Property ($1,200,000) at the time of loss is $960,000, which is less than the $1,000,000 limit of insurance. Therefore, the limit satisfies the Coinsurance condition and no coinsurance penalty applies.

DICE Analysis Step 4: Exclusions

The fourth DICE step is to determine whether the causes of loss are covered and, if so, if any exclusions affect coverage. In this case, it must be determined whether the windstorm that damaged the shingles and the windows and the water from the storm surge that damaged the building's interior are Covered Causes of Loss. The Causes of Loss—Broad Form indicates that windstorm is a Covered Cause of Loss. However, the Water exclusion may preclude coverage for losses related to the storm surge:

> g. Water
>
> (1) Flood, surface water, waves (including tidal wave and tsunami), tides, tidal water, overflow of any body of water, or spray from any of these, all whether or not driven by wind (including storm surge);
>
> (2) Mudslide or mudflow;
>
> (3) Water that backs up or overflows or is otherwise discharged from a sewer, drain, sump, sump pump or related equipment;
>
> (4) Water under the ground surface pressing on, or flowing or seeping through:
>
> (a) Foundations, walls, floors or paved surfaces;
>
> (b) Basements, whether paved or not; or
>
> (c) Doors, windows or other openings; or
>
> (5) Waterborne material carried or otherwise moved by any of the water referred to in Paragraph (1), (3) or (4), or material carried or otherwise moved by mudslide or mudflow.
>
> This exclusion applies regardless of whether any of the above, in Paragraphs (1) through (5), is caused by an act of nature or is otherwise caused. An example of a situation to which this exclusion applies is the situation where a dam, levee, seawall or other boundary or containment system fails in whole or in part, for any reason, to contain the water.
>
> But if any of the above, in Paragraphs (1) through (5), results in fire, explosion or sprinkler leakage, we will pay for the loss or damage caused by that fire, explosion or sprinkler leakage (if sprinkler leakage is a Covered Cause of Loss).

Knowledge to Action

Action Task: Refer to the Causes of Loss—Broad Form Water exclusion.

According to your analysis of the Water exclusion, is the water damage to the building from the storm surge covered?

Feedback: Because the Water exclusion specifies that flood and waves, "whether or not driven by wind," are not Covered Causes of Loss, the Water exclusion eliminates coverage for the water damage caused by the storm surge, even though it resulted from the windstorm. (If Jim had purchased a flood endorsement to the BPP or other applicable flood coverage, this damage would have been covered elsewhere.)

Because Jim's building did not require demolition of undamaged portions of the structure or entail increased construction costs, the Ordinance or Law exclusion is not applicable in this case.

Determination of Amount Payable

Now that you have completed the DICE analysis, you can determine the amount payable. Doing this involves applying the limit(s) of insurance available to pay for the loss and any applicable deductibles and conditions. In this case, the DICE analysis has revealed that the wind damage to the building will be covered under the policy but that the water damage to the building and the maintenance equipment will not be covered.

In this case, the first step in calculating the amount payable is to determine whether the policy's coverage applies on a replacement cost or an actual cash value basis. A review of the BPP's Valuation condition reveals that none of the alternative valuation methods described in that condition (such as selling price valuation for "stock") apply to Jim's loss.

Knowledge to Action

Action Task: Review the relevant portion of the commercial property declarations in Jim's policy to determine the valuation method applicable to Jim's building.

According to your analysis of the declarations page, does Jim's coverage apply on a replacement cost or an actual cash value basis?

Feedback: Jim's coverage applies on a replacement cost basis, as indicated by the check mark below Replacement Cost in the Optional Coverages section of the declarations page.

The next step in the calculation is to determine how the BPP's limit of insurance and deductible affect the amount payable for the covered losses.

Knowledge to Action

Action Task: Review the relevant portion of the declarations page in Jim's policy to determine the policy limit and deductible that will be used to calculate the amount payable.

According to your analysis of the declarations page, what are the relevant policy limits and deductible that will be used to calculate coverage?

Feedback: The declarations page shows a $1,000,000 limit of insurance for the covered Building and a $500 deductible.

Action Task: Review the Damage Estimate exhibit to determine the amount claimed for each of the three categories of damaged items.

Given the information you have developed thus far, what is the amount payable for each of the three categories of damaged items?

Feedback: The amount payable for the wind damage to the building, which is a Covered Cause of Loss to Covered Property, is $20,000, the full amount claimed. Jim will not recover for the water damage to the first floor and to the maintenance equipment, both of which are excluded despite being Covered Property because they were not caused by a Covered Cause of Loss. Therefore, before accounting for any applicable deductible, the total amount payable is $20,000.

Action Task: Review the policy's deductible as shown on the commercial property declarations page. Accounting for the deductible, what is the total amount payable?

Feedback: The $500 deductible is subtracted from the amount payable, thus making the new amount payable $19,500.

The exhibit illustrates how the amount payable is determined. See the exhibit "Determination of Amount Payable."

Determination of Amount Payable

Item	Description	Claimed	Coverage Limits/ Issues	Amount Payable
Wind damage to building	Destroyed roof shingles and broken windows	$20,000	Within coverage limit	$20,000
Water damage to building	Repairs to first floor	$95,000	Excluded	$0
Water damage to maintenance equipment	A lawnmower, an electric hedge trimmer, and a vacuum cleaner stored on the first floor sustained damage	$750	Excluded	$0
Subtotal				$20,000
Effect of Policy Deductible			Loss recovery reduced by $500	($500)
Total Amount Payable				$19,500

[DA07843]

SUMMARY

The Loss Conditions and Additional Conditions sections of the BPP state the duties of the insured and the insurer after a loss has occurred, establish procedures for adjusting claims, explain methods for establishing the value of damaged property, outline requirements for coinsurance, and explain the interests of a mortgageholder (mortgagee).

The BPP contains four optional coverages: Agreed Value, Inflation Guard, Replacement Cost, and Extension of Replacement Cost to Personal Property of Others. Optional Coverages only apply when an appropriate notation is made on the declarations page.

The Commercial Property Conditions Form contains these conditions:

- Concealment, Misrepresentation, or Fraud
- Control of Property
- Insurance Under Two or More Coverages
- Legal Action Against Us
- Liberalization
- Transfer of Rights of Recovery Against Others to Us
- No Benefit to Bailee
- Other Insurance
- Policy Period, Coverage Territory

The Common Policy Conditions form is attached to every CPP or monoline policy written subject to ISO Commercial Lines Manual rules. The form contains these conditions: Cancellation; Changes; Examination of Your Books and Records; Inspections and Surveys; Premiums; and Transfer of Your Rights and Duties Under This Policy.

Hundreds of endorsements can be used to modify commercial property coverage. Examples of the exposures that can be covered by endorsement include building ordinance or law, spoilage, flood, and earthquake. The BPP can be supplemented in either of two ways to address the problem of fluctuating personal property values: the Peak Season Limit of Insurance endorsement and the Value Reporting Form.

In addition to the BPP, several other commercial property forms are available for insuring special exposures.

The Builders Risk Coverage Form is designed to insure the interests of owners or contractors (or both) in buildings or other structures during construction. The form covers the building under construction and building materials and temporary structures at the building site. The builders risk form is usually issued with a limit equal to the projected value of the completed building.

The Condominium Association Coverage Form can be used to insure a condominium association against loss to its buildings, its personal property, and the personal property of others. The form covers fixtures, improvements, alterations, and appliances within condominium units if the condominium association agreement requires the association to insure them.

The Condominium Commercial Unit-Owners Coverage Form provides business personal property coverage for commercial (not residential) unit owners.

Just because damaged property qualifies as Covered Property does not mean that the loss is covered. The peril(s) causing the loss must also qualify as a Covered Cause of Loss. In this case, the property damaged directly by windstorm was covered, but the property damaged by flooding, even though it resulted from storm surge, was excluded.

ASSIGNMENT NOTE

1. Insurance Information Institute, "Few Homes Have Insurance Coverage for Earthquake or Tsunami, Although the U.S. Is At Risk for Both," March 23, 2011, www.iii.org/press_releases/few-homes-have-insurance-coverage-for-earthquake-or-tsunami-although-the-us-is-at-risk-for-both.htm (accessed July 11, 2011).

Segment B

Assignment 5
Business Income Insurance

Assignment 6
Commercial Crime and Equipment Breakdown Insurance

Assignment 7
Inland and Ocean Marine Insurance

Assignment 8
Business Owners, Farm Insurance and Other Specialty Coverages

Direct Your Learning

5

Business Income Insurance

Educational Objectives

After learning the content of this assignment, you should be able to:

- Describe the following aspects of the business income loss exposure:
  - Measurement of business income loss
  - Effect of business interruption on expenses
  - Property and perils involved in business income losses
- Summarize the provisions of the Business Income and Extra Expense insuring agreements in the ISO business income coverage (BIC) forms.
- Explain how each of the additional coverages and the coverage extension supplement the business income coverage (BIC) forms.
- Summarize the Limits of Insurance, Loss Conditions, and Additional Condition (Coinsurance) of the business income coverage (BIC) forms.
- Explain how the optional coverages each modify the business income coverage (BIC) forms.
- Given a case, determine whether, and for what amount, a described loss would be covered either by the Business Income (and Extra Expense) Coverage Form or the Business Income (Without Extra Expense) Coverage Form.

Outline

Business Income Insurance

5

BUSINESS INCOME LOSS EXPOSURES

Commercial property coverage forms are tailored to insure buildings and personal property against damage by covered perils. However, the loss in value of the property and the expense of restoring it are not the only losses that a business may sustain.

Almost all of a commercial firm's property is acquired because of the income that it will generate or facilitate. This income can be lost when property is damaged or destroyed.

To evaluate the coverage needs an organization faces and determine how business income policy provisions are applied, an insurance practitioner should first understand how business income losses are measured, how a business interruption affects expenses, and the property and perils that business income losses can involve.

Measurement of Business Income Losses

Simply described, **business income insurance** covers the reduction in an organization's income when operations are interrupted by damage to property caused by a covered peril. The exact insurance recovery, of course, is determined by the terms and conditions of the policy. Because the severity of a business income loss is directly related to the length of time required to restore the property, business income coverage is considered a "time element" coverage. It is also called a "business interruption" coverage, because the loss of business income results from the interruption of the insured's business.

Business income insurance
Insurance that covers the reduction in an organization's income when operations are interrupted by damage to property caused by a covered peril.

Business income losses are measured in terms of **net income**, which is the difference between revenues (such as money received for goods or services) and expenses (such as money paid for merchandise, rent, and insurance). It can be expressed by the formula:

Net income
The difference between revenues (such as money received for goods or services) and expenses (such as money paid for merchandise, rent, and insurance).

$$\text{Revenues} - \text{Expenses} = \text{Net income}$$

Profit is net income that results when revenues exceed expenses. **Net loss** is the net income that results when expenses exceed revenues. For accounting purposes, the amount of a net loss appears in parentheses or is preceded by a minus sign (–).

Profit
Net income that results when revenues exceed expenses.

Net loss
Net income that results when expenses exceed revenues.

Business income insurance covers the reduction in a firm's net income caused by accidental property damage. This reduction can be calculated by subtracting the amount of net income that a firm actually earned in a period of interruption from the amount of net income that the firm could reasonably have been expected to earn during the same period.

The following simplified example illustrates these concepts. Locksey Hardware Store suffered a partial fire loss and was closed for three months until the building could be repaired and the personal property replaced. During the three-month interruption, Locksey's revenue was reduced to nil, some ordinary expenses (payroll, electricity, and so on) were temporarily reduced or eliminated, and Locksey incurred some additional expenses (such as overtime labor and express freight on merchandise) to reopen the store as soon as possible. See the exhibit "Locksey's Revenue, Expenses, and Profit."

Locksey's Revenue, Expenses, and Profit

	Expected	Actual
Revenue	$300,000	$ 0
Expenses	240,000	120,000
Net profit (or loss)	$ 60,000	($120,000)

[DA02477]

The "Expected" column shows the revenue, expenses, and profit that Locksey could reasonably have expected during the three-month period, had no business interruption occurred. The "Actual" column shows its actual revenue, expenses, and net loss (indicated by parentheses) during the three-month period of interruption.

Locksey's business income loss is the $180,000 difference between the $60,000 profit it expected and the $120,000 net loss it actually experienced during the period of interruption.Locksey's loss can also be calculated by adding the $60,000 net income it would have earned to the $120,000 expenses that it actually incurred during the period.

For the sake of simplicity, this example assumes that Locksey's revenue returned to its normal level as soon as it reopened, which is seldom the case. In reality, Locksey's business income loss could have continued for several months after the store reopened.

Continuing expenses

Expenses that continue to be incurred during a business interruption.

Noncontinuing expenses

Expenses that will not continue during a business interruption.

Effect of Business Interruption on Expenses

During a business interruption, some of the organization's expenses (called **continuing expenses**) will continue, and other expenses (called **noncontinuing expenses**) will not continue. A business can also incur extra expenses during a business interruption. All changes in expenses must be considered when measuring a business income loss.

Continuing Expenses

If business is interrupted for only a short time, payroll of key employees, debt repayments, taxes, insurance, and many other expenses will continue during the interruption. If a longer interruption of business occurs, many expenses can be reduced or eliminated. Workers can be laid off, taxes are reduced (because of reduced income), and insurance premiums are smaller. It is often difficult to predict which expenses will continue and which will not.

Any reduction in expenses during a business interruption lessens the severity of the resulting business income loss. Nevertheless, continuing expenses can be, and ordinarily are, a significant part of business income losses. If, for example, an organization generates no revenue during a business interruption, its business income loss will be its lost profit for the period of interruption, plus the continuing expenses for that period, plus any extra expenses. In many cases, a company's continuing expenses exceed the profit that the company would have earned during the period.

Extra Expenses

Extra expenses are expenses, in addition to ordinary expenses, that an organization incurs to mitigate the effects of a business interruption. These are examples of extra expenses:

Extra expenses
Expenses, in addition to ordinary expenses, that an organization incurs to mitigate the effects of a business interruption.

- In order to reopen an assembly line that had been shut down because of an explosion, a factory owner pays the additional costs of overtime labor and overnight air shipment of repair parts.
- After sustaining fire damage to its warehouse, a wholesale distributor rents a similar warehouse and continues its operations within two weeks instead of shutting down entirely for several months.
- To continue classes while an elementary school building is rebuilt following hurricane damage, a school district rents mobile classrooms and situates them on the school's playground.

Extra expense measures often pay for themselves. For example, the extra cost of overtime labor and air freight of needed parts may have been considerably less than the income that would have been lost had such measures not been taken. Such measures actually reduce the business income loss, and most organizations will readily undertake measures that reduce loss.

Some organizations will incur extra expenses even when such expenditures exceed any reduction in the business income loss. For example, after a property loss occurs, a hospital might incur substantial extra expenses to maintain essential services for its patients even though such expenses increase its business income loss. The decision to incur such extra expenses depends on the organization's objectives. For some organizations, maintaining continuous service to customers may be more important than reducing the business income loss.

Property and Perils Involved in Business Income Losses

Business income losses typically result from physical damage to the affected organization's own buildings or personal property. However, a tenant's operations can be interrupted by damage to the building in which the tenant is located even though the part of the building the tenant occupies has not been damaged. For example, an explosion that debilitates heating, air conditioning, and ventilating equipment makes offices in sealed high-rise buildings uninhabitable in very hot or very cold weather, even though the offices themselves are not damaged.

In some cases, a physical loss at one location can cause a business interruption elsewhere. For example, a business may have to close because of damage to off-premises property that provides utilities such as electricity, water, or communications. Alternatively, one business may depend on another business as a major customer or as a key supplier. A business may be dependent simply because it is near a key facility or "magnet" property that attracts customers to the site (such as a major department store in a shopping mall). Damage to these kinds of properties could cause a business income loss at a location where no physical damage occurred.

The causes of loss for business income losses associated with property exposures are typically the same as those for physical damage losses. Thus, a fire or a windstorm that damages property may also cause a business income loss. A business income loss can also result when there has been no physical damage to buildings or personal property. For example, the closing of a road or a labor strike can cause a business income loss. However, such risks are generally not insurable. Any number of other events that are not covered by business income insurance can reduce an organization's net income. Prudent organizations use risk management techniques to avoid or lessen business income loss exposures that cannot be transferred by insurance. In order for business income insurance to apply, this must occur: an interruption of operations caused by property damage from a covered peril to property at locations or situations described in the policy resulting in a loss of business income and/or extra expense.

If any of these conditions are not met, there is no coverage under business income coverage.

BIC INSURING AGREEMENTS

A producer, underwriter, or risk management professional must understand what each business income coverage form covers in order to recommend the correct form to an insured who has business income that may be lost if a covered peril occurs.

Insurance for most business income exposures can be provided under either of the two Insurance Services Office (ISO) coverage forms for providing business income coverage:

- The Business Income (and Extra Expense) Coverage Form covers both business income and extra expense losses (even if the extra expenses do not reduce the business income loss).
- The Business Income (Without Extra Expense) Coverage Form covers business income loss but covers extra expenses only to the extent that they reduce the business income loss.

The Business Income insuring agreement is found in both of these forms and the Extra Expense insuring agreement is found only in the Business Income (and Extra Expense) Coverage Form. Either BIC form can be included in a commercial property coverage part, with or without another commercial property coverage form such as the Building and Personal Property Coverage Form. The causes of loss included in business income coverage can be designated by either the same causes of loss form that applies to other coverage forms or by a different causes of loss form that applies only to business income coverage.

Because the two ISO business income forms are similar in all respects except extra expense coverage, this section applies equally to both forms unless otherwise specified. The abbreviation "BIC" is used to refer to both forms. The phrases "BIC and extra expense" and "BIC without extra expense" are used to distinguish between the two forms.

Business Income Insuring Agreement

The BIC allows an insured to choose any one of these three options for business income coverage:

- Business income including rental value
- Business income other than rental value
- Rental value only

The option chosen by the insured should always be clearly indicated on the declarations page.

The first option covers both loss of rental value and loss of other business income. An insured that owns and operates out of a multi-tenant office building that it rents in part to other tenants might choose this. If the building became physically damaged and unable to be occupied, the insurer would pay for both the insured's loss of rental income from tenants and the insured's loss of business income from its own business.

The second option covers business income other than rental value. A business that has no rental income to lose might choose this.

The third option is less expensive, but it covers rental value only. This option might be purchased by a landlord whose only income is derived from renting property to others.

The insurer agrees to pay the actual loss of business income sustained by the named insured because of the necessary "suspension" of the named insured's "operations" during the "period of restoration." (The BIC definition of these terms is discussed in subsequent paragraphs.) The suspension must result from direct physical loss or damage to real or personal property caused by a covered cause of loss and occurring at the "premises" described in the declarations.

If the insured is a tenant, the definition of premises is broadened to include "any area within the building or on the site...if that area services, or is used to gain access to, the described premises." Thus, if fire damages the elevator motors in the basement of a building, a tenant on the thirtieth floor would be covered for any resulting business income loss even if no damage occurs above the first floor.

The BIC defines business income as the sum of these two items:

- Net profit or loss that would have been earned or incurred if the suspension had not occurred
- Normal operating expenses, including payroll, that continue during the suspension

The amount of profit or loss that would have been earned or incurred if the suspension had not occurred must be estimated based on past and prospective performance of the business.

The continuing expenses can be determined during the suspension. These expenses may include salaries of key employees, property taxes, and interest expenses.

The terms "operations," "period of restoration," and "suspension" are defined in the BIC's Definitions section. The "operations" of the insured are (1) the business activities of the insured that occur at the premises described in the declarations or (2) in the case of rental value coverage, the "tenantability" (suitability for occupancy) of the described premises.

The "period of restoration" is the period during which business income loss is covered under the BIC forms. For business income coverage, it begins seventy-two hours after the physical loss occurs and ends when the property is (or should have been) restored to use with reasonable speed. With regard to extra expense coverage, it begins immediately after the physical loss occurs. In both cases, the period of restoration ends on the date when the property should be restored with reasonable speed and similar quality or when the business is resumed at a new, permanent location. Thus, for business income coverage, there is no coverage for the first three days following the physical loss. The seventy-two hour deductible can be reduced to twenty-four hours or eliminated entirely by endorsement for an additional premium.

Inside the Premises - Robbery or Safe Burglary of Other Property is subject to a special limit of $5,000 per occurrence for these types of property - Special limit

(1) Precious metals, precious or semiprecious stones, pearls, furs, or completed or partially completed

(2) Manuscripts, drawing, or records of any kind or the cost of reconstructing them.

Also outside the Premises are subject to the same & Computer & Fund transfer fraud

The period of restoration does not include any additional time that might be required to repair or reconstruct the building in order to comply with any building code or law unless the policy has been specifically endorsed to cover such additional time. The period of restoration also does not include any increased period required by ordinance or law to respond to or assess the effects of pollutants.

"Suspension" means the slowdown or cessation of business activities or, in the case of rental value coverage, that a part of the premises is rendered untenantable (unfit for occupancy).

Whichever cause of loss form applies to the BIC determines what qualifies as a covered cause of loss for purposes of business income coverage. All of the provisions in the causes of loss form apply to business income claims, including a set of exclusions that apply only to business income and/or extra expense losses.

In summary, these are the key requirements for a business income claim to be covered in the BIC:

- Actual loss of business income you sustain resulting from the necessary suspension of your operations during the period of restoration caused by direct physical loss of or damage to property at the described premises
- Loss or damage caused by a covered cause of loss

Apply Your Knowledge

Department Store (DS) is insured under a commercial package policy that includes the Business Income (and Extra Expense) Coverage Form. For each of the loss scenarios described, determine whether the circumstances of the loss satisfy the conditions imposed by the Business Income insuring agreement in DS's Business Income (and Extra Expense) Coverage Form.

DS sustained an actual loss of business income at the described store premises as a result of decreased shopper traffic for several months while nearby streets were blocked off as part of a subway construction project.

Feedback: No. The circumstances of the loss do not meet the conditions of the Business Income insuring agreement because there was no direct physical loss to property at the described premises by a Covered Cause of Loss.

DS sustained an actual loss of business income while the second floor of the described store was necessarily shut down for repairs after a fire (a Covered Cause of Loss) caused physical loss to that floor. Although sales continued on the ground and first floors of the store, DS's net income was reduced by approximately 30 percent until the second floor was restored to use.

Feedback: Yes. The circumstances of the loss meet all the conditions of the Business Income insuring agreement:

- DS sustained an actual loss of business income.
- The loss of business income was due to the necessary suspension of DS's operations. (Partial interruption qualifies as "suspension.")
- DS incurred loss of business income during the period of restoration (before the property was restored).
- The suspension of DS's operations was caused by direct physical loss or damage to property at the described premises.
- The loss or damage was caused by a Covered Cause of Loss.

Extra Expense Insuring Agreement

The BIC and extra expense coverage form contains a second insuring agreement—Extra Expense. The Extra Expense insuring agreement provides coverage for expenses that the named insured incurs to avoid or minimize the suspension of operations. Examples of such extra expenses include the costs to move to a temporary location, increased rent at the temporary location, rental of substitute equipment (furniture, fixtures, or machinery), and the cost of substitute services such as for data processing.

The BIC and extra expense coverage form covers such expenses in full, subject to the policy limit. With the exception of extra expense to repair or replace property, these expenses are not limited to the amount by which they reduce the extra expense loss; coverage applies even if the business income loss is not reduced at all.

Even with the BIC and extra expense coverage form, extra expenses to repair or replace property are treated differently. Such expenses are covered only to the extent that they actually reduce the business income loss. For example, a business owner may pay a contractor at an overtime rate to work around the clock to repair damaged property so that the business can reopen promptly. The additional cost paid to do so would be payable as extra expense, but only to the extent that it actually reduced the business income loss. Thus, if reopening earlier reduced the business income loss by $20,000, the insurer would pay the overtime charges up to that amount (and subject to the limit of insurance).

BIC ADDITIONAL COVERAGES AND COVERAGE EXTENSION

The business income coverage (BIC) forms include additional coverages and a coverage extension that supplement the basic insuring agreement(s) in ways that are often vital to insureds recovering from business income losses.

Each version of the BIC form contains four additional coverages and one coverage extension to insure several sources of business income loss that would not otherwise be covered. The Business Income (Without Extra Expense) Coverage Form contains one more additional coverage, Expenses to Reduce Loss. The additional coverages and extension are shown in the exhibit. See the exhibit "BIC Insuring Agreements, Additional Coverages, and Coverage Extension."

BIC Insuring Agreements, Additional Coverages, and Coverage Extension

	Business Income (and Extra Expense) Coverage Form	Business Income (Without Extra Expense) Coverage Form
Insuring Agreement(s)	• Business Income • Extra Expense	• Business Income
Additional Coverages	• Civil Authority • Alterations and New Buildings • Extended Business Income • Interruption of Computer Operations	• Expenses to Reduce Loss • Civil Authority • Alterations and New Buildings • Extended Business Income • Interruption of Computer Operations
Coverage Extension	• Newly Acquired Locations	• Newly Acquired Locations

[DA02479]

Expenses to Reduce Loss

Instead of containing an Extra Expense insuring agreement, the BIC without extra expense form contains an additional coverage titled Expenses to Reduce Loss. This addition covers necessary expenses incurred by the named insured to reduce business income loss, other than the cost of extinguishing a fire.

Thus, the insured can incur the same types of expenses that are covered under the BIC and extra expense form, but they are covered only to the extent that they reduce business income loss.

A danger of the BIC without extra expense form is that the insured may incur extra expenses other than the reduction in business income loss. A large, uninsured extra expense loss can therefore result.

The BIC and extra expense form greatly reduces this possibility. Because the rate for the BIC and extra expense form is not much greater than the rate for the BIC without extra expense form, many businesses opt for the broader coverage form.

Civil Authority

In almost all cases, coverage under the BIC is related to damage to property at the insured's premises. However, Civil Authority additional coverage insures loss of business income that results when damage is to property other than the insured's and when access to the insured's premises is prohibited by civil authority. The insured's premises must be within one mile of the damaged property and access to the insured's premises must be denied by the civil authority because of a dangerous physical condition or to enable the civil authority unimpeded access to the damaged property. For example, fire damage to another building may make it unsafe for customers to go to the insured's premises.

If damage to the other premises resulted from a cause of loss covered by the insured's policy, the resulting income loss at the insured's premises would be covered for the period of suspension, beginning seventy-two hours after the time of the action by civil authority, up to a maximum of four consecutive weeks after the time of the action. The maximum period of coverage can be increased to 60, 90, or 180 days by endorsement. If the seventy-two hour period in the definition of "period of restoration" is reduced or eliminated in the BIC, the endorsement makes the same change in the Civil Authority additional coverage.

Apply Your Knowledge

Jennifer's shoe store has coverage under the BIC. A tenant situated a few doors away from Jennifer's store in the same shopping center had a fire that weakened the roof supports for part of the building. The civil authorities prohibited access to Jennifer's store because they were concerned that the building's roof could collapse. It took three and a half weeks (twenty-four days) before the civil authorities allowed Jennifer's customers to visit her store again. Does Jennifer have a covered business income claim? Explain.

Feedback: Yes, the Civil Authority additional coverage insures losses that occur somewhere other than at the insured's premises. Jennifer's premises is within one mile of the damaged property. Access was denied by the civil authority because of a dangerous physical condition—the threat of the roof collapsing—and the time period of the prohibited access was less than the coverage's allotted four consecutive weeks and access was denied beyond the seventy-two hour waiting period.

Alterations and New Buildings

In most cases, business income losses result from the interruption of operations that are already underway. However, the BIC form also provides coverage for loss of income resulting from a delay in starting operations if the delay results from damage at the described premises by a covered cause of loss to one of these:

- New buildings or structures, either completed or under construction
- Alterations or additions to existing buildings
- Machinery, equipment, supplies, or building materials located on or within 100 feet of the described premises (provided they are used in the construction, alterations, or additions or are incidental to the occupancy of new buildings)

The period of restoration for losses to new or altered buildings begins on the date that operations would have begun had the damage not occurred. The BIC and extra expense form specifically states that this additional coverage includes necessary extra expenses.

Extended Business Income

Business income coverage ceases when the period of restoration ends—that is, on the date when the property at the described premises should be repaired, rebuilt, or replaced with reasonable speed and similar quality. However, all of the insured business's former customers may not return immediately upon restoration, especially if the interruption has been long.

The Extended Business Income (EBI) additional coverage addresses this possibility by extending the regular business income coverage to include business income losses that continue after the period of restoration ends. The coverage begins when the damaged property has been restored and ends when the insured's business returns to normal, subject to a maximum of sixty days. For example, if a restaurant is closed because of fire damage, its regular customers will patronize other restaurants. Time will be needed for the insured's income to return to normal levels even after the physical repairs are completed.

Interruption of Computer Operations

A coverage restriction found in each of the BIC forms, titled Additional Limitation—Interruption of Computer Operations, states that no coverage applies when a suspension of operations is caused by destruction or corruption of, or any other loss or damage to, electronic data. An exception to this restriction is provided under the additional coverage Interruption of Computer Operations.

The additional coverage provides $2,500 of coverage for loss of business income or extra expense when business operations are suspended because of an interruption of computer operations resulting from the destruction or corruption of electronic data caused by a covered cause of loss. The $2,500 is an aggregate limit for all losses sustained in any one policy year that applies in addition to the regular limit of insurance. If the insurer is willing to provide a higher limit, it is shown in the declarations.

The $2,500 limit is not a meaningful amount of coverage for most insureds covered by commercial package policies, because losses can easily exceed that amount. Inland marine and cyber risk coverages are available to provide greater coverage.

The Interruption of Computer Operations additional coverage does not apply when loss to electronic data involves only electronic data that are integrated in and operate or control a building's elevator, lighting, heating, ventilation, air conditioning, or security system. This type of loss is specifically excepted from the Additional Limitation—Interruption of Computer Operations and is therefore covered by the business income insuring agreement without any of the restrictions of the additional coverage, such as the $2,500 aggregate limit and the limitation to specified causes of loss.

Newly Acquired Locations

The BIC forms' only coverage extension expands coverage to property at premises acquired during the policy period if a coinsurance of 50 percent or more is shown in the declarations. Titled Newly Acquired Locations, this optional coverage for insureds does not include property at fairs or exhibitions.

The coverage at any newly acquired location is limited to $100,000. This is an additional amount of insurance above the limit stated in the declarations and is not subject to the Coinsurance condition. An additional premium is charged for the automatic coverage from the date of acquisition of the new property.

The Newly Acquired Locations coverage terminates on the earliest of (1) the expiration date of the policy, (2) the date on which the insured reports the acquisition to the insurer, or (3) thirty days after the date of acquisition. This extension is intended to provide temporary protection until the insured obtains permanent coverage.

BIC LIMIT OF INSURANCE AND CONDITIONS

The sometimes overlooked Limits of Insurance, Loss Conditions, and Additional Condition (Coinsurance) sections of the business income coverage (BIC) forms can be crucial in determining how much will be paid for a business income loss.

The Limits of Insurance, Loss Conditions, and Additional Condition (Coinsurance) sections of the Insurance Services Office (ISO) BIC forms contain policy provisions that guide both the insured and insurer when determining the amount payable for a business income loss. The Loss Conditions, in particular, also address these issues:

- Appraisal
- Duties in the Event of Loss
- Loss Determination
- Loss Payment

Limits of Insurance

The limit of insurance stated in the declarations is the maximum amount the insurer will pay for loss in any one occurrence.

Any amounts payable under these coverages of the BIC do not increase the limit of insurance:

- Extra Expense (in the Business Income [and Extra Expense] Coverage Form only)
- Expenses to Reduce Loss (in the Business Income [Without Extra Expense] Coverage Form only)
- Civil Authority
- Alterations and New Buildings
- Extended Business Income

The Interruption of Computer Operations additional coverage and the Newly Acquired Locations coverage extension are payable subject to their own limits. Any amounts the insurer pays for these two coverages do not reduce the limit of insurance shown in the declarations. Limits of insurance for business income can be written on either a specific or blanket basis. If they are written on a specific basis, a specific limit is set for each building insured. If they are written on a blanket basis, the limit applies to all buildings at one location or to all buildings at multiple locations. Writing coverage on a blanket basis can help a business with interdependent locations, with which a loss at one building could affect income at another building. For example, if a warehouse is damaged, it may be unable to supply goods to be sold at another building.

Loss Conditions

The Loss Conditions provide a forum to resolve disputes over amounts to be paid, require an insured to mitigate a loss, identify factors to apply when determining the amount of business income loss, and require prompt payment once an amount is agreed upon.

Appraisal

The Appraisal condition allows either the insured or the insurer to demand an appraisal of a loss if the insured and the insurer disagree on the amount of loss, but not in disputes as to coverage. The condition also describes the appraisal procedure to be followed in such cases.

Duties in the Event of Loss

The duties of the insured after loss—such as giving the insurer prompt notice of loss, protecting covered property from further loss, and cooperating with the insurer—are similar to the duties specified in the ISO Building and Personal Property Coverage Form, also known as the BPP. The BIC imposes one additional duty on any insured that intends to continue its business: to resume operations, in whole or in part, as quickly as possible.

Loss Determination

The amount of a business income loss can never be known precisely, but business income loss is determined on the basis of these items:

- Net income of the business before the loss occurred
- Probable net income of the business if no loss had occurred
- Operating expenses that must continue during the period of restoration to permit the insured to resume operations with the quality of service that existed prior to loss
- Other relevant sources of information

Not all expenses terminate when a business's operations are suspended. Continuous expenses include payroll and, depending on the insured's circumstances, utilities, rental payments, taxes, interest payable on loans, and similar items. Other relevant sources of information may include the insured's financial and accounting records, bills, invoices, notes, deeds, liens, and contracts.

The BIC states that the amount of loss will not be based on the net income that might have been earned as a result of an increase in business resulting from favorable business conditions caused by the effect of the covered cause of loss. This change was motivated by questions that arose following Hurricane Andrew in 1992. Insurers believed that the proper measure of damages for a hotel, for example, would be the room rentals that the hotel would normally have earned had the hurricane not occurred. The policy wording change makes it clear that the increase in business resulting from a catastrophe will not be included when estimating the likely net income.

Loss Payment

The insurer agrees to pay for a covered loss within thirty days after the date on which the amount of loss is agreed to (or an appraisal award is made).

The insured must have complied with all policy conditions, including filing a sworn statement of loss.

If the insured does not resume operations as quickly as possible, the insurer pays the loss based on the length of time it would have taken the insured to do so. If the insured does not resume operations at all (many businesses do not reopen after a serious fire or other damage), the period of restoration is based on the time it would have taken to resume operations as quickly as possible.

Additional Condition: Coinsurance

The BIC forms contain an additional condition establishing a coinsurance provision. The BIC coinsurance percentage may be 50, 60, 70, 80, 90, 100, or 125 percent. The policy may also be written with no coinsurance provision. The BIC loss payment calculation is:

$$\text{Loss payment} = \left(\frac{\text{Amount of insurance carried}}{\text{Amount of insurance required}}\right) \times \text{Loss amount}$$

The numerator of the fraction in this calculation is the amount of insurance carried. The denominator is the amount of insurance required; it is determined by multiplying the coinsurance percentage by the sum of the insured's net income (whether profit or loss) plus all operating expenses (less certain expenses specified in the form) that would have been incurred in the absence of a loss for the twelve-month period beginning at the inception or latest anniversary date of the policy.

Although the procedure is similar to that used with the BPP, the coinsurance basis used for business income insurance is significantly different. For other property coverages, the coinsurance basis is the same as the property covered. That is, if a building is the covered property, the coinsurance basis is either the replacement cost or the actual cash value of the building (depending on which valuation basis the policy provides). This is not the case with business income insurance. The item covered in business income insurance is net income plus continuing operating expenses; the coinsurance basis is the projected net income and all operating expenses except for certain deductible items.

Another difference between the item covered and the coinsurance basis is the period of time used in computing values. For coverage purposes, the time covered is the period of restoration plus thirty days of extended business income. For coinsurance purposes, coverage includes the estimated net income and expenses for one year, starting with the policy inception or anniversary. This makes calculating the amount of insurance needed to satisfy coinsurance more complicated for business income than for other property coverages.

To assist insureds in making the necessary calculations, ISO publishes a Business Income Report/Work Sheet. Completing this form requires a significant level of financial sophistication. Therefore, some small businesses prefer options that eliminate the coinsurance requirement.

The variety of coinsurance percentages from which the insured may choose reflects the fact that the maximum foreseeable loss for a given insured seldom equals the projected net income and operating expenses for twelve months. To be properly protected, insureds should carry, at minimum, an amount of insurance equal to their **probable maximum loss (PML)**.

Probable maximum loss (PML)
The largest loss that an insured is likely to sustain.

For some insureds, PML may constitute only a small fraction of the coinsurance basis. For example, a retail store operating in an area that contains numerous empty stores may be able to relocate and be fully operational within three months if its present location is totally destroyed. In contrast, a manufacturer that depends on sophisticated, special-order machinery might be shut down for eighteen months or more while waiting for replacement equipment if it sustains extensive damage to key equipment.

The retail store might need an amount of insurance equal to less than half its coinsurance basis and could thus choose 50 percent coinsurance; the manufacturer might need an amount of insurance much greater than its coinsurance basis. It could select 125 percent coinsurance, which would reduce the rate, because rates are lower when higher coinsurance percentages are selected.

Reality Check

Effect of Coinsurance Penalty

This hypothetical example shows how an insured's failure to comply with the BIC Coinsurance condition can result in an insufficient loss recovery, even when the amount of loss is less than the limit of insurance.

Karen operates a retail store. Her store is insured under a Commercial Package Policy that includes the BIC. She selected a coinsurance percentage of 80 percent and an amount of $200,000 for coverage of her business income losses. The sum of her store's net income plus all operating expenses that would be incurred in the absence of a loss for the twelve-month period beginning at the inception or latest anniversary date of the policy is $400,000. This amount, the coinsurance basis, is twice the amount of the insurance coverage she bought. So Karen was substantially underinsured when she had a fire at her store. She lost $100,000 in business income as a result of the fire.

Applying the coinsurance formula to determine how much the insurer will pay her, the $400,000 coinsurance basis is multiplied by 80 percent. The result is $320,000, which is the minimum amount of coverage she should have bought to avoid a coinsurance penalty. The $200,000 amount of insurance she did buy is divided by the $320,000 amount she should have bought. The result is 0.625, which is multiplied by the $100,000 business income loss. That result is $62,500, which is the amount Karen's insurer will pay for her $100,000 loss, despite the $200,000 of coverage she purchased.

The difference between $100,000 and $62,500 is $37,500. That amount is the coinsurance penalty assessed against the loss as a result of purchasing an inadequate amount of coverage. Options are available to Karen and other insureds to omit or suspend the Coinsurance condition, thereby avoiding coinsurance penalties.

[DA07853]

BIC OPTIONAL COVERAGES

Optional coverages that can be activated in either version of the business income coverage (BIC) forms allow the insured to obtain significant coverage enhancements.

The BIC forms each include four optional coverages that modify the basic coverage:

- Maximum Period of Indemnity
- Monthly Limit of Indemnity
- Business Income Agreed Value
- Extended Period of Indemnity

The first three optional coverages eliminate or suspend the Coinsurance condition, and the fourth optional coverage covers loss of business income that continues after the Extended Business Income additional coverage ends.

Maximum Period of Indemnity

The Maximum Period of Indemnity optional coverage negates the Coinsurance condition while limiting loss payment to the lesser of (1) the amount of loss sustained during the 120 days following the start of restoration or (2) the policy limit. The Maximum Period of Indemnity is not an additional coverage: It is a restriction of the period of restoration provided by the BIC, which, from the insured's point of view, has the advantage of avoiding any coinsurance penalty.

The period of restoration begins seventy-two hours after the time of direct physical loss. Therefore, an effective three-day deductible applies to these optional coverages in the same way that it applies to the standard BIC. (The seventy-two-hour period can be reduced to twenty-four hours or eliminated by endorsement.)

The coinsurance condition does not apply at any location to which the maximum period of indemnity is applicable. Therefore, this optional coverage should be used only when the insured is certain that any suspension of operations will last no more than four months.

Monthly Limit of Indemnity

Activated by inserting a fraction in the appropriate space in the declarations, the Monthly Limit of Indemnity optional coverage negates the Coinsurance condition while limiting the amount recoverable during any month of business interruption to the noted fraction of the insurance amount. This optional coverage applies only to business income coverage. Therefore, in the Business Income (and Extra Expense) Coverage Form, this optional coverage does not limit recovery for extra expense.

The Coinsurance condition does not apply to any location at which the monthly limit of indemnity is applicable. But this optional coverage is sometimes chosen because the insured does not want to disclose financial information to prove compliance with the Coinsurance condition or because the Coinsurance condition requires more insurance than the insured deems necessary.

Business Income Agreed Value

The Business Income Agreed Value optional coverage suspends the Coinsurance condition as long as the insured carries an amount of business income insurance that is equal to the value agreed on by the policyholder and the insurer. An insurer that is willing to provide this coverage—which, like the Maximum Period of Indemnity coverage, helps the insured avoid a potential coinsurance penalty—must take two steps to activate it.

Reality Check

Example of Applying the Monthly Limit of Indemnity Optional Coverage

This hypothetical example shows how the Monthly Limit of Indemnity optional coverage would limit payment of a business income loss.

If the fraction shown in the declarations is 1/4 and the policy limit is $100,000, the maximum amount the insured could recover for any business income loss during any period of thirty consecutive days is $25,000. The claim payment would be the lesser of the actual loss sustained or $25,000 for the applicable thirty-day period. So if the business is suspended for three months following the start of the restoration period, and the actual loss of income is $30,000 for each of those months, the claim payment is only $25,000 per month, or a total of $75,000.

[DA07851]

First, the insurer must secure from the insured a completed business income report/worksheet showing this information:

- The insured's actual data for the most recent twelve-month accounting period before the date of the worksheet
- Estimated data for the twelve months immediately following inception of the coverage

Second, the insurer must enter the agreed value into the declarations. The agreed value must be at least equal to the product obtained by multiplying the coinsurance percentage shown in the declarations by the estimated net income and operating expenses shown on the worksheet for the twelve months following the inception of the optional coverage.

The agreed value is effective for a period of twelve months or until the policy expires, whichever comes first. The insured must submit a new worksheet to the insurer every twelve months for the agreed value coverage to remain in effect.

The Coinsurance condition is suspended while this optional coverage is in place. However, during this period, the insured must carry an amount of insurance at least equal to the agreed value if losses are to be paid in full. The Coinsurance condition is automatically reinstated if the agreed value coverage lapses. This could happen, for example, if the insured renews a policy but does not submit a new worksheet.

Extended Period of Indemnity

The Extended Period of Indemnity optional coverage extends the duration of the Extended Business Income (EBI) additional coverage to include business income losses that continue for more than sixty days after the property

Reality Check

Example of Applying the Business Income Agreed Value Optional Coverage

This hypothetical example illustrates the operation of the Business Income Agreed Value optional coverage.

ABC Corporation has a BIC with an agreed value of $200,000. If ABC carries insurance of $200,000 or more, its covered losses will be paid in full, without any possibility of a coinsurance penalty, up to the amount of insurance. However, if ABC carries only $150,000 of insurance, the Coinsurance condition will be reinstated and, consequently, only three-fourths of its covered losses will be paid (calculated as $150,000/$200,000 = 0.75).

[DA07852]

is restored. The period of indemnity can be extended up to 730 days, or two years. The actual number of days selected depends on the insured's estimate of the amount of time it would take for revenues to return to normal after the property is restored.

Many insureds, such as restaurants and clothing stores, depend on strong customer relationships and repeat business and would be unlikely to return to normal income levels within sixty days of reopening after a severe loss. For such insureds, this optional coverage can be highly attractive.

DETERMINING WHETHER THE BIC FORM COVERS A LOSS

Knowing how to apply business income coverage to the facts of a case is an important skill. This case study will help you make the transition from knowing policy language to applying policy language to losses to determine whether coverage applies. As you progress through this case study, you can check your understanding of the coverage provided by answering the Knowledge to Action questions.

Case Facts

Given the facts presented by the case, will the business income loss be covered? If so, what amount will the insurer pay for the claim? When answering the questions in this case-based activity, consider only the information provided as part of this case.

Fancy Wear Boutique (FWB), a retail clothing store in Chicago, is insured under a commercial package policy that includes the Business Income (and Extra Expense) Coverage Form, the Causes of Loss—Special Form, the

Commercial Property Conditions, and the Common Policy Conditions (as well as other forms that are not relevant to this case).

The Commercial Property Coverage Part Declarations Page describes the insured premises at the address of the store building owned by FWB and shows a $1 million Business Income limit of insurance for the location, subject to option (2), Business Income Other Than "Rental Value." The declarations also show that FWB had purchased the Business Income Agreed Value optional coverage and that the value agreed to by the insurer and FWB was $1 million. None of the other optional coverages of the Business Income (and Extra Expense) Coverage Form are in effect. Moreover, no endorsements apply to FWB's Business Income (and Extra Expense) Coverage Form or Causes of Loss—Special Form. The one-year policy period shown in the declarations began on January 1, 20X1.

On April 1, 20X1, FWB suffered a total direct physical loss to its store building and contents when a tornado touched down on FWB's premises but did not cause widespread damage in the immediate area. Replacement of the building and its contents was accomplished with reasonable speed and required one year. As a result of FWB's direct physical loss, both the revenues and normal operating expenses that FWB expected to experience were reduced as shown in the table. The resulting loss of business income that FWB sustained while operations were suspended at the described premises was $680,000. The business income loss for the first seventy-two hours following the physical loss totaled $4,000. See the exhibit "FWB's Expected and Actual Revenues, Expenses, Net Income."

FWB's Expected and Actual Revenues, Expenses, Net Income

	Expected	Actual
Revenues	$2,000,000	$1,000,000
Expenses	750,000	430,000
Net Income	$1,250,000	$570,000

Business income loss = $1,250,000 – $570,000
= $680,000

[DA07918]

To keep its business operating during the period of restoration, FWB rented and moved into a nearby building one month after the tornado occurred and continued operating the boutique at this location for the duration of the restoration period. During this period, FWB incurred additional costs totaling $34,000 ($20,000 for rent, $3,000 for moving expenses, $5,000 for leased equipment, and $6,000 for additional advertising expenses). FWB would not have incurred any of these expenses had the tornado damage not occurred.

After the period of restoration ended and FWB resumed operations at the insured premises, the boutique continued to sustain loss of business income for sixty days, in these amounts:

- First period of sixty days after reopening: $15,000
- Second period of sixty days after reopening: $10,000

All loss of business income that occurred after FWB reopened its store resulted from changes in customers' shopping behavior during FWB's year-long suspension of normal operations while temporarily relocated. The additional loss of business income did not result from unfavorable business conditions caused by the impact of the tornado in FWB's area. Moreover, there was nothing more that FWB could reasonably have done to restore its normal business income level any sooner than it did.

FWB and the insurer agreed on all loss determinations, and FWB fulfilled all its post-loss duties under the policy.

Necessary Reference Materials

To determine whether FWB's policy provides coverage for business income loss incurred as a result of the tornado, you need copies of the policy forms, and the declarations pages themselves. There are no endorsements that affect Business Income coverage, but if there were, they would need to be reviewed to see how they affect the Business Income (and Extra Expense) Coverage Form.

You will need to have copies of the following forms available for your reference while working on this coverage case:

- Business Income (and Extra Expense) Coverage Form (CP 00 30 10 12)
- Causes of Loss—Special Form (CP 10 30 10 12)
- Commercial Property Conditions (CP 00 90 07 88)

Determination of Coverage

When examining the policy forms to determine whether coverage applies to the losses, you can apply the four steps of the DICE method. This involves analyzing the policy declarations, insuring agreement, conditions, and exclusions and determining whether any information found at each step precludes coverage at the time of the loss. You should also examine other categories of policy provisions such as the insured's duties, general provisions, endorsements (if applicable), and terms defined in the policy in relation to the declarations, insuring agreements, conditions, and exclusions.

DICE Analysis Step 1: Declarations

The first DICE step is to review the declarations pages to determine whether it covers the person or the property at the time of the loss. Action Task: Review the declarations in FWB's policy. See the exhibit "Excerpt From FWB's Declarations Page."

A basic requirement, expressed in the Policy and Coverage Territory provision in the Commercial Property Conditions, is that the loss or damage must commence during the policy period shown in the declarations and must commence within the coverage territory in order for coverage to apply. The facts of FWB's claim satisfy this requirement because the business income loss commenced on April 1, 20X1, which is within the policy period stated in the declarations; and the loss commenced at the described premises, which is within the coverage territory. Even though the business income and extra expense loss continued for several months after the policy period ended, FWB's claim for the entire business income and extra expense claim would be covered under the policy in effect at the time the loss commenced. This result is supported by this sentence in the policy definition of period of restoration: "The expiration date of this policy will not cut short the 'period of restoration.' "

DICE Analysis Step 2: Insuring Agreement

The second DICE step is to review the insuring agreement to determine whether it is applicable to the described loss. The Business Income (and Extra Expense) Coverage form has two insuring agreements—one for the business income and a second for extra expense. You should determine what part of the loss is covered under the Business Income insuring agreement and what part is covered under the Extra Expense insuring agreement.

To be covered under the Business Income insuring agreement, a loss must be an actual loss of business income as defined and must meet several requirements imposed by the Business Income insuring agreement.

During its suspension of operations at the described premises, FWB sustained a $680,000 loss of business income, as defined in the Business Income insuring agreement. Because the claim is for business income other than rental income, the loss falls within option (2), Business Income Other Than "Rental Value," shown in the declarations. (A claim for loss of rental income, for example, would not be covered under FWB's business income coverage.)

Excerpt From FWB's Declarations Page

COMMERCIAL PROPERTY
CP DS 00 10 00

COMMERCIAL PROPERTY COVERAGE PART DECLARATIONS PAGE

POLICY NO. 00123456 **EFFECTIVE DATE** 01 / 01 / 20X1 ☐ **"X" If Supplemental Declarations Is Attached**

NAMED INSURED Fancy Wear Boutique

DESCRIPTION OF PREMISES

Prem. No.	Bldg. No.	Location, Construction And Occupancy
001	001	1234 Main St., Chicago, IL Joisted Masonry Clothing or Wearing Apparel Store

COVERAGES PROVIDED **Insurance At The Described Premises Applies Only For Coverages For Which A Limit Of Insurance Is Shown**

Prem. No.	Bldg. No.	Coverage	Limit Of Insurance	Covered Causes Of Loss	Coinsurance*	Rates
001	001	Building	600,000	Special	80%	See Sched.
		Your Business Personal Property	700,000	Special		
		Personal Property of Others	50,000	Special		
		Business income/Extra Expense	1,000,000	Special		
		Option (2) Business Income Other Than Rental Value				
		Business Income Agreed Value optional coverage	1,000,000			

CP DS 00 10 00 Page 1 of 1 ☐

[DA07919]

Furthermore, the circumstances of the claim meet the other applicable requirements imposed by the insuring agreement:

- The actual loss of FWB's business income was due to the necessary suspension of FWB's operations.
- The suspension was caused by direct physical loss of or damage to property (in this case, building and contents) at the premises described in the declarations and for which a Business Income limit of insurance is shown.
- The loss or damage was caused by a Covered Cause of Loss (in this case, tornado, a type of windstorm that is not excluded by the Causes of Loss—Special Form and is therefore covered).

The Business Income insuring agreement states that the insurer will pay actual loss of Business Income only during the "period of restoration." According to the policy definition of this term, the period of restoration, for purposes of Business Income coverage (as opposed to Extra Expense coverage), begins "seventy-two hours after the time of direct physical loss or damage." Because FWB sustained $4,000 of business income loss during those first seventy-two hours (three days), that sum will be deducted from the covered amount of business income loss.

For expenses to be covered under the Extra Expense insuring agreement, the circumstances of the claim must meet the requirements imposed by that agreement. The requirements of the insuring agreement are satisfied by these case facts:

- FWB incurred $34,000 in additional costs during the period of restoration to continue its operations at a substitute store.
- FWB would not have incurred these costs if there had been no direct physical loss or damage or if the loss or damage had not been caused by or resulted from a Covered Cause of Loss (in this case, tornado).

Knowledge to Action

Do any additional coverages or coverage extensions apply?

Feedback: Yes, but the only additional coverage or coverage extension of the Business Income (and Extra Expense) Coverage Form that applies to FWB's claim is the Extended Business Income (EBI) additional coverage. EBI applies to the claim because FWB continued to sustain loss of Business Income after its property was replaced and operations resumed. Moreover, as explained in the case facts, the additional loss of business income did not result from "unfavorable business conditions caused by the impact of the Covered Cause of Loss in the area where the described premises are located."

Although EBI applies to FWB's claim, it is limited to the sixty consecutive days immediately following the date the property was replaced and operations resumed. FWB could have lengthened this sixty-day period by purchasing the Extended Period of Indemnity optional coverage, but chose not to obtain that optional coverage.

DICE Analysis Step 3: Conditions

The third DICE step is to review the policy conditions to determine whether they preclude coverage at the time of the loss.

Numerous policy conditions are associated with FWB's business income and extra expense coverage. In addition to the conditions contained in the Business Income (and Extra Expense) Coverage Form, the Commercial Property Conditions and Common Policy Conditions also apply. In investigating the loss, the insurer must ascertain that the insured and the insurer have performed their respective duties imposed by these conditions and that the circumstances of the loss satisfy any other applicable conditions.

As stated in the case facts, the insurer determined that FWB performed all the duties required by the Duties in the Event of Loss condition. Because the insurer and FWB agreed on the determination of the amount of Business Income loss and the amount of Extra Expense incurred, the Appraisal condition was not applicable.

Also, because FWB has a $1 million limit, which satisfies the requirement in the Business Income Agreed Value optional coverage that FWB has purchased, the Coinsurance condition is suspended and therefore there is no possibility of a coinsurance penalty that would reduce the recovery amount. No other conditions had any negative effect on coverage.

Due to FWB complying with all the terms of the coverage part, once the insurer and FWB agree on the amount of loss, the insurer must pay the claim within thirty days after receiving FWB's sworn proof of loss.

Knowledge to Action

Of the following conditions required of the insured, FWB, which are found only as a condition of business income coverage?

a. Timely reporting of claim to the insurer

b. Cooperating with the insurer in investigation of claim

c. Providing a sworn proof of loss statement to the insurer

d. Resuming operations, in whole or in part, as quickly as possible

Feedback: d. Resuming operations is a condition that is unique to business income coverage.

DICE Analysis Step 4: Exclusions

The fourth DICE step is to review the policy exclusions to determine whether they exclude or limit coverage of the loss. The case facts presented provide no indication that any exclusion applies.

Determination of Amounts Payable

Now that you have completed the DICE analysis, you can determine the amounts payable. This involves analyzing the limit(s) of insurance available to pay for the loss and any deductibles that apply. It also involves determining whether more than one policy provides coverage for the same loss. FWB has no other policy that would cover this business income loss and therefore the Other Insurance provisions do not need to be considered.

The full amount of business income loss sustained before FWB's property was restored ($680,000) is covered, minus the amount sustained during the first three days after the physical loss occurred ($4,000), which results in the covered amount of $676,000 of business income loss.

All of FWB's $34,000 in additional costs are covered as extra expense. The period of restoration for Extra Expense coverage begins immediately after the direct physical loss occurs; there is no deductible for loss sustained during the first seventy-two hours, as in the case of business income coverage.

Only the $15,000 of business income loss sustained during the first sixty days following resumption of operations is insured under the EBI coverage extension. The additional $10,000 of business income loss sustained after the initial sixty-day period is not covered. FWB could have covered the additional income loss by purchasing the Extended Period of Indemnity optional coverage. See the exhibit "Amounts Payable to FWB."

Amounts Payable to FWB

Type of Loss	Amount of Loss Covered
Business Income	$676,000
Extra Expense	34,000
EBI	15,000
Total	$725,000

[DA07920]

The limit of insurance for FWB's Business Income (and Extra Expense) Coverage Form is $1 million, which is the maximum amount payable for loss in any one occurrence. Because the covered amount of FWB's losses is $725,000, the limit of insurance does not reduce the amount payable. As discussed in connection with Step 3, the Business Income Agreed Value optional coverage is in effect, suspending the Coinsurance condition and therefore eliminating any possibility of a coinsurance penalty that would reduce the amount payable.

SUMMARY

A business income loss can sometimes be more devastating for an insured than the associated property loss. A business income loss is measured as the reduction in the insured's net income—the difference between expected net income had no loss occurred and actual net income after the loss. The causes of loss are often the same as for direct property losses.

Using either the Business Income (and Extra Expense) Coverage Form or the Business Income (Without Extra Expense) Coverage Form, most business income exposures can be insured. The Business Income insuring agreement is found in both of these forms, while the Extra Expense insuring agreement is found only in the Business Income (and Extra Expense) Coverage Form.

The basic coverage provided by the BIC form is supplemented by these additional coverages and one coverage extension:

- Expenses to Reduce Loss (BIC without extra expense only)
- Civil Authority
- Alterations and New Buildings
- Extended Business Income
- Interruption of Computer Operations
- Newly Acquired Locations

The amount payable by an insurer for a business income loss is determined in part by the BIC's Limits of Insurance, Loss Conditions, and Additional Condition (Coinsurance) sections. In particular, purchasing a limit of insurance that satisfies the BIC Coinsurance condition can help ensure an adequate recovery for business income losses.

The BIC includes four optional coverages that can be used to prevent application of a coinsurance penalty or to prolong business income coverage beyond the period of restoration.

The four optional coverages include:

- Maximum Period of Indemnity
- Monthly Limit of Indemnity

- Business Income Agreed Value
- Extended Period of Indemnity

You should now be able to apply policy language to business income losses to determine whether the losses are covered and the amount for which they are covered.

Direct Your Learning

6

Commercial Crime and Equipment Breakdown Insurance

Educational Objectives

After learning the content of this assignment, you should be able to:

- Describe the basic characteristics of the ISO commercial crime program and financial institution bonds.
- Summarize the seven insuring agreements of the Commercial Crime Coverage Form in terms of these elements:
  - Covered causes of loss
  - Covered property
  - Where coverage applies
- Apply the Commercial Crime Coverage Form's Limit of Insurance and Deductible provisions to a claim.
- Identify losses that the Commercial Crime Coverage Form excludes.
- Explain how the Commercial Crime Coverage Form's conditions address each of these issues:
  - Interests insured
  - Where coverage applies
  - When coverage applies
  - Claim-related duties and procedures
  - Conditions applicable to Employee Theft only
- Given a case, determine whether, and for how much, a described loss would be covered by the Commercial Crime Coverage Form.
- Describe equipment breakdown insurance in terms of these elements:
  - Why equipment breakdown insurance is needed
  - Insuring agreements included in equipment breakdown coverage forms
  - Conditions that distinguish equipment breakdown insurance from other types of insurance

Outline

Commercial Crime and Equipment Breakdown Insurance

6

OVERVIEW OF COMMERCIAL CRIME INSURANCE

Organizations use various techniques to manage their loss exposures resulting from criminal acts such as robbery, burglary, and other forms of theft. Among these techniques are avoidance (for example, paying employees by check or direct deposit instead of in cash), risk control (for example, installing burglar alarms), and insurance.

Many types of insurance provide coverage against some property losses that result from criminal acts. Because crime loss exposures can vary significantly among policyholders and require special underwriting skills, insurers prefer to insure certain types of crime-related property loss under separate commercial crime insurance forms. These forms allow organizations to cover crime losses that are not insured under other insurance policies.

Briefly described, commercial crime insurance covers money, securities, and other property against a variety of criminal acts, such as employee theft, robbery, forgery, extortion, and computer fraud. Many insurers use Insurance Services Office, Inc. (ISO) commercial crime forms. Financial institution bonds are used to meet the crime insurance needs of banks, insurance companies, and other types of financial institutions.

ISO Commercial Crime Program

The ISO commercial crime program includes crime coverage forms that can be added to a commercial package policy, as well as crime policy forms that can be written as monoline crime policies. The principal difference between the coverage forms and the policy forms is that the policy forms include the conditions contained in the ISO Common Policy Conditions form, thus eliminating the need to attach them to a monoline crime policy. Each coverage form and policy form comes in two versions: a discovery form and a loss sustained form. See the exhibit "Crime Forms: Discovery Form Versus Loss Sustained Form."

The ISO commercial crime coverage forms and policy forms are designed for insuring any type of nongovernment commercial or not-for-profit entity other than a financial institution. A separate set of ISO government crime coverage forms and policy forms is used to insure government entities, such as states, counties, and public utilities. See the exhibit "ISO Crime Forms and Policies."

Crime Forms: Discovery Form Versus Loss Sustained Form

Discovery Form	Loss Sustained Form
Form that covers losses discovered during the policy period even though they may have occurred before the policy period.	Form that covers losses actually sustained during the policy period and discovered no later than one year after policy expiration.

[DA07817]

Financial Institution Bonds

Few industries have crime loss exposures equal to those faced by banks and other financial institutions. A financial institution bond is an insurance policy that covers the crime loss exposures of financial institutions. Financial institution bonds were developed by the Surety & Fidelity Association of America (SFAA) and are called "bonds" because one of the key coverages that they provide is employee dishonesty insurance, which was traditionally called a "fidelity bond."

Although banks are the most common type of financial institution, other entities—such as savings and loan associations, credit unions, stockbrokers, finance companies, and insurance companies—are also eligible to be insured under financial institution bonds. Entities eligible for financial institution bonds are not eligible for the ISO commercial crime program.

The most widely used financial institution bond is Standard Form No. 24, used to insure banks and savings and loan associations. For many years, this form was called the "bankers blanket bond," a term still often used informally to refer to this coverage. The forms used for other types of financial institutions are similar to Form 24. ISO also publishes financial institution forms similar to the SFAA forms, and many of the insurers that specialize in financial institution coverage have developed their own forms.

ISO Crime Forms and Policies

Form	Form #	Type of Form	Description
Commercial Crime Coverage Form	CR 00 20	Discovery*	Designed for attachment to another policy to provide crime coverage (eight insuring agreements) for organizations other than financial institutions** and government entities.
Commercial Crime Coverage Form	CR 00 21	Loss sustained***	Designed for attachment to another policy to provide crime coverage (eight insuring agreements) for organizations other than financial institutions and government entities.
Commercial Crime Policy	CR 00 22	Discovery	Designed as a stand-alone policy to provide crime coverage (eight insuring agreements) for organizations other than financial institutions and government entities.
Commercial Crime Policy	CR 00 23	Loss sustained	Designed as a stand-alone policy to provide crime coverage (eight insuring agreements) for organizations other than financial institutions and government entities.
Government Crime Coverage Form	CR 00 24	Discovery	Designed for attachment to another policy to provide crime coverage (nine insuring agreements) for government entities.
Government Crime Coverage Form	CR 00 25	Loss sustained	Designed for attachment to another policy to provide crime coverage (nine insuring agreements) for government entities.
Government Crime Policy	CR 00 26	Discovery	Designed as a stand-alone policy to provide crime coverage (nine insuring agreements) for government entities.
Government Crime Policy	CR 00 27	Loss sustained	Designed as a stand-alone policy to provide crime coverage (nine insuring agreements) for government entities.
Employee Theft and Forgery Policy	CR 00 28	Discovery	Designed to provide only employee theft and forgery or alteration coverage in a monoline policy.
Employee Theft and Forgery Policy	CR 00 29	Loss Sustained	Designed to provide only employee theft and forgery or alteration coverage in a monoline policy.

* Loss is discovered during the policy period and sustained during the policy period, before it, or both.

**Financial institutions include banks, savings and loan associations, credit unions, insurers, and similar institutions. These organizations obtain their crime insurance under financial institution bonds (a specialized policy).

***Loss is sustained during the policy period and discovered no longer than one year after the policy period.

[DA05994]

COMMERCIAL CRIME INSURING AGREEMENTS

The Insurance Services Office, Inc. (ISO) Commercial Crime Coverage Form offers optional insuring agreements that enable organizations to customize crime coverage to meet their business needs.

The ISO Commercial Crime Coverage Form includes these insuring agreements, numbered in the form as shown:

1. Employee Theft
2. Forgery or Alteration
3. Inside the Premises—Theft of Money and Securities
4. Inside the Premises—Robbery or Safe Burglary of Other Property
5. Outside the Premises
6. Computer and Funds Transfer Fraud
7. Money Orders and Counterfeit Money

Insureds may select one or more of these insuring agreements and can add other crime coverages by endorsement.

Employee Theft

Insuring Agreement 1 covers an employer against theft of its property by its own employees. The scope of the coverage is determined by policy definitions of various terms. See the exhibit "Summary of Employee Theft Coverage."

Summary of Employee Theft Coverage

Cause of Loss	"Theft" committed by any "employee."
Property Covered	"Money," "securities," and "other property."
Where Coverage Applies	Covered territory is the United States (including its territories and possessions), Puerto Rico, and Canada. Coverage also applies to loss caused by an employee who is temporarily outside the covered territory for not more than ninety consecutive days.

[DA02511]

The policy defines "theft" as the unlawful taking of "money," "securities," or "other property" to the deprivation of the insured. No police report or criminal conviction is required for coverage to apply. The Employee Theft insuring agreement also states that the term "theft" includes forgery—thereby clarifying that forgery committed by an employee is covered under this insuring agreement, not under the Forgery or Alteration insuring agreement.

The policy definition of "employee" is a natural person (not a corporation) who is currently employed by the insured or who was employed by the insured within the past thirty days; who is compensated by the insured by salary, wages, or commissions; and who is subject to the control and direction of the insured. The definition includes further details that are not discussed here.

The policy defines these types of covered property:

- "Money" means currency, coins, and bank notes in current use with a face value, and travelers' checks, register checks, and money orders held for sale to the public. Under insuring agreements 1, 2, and 6, money also includes deposits in the named insured's account at any financial institution as defined in the form.
- "Securities" means negotiable and nonnegotiable instruments or contracts representing money or other property, such as stocks, bonds, tokens, tickets, stamps, and evidences of debt issued in connection with credit cards other than cards issued by the insured.
- "Other property" means all other tangible property that has intrinsic value. Computer programs, electronic data, and other specified property are excluded. "Tangible" means "possible to touch." Copyrights, patents, intellectual property, and other intangible items are not covered property under the crime coverage form.

The Employee Theft insuring agreement extends the coverage territory to include loss caused by any employee while temporarily outside the regular policy territory (the United States, including its territories and possessions, Puerto Rico, and Canada) for up to ninety consecutive days.

Forgery or Alteration

Insuring Agreement 2 covers loss sustained for these reasons:

> "forgery" or alteration of checks, drafts, promissory notes, or similar written promises, orders or directions to pay a sum certain in "money" that are:
>
> (1) Made or drawn by or drawn upon you; or
>
> (2) Made or drawn by one acting as your agent;
>
> or that are purported to have been so made or drawn.[1]

The coverage pays losses of the insured or its representatives resulting from forgery or alteration of checks and similar instruments; it does not pay losses resulting from the insured's knowing acceptance of instruments that have been forged or altered by others. See the exhibit "Summary of Forgery or Alteration Coverage."

Summary of Forgery or Alteration Coverage

Causes of Loss	"Forgery" and alteration
Property Covered	Checks, drafts, promissory notes, or similar instruments made or drawn by the insured or the insured's agent
Where Coverage Applies	Worldwide

[DA07838]

Forgery or alteration coverage does not apply to loss resulting from dishonest acts of the insured or of its partners, members, directors, trustees, representatives, or employees. Forgery committed against the insured by the insured's employees is covered under the Employee Theft insuring agreement, not under the Forgery or Alteration insuring agreement.

Inside the Premises—Theft of Money and Securities

Insuring Agreement 3 covers money and securities inside the "premises" or "financial institution premises" against theft, disappearance, or destruction.

Under this insuring agreement, "premises" means the interior of any commercial building the named insured occupies. The form defines financial institution premises as the interior of that portion of any building occupied by a financial institution. For purposes of Insuring Agreement 3, the form defines "financial institution" as "(1) A bank, savings bank, savings and loan association, trust company, credit union or similar depository institution; or (2) An insurance company."[2]

The insuring agreement extends coverage to apply to loss or damage to the premises if the insured is the owner or is liable for the damage, and to containers that hold covered property if damage is caused by safe burglary or attempted safe burglary.

The policy definition of theft includes any type of "unlawful taking" of covered property "to the deprivation of the insured." Hence, an insured loss (subject to exclusions) can be caused by burglary, robbery, observed or unobserved theft, or any other unlawful taking of money or securities. However, for this coverage to apply, the thief must be present inside the premises or the banking premises; thus, theft committed through a remote computer is not covered.

Disappearance or destruction includes losses regardless of whether they are caused by unlawful acts. For example, coverage is provided for money and securities destroyed by fire, and disappearance of property is covered regardless of whether theft appears to be the cause. See the exhibit "Summary of Inside the Premises—Theft of Money and Securities Coverage."

Summary of Inside the Premises—Theft of Money and Securities Coverage

	Basic Coverage	Extension for Damage to Premises	Extension for Containers
Covered Causes of Loss	"Theft," disappearance, destruction	Actual or attempted "theft" of "money" or "securities"	Actual or attempted "theft" or unlawful entry
Covered Property	"Money," "securities"	The "premises" or their exterior	Locked safe, vault, cash register, cash box, or cash drawer
Where Coverage Applies	Inside the "premises" or "financial institution premises" (The thief must be present inside the premises.)	At the "premises"	Inside the "premises"

[DA02514]

Inside the Premises—Robbery or Safe Burglary of Other Property

Insuring Agreement 4 covers "other property" from actual or attempted "robbery" of a "custodian" and actual or attempted "safe burglary."

According to the policy definition, the unlawful taking of property is considered "robbery" if the person taking the property has caused or threatened to cause bodily harm to the person having care or custody of the property or if the custodian witnesses an obviously unlawful act (for example, seeing someone run out of the store with property for which he or she has not paid). See the exhibit "Summary of Inside the Premises—Robbery or Safe Burglary of Other Property Coverage."

Summary of Inside the Premises—Robbery or Safe Burglary of Other Property Coverage

	Basic Coverage	Extension for Damage to Premises	Extension for Containers
Covered Causes of Loss	Actual or attempted "robbery" of a "custodian" or "safe burglary"	Actual or attempted "robbery" or "safe burglary" of "other property"	Actual or attempted "robbery" or "safe burglary"
Covered Property	"Other property"	The "premises" or their exterior	Locked safe or vault
Where Coverage Applies	Inside the "premises"	At the "premises"	Inside the "premises"

[DA02521]

For robbery coverage to apply, the property must be inside the premises when taken from the named insured, the named insured's partners, or any employee who is a custodian as defined in the policy. A custodian may be a salesperson or cashier working inside the insured's store but cannot be a watchperson (hired exclusively to have care and custody of property inside the premises with no other duties) or janitor (a doorkeeper or person who cleans or maintains the premises).

The other covered peril, "safe burglary," is the unlawful taking of a safe or vault from inside the premises or of property from within a locked safe or vault by a person unlawfully entering the safe or vault as evidenced by marks of forcible entry. Coverage is only provided if a burglar leaves marks of forcible entry into the safe or vault. In an actual or attempted robbery or safe burglary, coverage extends for resulting damage to the premises and for loss of or damage to a locked safe or vault located inside the premises.

Outside the Premises

Insuring Agreement 5 covers money, securities, and other property while outside the premises and in the care and custody of either a "messenger" or an armored vehicle company. The policy defines "messenger" as the named insured, a relative of the named insured, any partner or member of the named insured, "or any 'employee' while having care and custody of property outside the 'premises.'"[3] For example, an employee who takes cash and checks to the bank for deposit in the insured's account is a messenger.

The perils insured against vary by the type of property involved in the loss. Money and securities are covered against theft, disappearance, or destruction. Other property is covered against actual or attempted robbery. See the exhibit "Summary of Outside the Premises Coverage."

Summary of Outside the Premises Coverage

	Coverage for "Money" and "Securities"	Coverage for "Other Property"
Covered Causes of Loss	"Theft," disappearance, destruction	Actual or attempted "robbery"
Where Coverage Applies	Outside the "premises" while in care or custody of a "messenger" or an armored car company and inside the United States (including its territories and possessions), Puerto Rico, and Canada	Outside the "premises" while in care or custody of a "messenger" or an armored car company and inside the U.S. (including its territories and possessions), Puerto Rico, and Canada

[DA02522]

Computer and Funds Transfer Fraud

Insuring Agreement 6 covers two types of loss that were, before the introduction of the 2012 editions of the ISO commercial crime forms, covered by separate Computer Fraud and Funds Transfer Fraud insuring agreements.

The first part of the Computer and Funds Transfer Fraud insuring agreement covers loss resulting directly from fraudulent entry of electronic data or computer program into, or change of electronic data or computer program within, a computer system owned, leased, or operated by the named insured. The fraudulent entry or change must cause either of these results:

- Money, securities, or other property to be transferred, paid, or delivered
- The named insured's account at a financial institution to be debited or deleted

The second part of the insuring agreement covers loss resulting directly from a fraudulent instruction directing a financial institution to debit the named insured's transfer account and transfer, pay, or deliver money or securities from that account. See the exhibit "Summary of Computer Funds and Transfer Fraud Coverage."

Summary of Computer Funds and Transfer Fraud Coverage

	Coverage for Computer Fraud	Coverage for Funds Transfer Fraud
Covered Cause of Loss	Use of a computer to fraudulently cause a transfer of covered property or cause the named insured's account at a financial institution to be debited or deleted.	Fraudulent instruction directing a financial institution to debit the named insured's transfer account and transfer covered property from that account.
Covered Property	"Money," "securities," and "other property."	"Money" or "securities."
Where Coverage Applies	Coverage applies to loss resulting directly from an occurrence taking place anywhere in the world.	

[DA11294]

Money Orders and Counterfeit Money

Insuring Agreement 7 covers loss from money orders that are not paid when presented and "counterfeit money" that the insured has accepted in good faith in exchange for merchandise, money, or services. See the exhibit "Summary of Money Orders and Counterfeit Money Coverage."

Summary of Money Orders and Counterfeit Money Coverage

Covered Cause of Loss	Good-faith acceptance of: (1) Money orders that are not paid upon presentation or (2) "Counterfeit money"
Covered Property	Money orders issued by any post office, express company, or financial institution; and "counterfeit money" acquired during the regular course of business
Where Coverage Applies	United States (including its territories and possessions), Puerto Rico, and Canada

[DA02525]

COMMERCIAL CRIME LIMITS AND DEDUCTIBLE

Applying an insurance policy's limit of insurance and deductible to a claim covered under the policy is crucial to determining the amount payable. The Insurance Services Office, Inc. (ISO) Commercial Crime Coverage Form contains provisions that specify the manner in which the policy's limits and deductible(s) should be applied.

The Commercial Crime Coverage Form's Limit of Insurance provision states that the most the insurer will pay for all loss resulting directly from an "occurrence" (as defined in the policy) is the applicable limit shown in the declarations. Therefore, whether an act meets the policy's definition of occurrence and the limit that applies to the claim that stems from that act are components of the determination of the amount payable. The Deductible provision, which indicates how the deductible shown in the policy's declarations affects the insurer's payment, must also be applied to the claim.

Limit of Insurance

Under the Commercial Crime Coverage Form, a separate limit of insurance can be shown in the declarations for each insuring agreement that the insured selects. If a loss is covered under more than one insuring agreement, the insurer will pay no more than the highest limit of the insuring agreements that apply.

Definition of Occurrence

The definition of "occurrence" is key in determining how much the insurer is obligated to pay for a covered crime loss. Slightly different definitions of occurrence apply to employee theft coverage, forgery or alteration coverage, and all other coverages. Each of these definitions states that "occurrence" includes an individual act, the combined total of all separate acts (whether or not related), or a series of acts (whether or not related).

As defined for employee theft, the definition of occurrence requires that the act or acts must be committed by an employee (as defined in the form) acting alone or in collusion with others. Thus, if the employee theft limit is $100,000, the most the insurer would be required to pay for one instance of embezzlement—regardless of how many employees might have been involved in the crime—is $100,000. In addition, because of the definition of occurrence, the applicable limit is the most the insurer will pay for an individual act or a series of acts involving the same employee.

The definition of occurrence that applies to forgery or alteration requires that the act or acts must be committed by a person acting alone or in collusion with others and must involve one or more instruments. Therefore, if one person or a ring of perpetrators forged multiple documents, the resulting loss would be considered as having been caused by a single occurrence, and the insurer would pay no more for the combined loss than the forgery or alteration limit.

The definition of occurrence that applies to all coverages other than employee dishonesty and forgery or alteration includes not only acts but also events. The word "event" is included because some of the perils covered by these other coverages are events rather than acts committed by persons. For example, money and securities can be covered for theft, disappearance, or destruction. Although theft is an act committed by persons, disappearance and destruction can be caused by events such as windstorm or earthquake.

Each definition of occurrence comes in two different versions: one for the loss sustained forms and another for the discovery forms. The difference is found at the end of each definition:

- The loss sustained forms state that the act must be committed (or the event must occur) "during the Policy Period shown in the Declarations, except as provided" in the conditions pertaining to loss sustained under prior insurance
- The discovery forms state that the act must be committed (or the event must occur) "during the Policy Period shown in the Declarations, before such Policy Period or both."[4]

Special Limits of Insurance

In addition to the limits of insurance shown in the policy declarations for each insuring agreement, three of the insuring agreements are subject to special limits that apply only to specified types of covered property.

Inside the Premises—Robbery or Safe Burglary of Other Property is subject to a special limit of $5,000 per occurrence for these types of property:

> (1) Precious metals, precious or semiprecious stones, pearls, furs, or completed or partially completed articles made of or containing such materials that constitute the principal value of such articles; or
>
> (2) Manuscripts, drawings, or records of any kind or the cost of reconstructing them or reproducing any information contained in them.[5]

Outside the Premises coverage is subject to a special limit of $5,000 per occurrence for the types of property listed in items (1) and (2). Computer and Funds Transfer Fraud coverage is subject to a special limit of $5,000 per occurrence for loss of or damage to the types of property listed in item (2).

Deductible

No loss in any one occurrence is payable by the insurer unless the amount of loss exceeds the deductible shown in the declarations. If the amount of loss exceeds the deductible, the insurer will pay the amount of the loss in excess of the deductible, up to the limit of insurance.

To illustrate application of the deductible with a hypothetical case, assume that Tri-State Supply Company has employee theft coverage with a $100,000 limit and a $1,000 deductible. If one employee stole $5,000 of covered property, the insurer would pay the amount of loss in excess of the $1,000 deductible, or $4,000. If the amount of loss exceeded the limit of insurance by the deductible amount or more, the insured would be able to recover the full amount of insurance. For example, on a loss of $101,000 or more, the insurer would pay the full $100,000 limit in excess of the $1,000 deductible. In other words, the deductible is taken off the amount of the loss, not off the limit.

Apply Your Knowledge

An independent audit of the accounting records of a business insured under a Commercial Crime Coverage Form reveals that several employees in the organization's accounting department colluded over five years (and five policy periods) to embezzle $200,000 annually. The policy's limit of insurance is $500,000, with a per-occurrence deductible of $1,000. The insured submits a claim to its insurer for $1,000,000, the total that was stolen. Will the Commercial Crime Coverage Form apply to this claim and, if so, what amount will the insurer pay for this loss?

Feedback: Yes, the Commercial Crime Coverage Form will apply to this claim. The definition of "occurrence" applicable to employee theft coverage requires that the act or acts be committed by an employee, whether acting alone or in collusion with others, and that the act must be committed "during the Policy Period shown in the Declarations, before such Policy Period, or both." The facts of the claim meet this condition, as the theft occurred over a number of years prior to the discovery during the audit. Additionally, the definition of occurrence states the limit of insurance is the most the insurer will be liable for as a result of an individual act or a series of acts involving the same employee. In this circumstance, the most the insurer will pay for the act of employee theft, regardless of how many employees were involved and—equally importantly—regardless of the number of acts of employee theft, is $500,000. Finally, the amount of loss the insurer is obligated to pay under the Commercial Crime Coverage Form is the amount in excess of the deductible. The amount of the loss, $1,000,000, exceeds the limit of $500,000, so the insurer will pay the full limit in excess of the $1,000 deductible. The deductible is subtracted from the amount of the loss, not the limit of insurance.

COMMERCIAL CRIME EXCLUSIONS

As with most insurance coverage forms, the Commercial Crime Coverage Form excludes losses that are best covered under other insurance, are not insurable, or are not anticipated in the policy premium.

In the Insurance Services Office, Inc. (ISO) Commercial Crime Coverage Form, the basic crime insuring agreements are subject to several exclusions. The exclusions are divided into different groups, depending on whether they apply to all or only some insuring agreements.

Exclusions are presented in the coverage form and described in this section based on these groupings:

- General exclusions
- Exclusions applicable only to employee theft
- Exclusions applicable to inside the premises and outside the premises
- Exclusions applicable only to computer and funds transfer fraud

General Exclusions

Eleven general exclusions are applicable to any of the crime insuring agreements:

- Acts Committed by You, Your Partners or Your Members—The exclusion eliminates coverage for loss resulting from theft or any other dishonest act committed by the named insured, the named insured's partners, or (if the named insured is a limited liability company) the named insured's members, whether acting alone or in collusion with other persons.
- Acts Committed by Your Employees Learned of by You Prior to the Policy Period—The exclusion eliminates coverage for loss resulting from theft or any other dishonest act committed by an employee if the named insured, the named insured's partners, or the named insured's members, or any managers, officers, directors, or trustees, not in collusion with the employee, knew that the employee had committed theft or a dishonest act before the policy's effective date. This exclusion prevents the insurer from having to cover employee theft committed by employees who are known, prior to the policy period, to have committed any type of dishonest act.
- Acts Committed by Your Employees, Managers, Directors, Trustees or Representatives—The commercial crime form excludes theft or other dishonest acts committed by the named insured's employees, managers, directors, trustees, or authorized representatives. The exclusion applies regardless of whether such persons acted alone or in collusion with others and while such persons performed services for the named insured or otherwise. The exclusion states that it does not apply to loss covered under the Employee Theft insuring agreement.
- Confidential or Personal Information—The form excludes losses resulting from the use of another person's or organization's confidential or personal information, including, but not limited to, patents, trade secrets, processing methods, customer lists, credit card information, or health information.
- Data Security Breach—The form excludes fees, costs, fines, penalties, and other expenses the insured incurs related to the access to or disclosure of

another person's or organization's confidential or personal information, which includes, but is not limited to, patents, trade secrets, processing methods, customer lists, financial information, credit card information, health information, or any other type of nonpublic information.

- Governmental Action—Like virtually any policy covering property loss, the commercial crime form excludes loss resulting from seizure or destruction of property by order of government authority.
- Indirect Loss—The form lists three examples of indirect loss that are not covered: (1) business income losses; (2) payment of damages for which the insured is legally liable (other than compensatory damages arising directly from a loss covered by the policy); and (3) expenses incurred in establishing either the existence or the amount of loss under the policy. The exclusion is not limited to just those three types of indirect loss; any indirect loss is excluded.
- Legal Fees, Costs and Expenses—The form excludes fees, costs, and expenses related to any legal action except when covered under the Forgery and Alteration insuring agreement.
- Nuclear Hazard—The exclusion eliminates coverage for loss or damage caused by any nuclear reaction, radiation, or radioactive contamination.
- Pollution—This exclusion eliminates coverage for any loss or damage that in any way results from pollution, which the exclusion defines as "the discharge, dispersal, seepage, migration, release or escape of any solid, liquid, gaseous, or thermal irritant or contaminant." Pollution includes residuals of pollutants, such as smoke, vapor, fumes, and so forth, along with materials to be recycled, reconditioned, or reclaimed.
- War and Military Action—This exclusion eliminates coverage for loss or damage resulting from war or civil war, whether declared or undeclared; warlike actions by a military force; or acts of rebellion or revolution, including governmental action to defend against such acts.

Exclusions Applicable Only to Employee Theft

This group of exclusions applies only to the Employee Theft insuring agreement:

- Inventory Shortages—The insurer will not pay for any loss that depends on inventory or profit-and-loss calculations to prove either the existence or the amount of the loss. An inventory shortage is the difference between a physical inventory and the inventory shown in the insured's books and records. An inventory shortage may occur for reasons other than employee theft. For example, there may have been bookkeeping or arithmetic errors, obsolete inventory may have been discarded, or samples may have been sent to customers but not deleted from the inventory records. Therefore, insurers will not accept an inventory calculation as proof that the insured has sustained an employee theft loss. However, if an insured establishes without inventory computations that it has sustained a loss, the form allows the insured to offer inventory records and actual physical count of inventory in support of the amount of loss claimed.

- Trading—An employer may sustain a large financial loss resulting from an employee's unauthorized trading in stocks, bonds, futures, commodities, or other similar items. Because employee theft coverage rates do not contemplate such losses, the form excludes loss resulting from trading, whether the trading occurs in the named insured's name or in a "genuine or fictitious account."
- Warehouse Receipts—The Warehouse Receipts exclusion eliminates coverage for "loss resulting from fraudulent or dishonest signing, issuing, canceling or failing to cancel, a warehouse receipt or any papers connected with it." Such a loss may occur, for example, when an employee releases merchandise without canceling the receipt or issues a receipt without having received the merchandise. The customer could then make a claim for missing goods based on the erroneous receipts. Such claims would not be covered because of this exclusion.

Exclusions Applicable Only to Inside the Premises and Outside the Premises

These eight exclusions apply specifically to the Inside the Premises—Theft of Money and Securities; Inside the Premises—Robbery or Safe Burglary of Other Property; and Outside the Premises insuring agreements:

- Accounting or Arithmetical Errors or Omissions—The form excludes losses resulting from accounting or arithmetical errors or omissions. Although many losses of this type are within the policy deductible, some losses could be sizable. The exposure falls within the general category of business risks that should be addressed by loss control measures, with any losses retained by the business.
- Exchanges or Purchases—Loss resulting from giving or surrendering property in an exchange or purchase is excluded. Thus, a fraudulent transaction that involves the loss of money, securities, or other property is not covered. For example, the loss sustained when a purchaser pays with a forged cashier's check is excluded from coverage.
- Fire—The three insuring agreements do not cover loss or damage resulting from fire, regardless of its cause. However, the exclusion does not apply to fire damage to a safe or vault. The exclusion also does not apply (under Inside the Premises—Theft of Money and Securities) to money or securities damaged or destroyed by fire. Nearly all organizations have commercial property insurance to cover the fire losses that the crime form excludes; money, however, is not covered under commercial property coverage forms.
- Money Operated Devices—Loss of property from money-operated devices (such as vending machines, amusement devices, or change machines) is not covered unless a continuous recording instrument inside the machine

keeps track of the amount of money deposited. In the absence of a recording device, establishing the amount of the loss would be difficult or impossible.

- Motor Vehicles or Equipment and Accessories—The form excludes loss of or damage to motor vehicles, trailers, or semi-trailers, or for equipment and accessories attached to them. Theft of automobiles and related equipment can be insured under automobile physical damage coverage, and theft of mobile equipment can be insured under inland marine forms.
- Transfer or Surrender of Property—Loss of or damage to property after it has been transferred or surrendered to a person or place outside the premises or financial institution premises is excluded under several specified circumstances. For example, loss of property that the insured has voluntarily sent to an imposter on the basis of unauthorized instructions is excluded.
- Vandalism—Coverage extensions stated in the two inside the premises insuring agreements cover damage to the premises and their exterior and loss of or damage to various types of receptacles containing covered property if directly caused by a covered peril. The Vandalism exclusion eliminates coverage for damage to those types of property by vandalism or malicious mischief. Commercial property forms normally include coverage for damage to such property by vandalism or malicious mischief, including building damage caused by the breaking in or exiting of burglars.
- Voluntary Parting With Title to or Possession of Property—The voluntary parting exclusion eliminates coverage when the insured or an agent of the insured is tricked into voluntarily surrendering property to a thief. For example, a business owner tells the firm's cashier that a bank messenger is to pick up money at a given time each day. If a wrongdoer impersonates the messenger and succeeds in getting the cashier to part with the money voluntarily, the loss would not be covered by Inside the Premises—Theft of Money and Securities.

Exclusions Applicable Only to Computer and Funds Transfer Fraud

These five exclusions apply only to the Computer and Funds Transfer Fraud insuring agreement:

- Authorized Access—Loss resulting from fraudulent entry of or a fraudulent change to electronic data or a computer program in any computer system that is owned, leased, or operated by the insured that is executed by a person or organization with authorized access to the insured's computer system is excluded. The exclusion does not apply if the fraudulent entry or change is made by an employee acting on a fraudulent instruction from a computer software contractor who has a written agreement with the insured. It also does not apply to losses that may be covered under the Employee Theft Insuring Agreement.

- Credit Card Transactions—Loss resulting from the use or purported use of credit, debit, charge, access, convenience, identification, stored-value, or other cards or the information contained on such cards is excluded.
- Exchanges or Purchases—Loss resulting from the giving or surrendering of property in any exchange or purchase is excluded. For example, this exclusion may apply to an Internet-based transaction in which an insured knowingly exchanges a product for compensation whose value is less than the value the insured intended to receive in exchange for that product.
- Fraudulent Instructions—Loss resulting from an employee or financial institution acting upon a fraudulent instruction to transfer, pay, or deliver money, securities, or other property or from an employee or financial institution acting upon a fraudulent instruction to debit or delete the insured's account is excluded. However, the exclusion does not apply if the loss results directly from a fraudulent instruction that directs a financial institution to debit the insured's transfer account and pay, transfer, or deliver money or securities from that account. It also does not apply if the fraudulent entry or change is made by an employee acting on a fraudulent instruction from a computer software contractor who has a written agreement with the insured.
- Inventory Shortages—A separate Inventory Shortages exclusion applies to computer fraud coverage. Unlike the general exclusion, this exclusion does not include the wording permitting the insured to use inventory records in support of the amount of loss claimed.

Apply Your Knowledge

Identify any exclusions of the Commercial Crime Coverage Form that would apply to these losses. In each case, the insured has purchased all of the insuring agreements under this coverage form:

Tom, an employee of the insured, commits an act that meets all of the requirements under the Employee Theft insuring agreement. The insurer's claims investigation reveals that Tom had been arrested for shoplifting before the policy period began. However, Tom's employer had no knowledge of Tom's prior dishonesty until it was revealed by the investigation. Would the Acts of Employees Learned of by You Prior to the Policy Period exclusion eliminate coverage for this loss?

Feedback: No. The exclusion applies only if the insured learns of the prior dishonest act before the beginning of the policy period. In this case, Tom's employer did not know about Tom's prior dishonest act before the policy period, so the exclusion does not apply.

Vandals set the insured's building on fire. In addition to damaging the building and its contents, the fire destroys $5,000 of money that was in the insured's building. The loss of money meets all the requirements under the Inside the Premises—Theft of Money and Securities insuring agreement, which covers money and securities against theft, disappearance, or destruction. Would the Fire exclusion eliminate coverage for this loss?

Feedback: No. The Fire exclusion does not apply to loss of or damage to money or securities.

A thief breaks into and steals money from vending machines located in a convenience store. The vending machines do not contain recording instruments to track the money that was deposited. The loss of money meets all the requirements under the Inside the Premises—Theft of Money and Securities insuring agreement. Would the Money Operated Devices exclusion eliminate coverage for this loss?

Feedback: Yes. The Money Operated Devices exclusion eliminates coverage from such devices that do not have a continuous recording instrument inside them to keep track of the amount of money deposited.

COMMERCIAL CRIME CONDITIONS

The Insurance Services Office, Inc. (ISO) Commercial Crime Coverage Form includes numerous policy conditions that affect the application or extent of coverage provided.

As with all insurance policies, conditions are included in the ISO Commercial Crime Coverage Form that extend or eliminate coverage under various circumstances. Some conditions apply only to certain insuring agreements. Other conditions apply to all of the insuring agreements. The latter group, although listed alphabetically in the form, are presented here in logical order followed by two conditions that apply only to the Employee Theft insuring agreement.

Interests Insured

Several conditions help to clarify issues concerning the interests insured under a crime policy.

The Ownership of Property; Interests Covered condition states that the insurance applies only to property owned, leased, or held by the named insured, or for which the insured is legally liable, provided that the insured was liable for the property before the loss occurred. However, the insurance is for the insured's benefit only; any claim must be made by the insured. If the insured does not want to present a claim, the owner of the property cannot make a direct claim on the insurance. Coverage for theft by the insured's employee of client's property may be added by endorsement.

The Joint Insured condition appoints the first named insured as agent for all other insureds with regard to all transactions under the policy. It also provides that an employee of any insured is considered to be an employee of every insured and that knowledge possessed by any insured or any partner, officer, or limited liability company (LLC) member of any insured is considered to be known to all insureds.

If, during the policy period, the insured adds additional premises or employees other than by consolidation, merger, or acquisition, the Additional Premises or Employees condition states that policy coverage will be extended automatically.

No notice is required, and no additional premium is charged for the remainder of the policy period. On renewal, the insured must give the insurer full information, and the renewal premium will reflect the revised exposure.

If the insured acquires additional employees or premises by consolidation, merger, or acquisition, the Consolidation—Merger or Acquisition condition states that coverage will be extended automatically for ninety days to the new employees or premises. If the insured wishes to extend coverage beyond ninety days, the insured must notify the insurer of the consolidation, merger, or acquisition promptly and pay the appropriate additional premium.

Where Coverage Applies

Many of the crime insuring agreements limit coverage to occurrences inside the premises described in the policy. When coverage is not restricted to the premises, the Territory condition defines the geographical scope of coverage. This condition limits coverage for all insuring agreements to acts committed or events occurring within the United States (including its territories and possessions), Puerto Rico, and Canada. The territorial provision for employee theft coverage is extended to include coverage for loss caused by employees temporarily outside the coverage territory for not more than ninety days. The territorial provisions for forgery or alteration coverage and computer and funds transfer fraud coverage are extended to cover loss resulting from occurrences taking place anywhere in the world.

When Coverage Applies

Three conditions are principally concerned with determining when a loss must occur in order to be covered under the loss sustained version of the Commercial Crime Coverage Form:

- Extended Period to Discover Loss
- Loss Sustained During Prior Insurance Issued by Us or Any Affiliate
- Loss Sustained During Prior Insurance Not Issued by Us or Any Affiliate

Extended Period to Discover Loss

Under the loss sustained form, the insurer will pay for loss that the named insured sustains through acts committed or events occurring during the policy period. Moreover, coverage applies only to acts discovered during the policy period or within one year after the policy is canceled. However, the discovery period terminates immediately as of the effective date of any other insurance that the insured obtains (from any insurer) that replaces coverage in whole or in part. See the exhibit "Discovery Form."

Discovery Form

All of the ISO crime forms are available in loss sustained and discovery versions. The discovery form covers losses regardless of when they occurred if they are first discovered during the policy period or during the sixty-day discovery period that applies to most claims under the discovery form.

To limit the broad coverage for prior occurrences that discovery forms provide, the insurer may attach a retroactive date endorsement. This endorsement states that coverage is limited to losses the insured sustains through acts committed or events occurring after the retroactive date shown in the policy schedule. For coverage to apply, the loss must still be discovered during the policy period or the extended loss discovery period.

[DA07834]

Loss Sustained During Prior Insurance Issued by Us or Any Affiliate

Some losses occurring before the current policy period of a loss sustained crime policy may be covered by the policy currently in effect. Under the Loss Sustained During Prior Insurance Issued by Us or Any Affiliate condition, the insurer agrees to pay a loss that meets these criteria:

- The loss is discovered during the policy period shown in the declarations.
- The loss occurred while prior insurance, issued by the same insurer or an affiliated insurer, was in effect.
- The current insurance became effective when the prior insurance was canceled.
- The loss would have been covered by the present insurance if the insurance had been in force at the time of loss.

If these requirements are met, the current policy applies, but the most the insurer will pay is the amount recoverable under the prior insurance, if it had remained in effect.

The same condition also contains provisions for settling covered losses that occurred over more than one policy period. Such losses typically are associated with employee theft, in which an employee may have embezzled funds for years before the employer discovers the loss.

Coverage must be continuous; that is, the renewal policy must have commenced when the prior policy expired, but no limit of insurance accumulates from year to year. A policy in force for ten years with a $50,000 limit will pay a maximum of $50,000 for any one covered loss, not ten times $50,000. This is important to consider when selecting the amount of insurance for employee theft coverage. A dishonest employee often steals smaller amounts on numerous occasions over many years that can accumulate in significant losses.

This condition is found in the loss sustained form only; it is not needed in the discovery form because the discovery form covers loss, regardless of when it occurred, that is discovered during the current policy period.

Loss Sustained During Prior Insurance Not Issued by Us or Any Affiliate

If the prior insurance was not provided by the current insurer or an affiliate, the Loss Sustained During Prior Insurance Not Issued by Us or Any Affiliate condition applies. Under this condition, which is found in the loss sustained form but not in the discovery form, the insurer agrees to pay a loss that meets all of these criteria:

- The loss is discovered during the policy period shown in the declarations.
- The loss occurred while prior insurance, issued by another unaffiliated insurer, was in effect.
- The current insurance became effective when the prior insurance was canceled or terminated.
- The loss would have been covered by the present insurance if the insurance had been in force at the time of loss.

If these requirements are met, the insurer will pay the *lesser* of the amount recoverable under the present insurance or the prior insurance (if it had remained in effect).

Reality Check

Loss Sustained During Prior Insurance Not Issued by Us

This hypothetical example illustrates why an insurer would be willing to cover a loss that occurred during the prior policy period of another insurer.

Joanie, the proprietor of an electronics store, was alarmed when her commercial crime insurer raised the premium on her loss sustained crime policy by 20 percent. She consulted Mark, her insurance agent, because she wanted to change insurers. However, she was concerned that she would not be covered for any crime loss that occurred when that policy was in effect but was not discovered until after the policy was canceled.

Mark explained that another insurer offers loss sustained coverage using ISO's Commercial Crime Coverage Form. He told Joanie that the form has a condition that would cover a loss sustained during prior insurance not issued by the new insurer if the loss met specified criteria.

After Mark explained the criteria and quoted Joanie a lower premium on the new crime policy, Joanie was surprised that the new insurer would be willing to cover such a loss. Mark explained that without the offer of such coverage, it would be nearly impossible to persuade an insured to switch to a new insurer. In effect, providing this coverage for a prior period is one of an insurer's costs of acquiring new policyholders.

[DA07835]

The essential difference between these two provisions concerns the available limits. If the loss is covered by both the current insurance and prior insurance issued by the same or an affiliated company, the highest limit in force under any of the policies covering the loss will be available to the insured. If the loss occurred under prior insurance issued by another insurer, recovery is limited to, at most, the applicable limit in the policy in effect at the time of the loss.

Claim-Related Duties and Procedures

Several conditions establish the duties and procedures to follow after a loss involving covered property.

The insured's duties stated in the Duties in the Event of Loss condition in a crime policy are essentially the same as such duties under other property policies. After discovering a loss or a situation that may result in a loss, the insured has these duties:

- Notify the insurer as soon as possible and, except for employee theft and forgery and alteration losses, notify the police if the insured believes that the loss involves a violation of law
- Submit a detailed, sworn proof of loss within 120 days

- Cooperate with the insurer in its investigation of the loss
- Produce all pertinent records for the insurer to examine
- Submit to examination under oath if requested by the insurer
- Secure all rights of recovery that the insured has against others responsible for the loss and do nothing to impair those rights.

The Records condition in a crime policy requires the insured to keep sufficient records to enable the insurer to verify the amount of loss.

Under the Valuation—Settlement condition of a crime policy, the value of a covered loss is determined differently for each of the three categories of covered property:

- Money is valued at its face value. If foreign money is lost, the insured has the option of receiving payment for the loss at the face value of the money or at its equivalent U.S. value on the date of the loss.
- Securities are valued as of the close of business on the day the loss is discovered. In many cases, duplicate securities can be issued if the insured posts a bond. The insurer will pay the cost of the bond as part of the loss. The insurer has the option of paying the market value of lost securities or replacing them in kind. If securities are replaced, the insured must assign to the insurer all rights, title, and interest in the lost securities.
- If property other than money and securities is lost or damaged, the insurer has the option of paying the replacement cost of the property, repairing the property, or replacing it. If the property is not promptly repaired or replaced as soon after the loss or damage as possible, the insurer will pay the loss on an actual cash value basis.

The Recoveries condition of a crime policy specifies how any subrogation or salvage recoveries will be divided between the insurer and the insured. First the insured is reimbursed for its covered loss that exceeded the limit of insurance.

The remaining amount of the recovery is paid to the insurer until it has recovered all that it paid. Any remaining value is paid to the insured to reimburse it for the deductible amount and for any loss not covered by the insurance.

As with most insurance policies, the crime general provisions include a subrogation provision. Under the Transfer of Your Rights Against Others to Us condition, for any loss the insurer pays to the insured, the insured must transfer its rights of recovery against others to the insurer. Moreover, the insured must do nothing after loss to impair those rights. (The insured is permitted to waive its rights of action against other parties if the waiver is made before loss occurs.)

The Other Insurance condition is split into two parts: primary and excess.

If the insurance is written as primary, a loss will be shared on a pro rata by limits basis with other insurance subject to the same terms and conditions.

If the other insurance is not subject to the same terms and conditions, the insurance will apply as excess coverage over any other insurance available to the insured to cover a loss. Often, the other policy will have a similar clause. When two or more policies cover a loss and all policies purport to be excess over other insurance, courts usually require the insurers to contribute on a pro rata basis if the insurers are unable to agree on a mutually acceptable method.

If the insurance is written on an excess basis, the insurer will only pay the amount of loss that exceeds the limit and deductible of the other insurance.

Conditions Applicable to Employee Theft Only

The Termination as to Any Employee condition and the Employee Benefit Plans condition apply only to the Employee Theft insuring agreement.

The first part of the Termination as to Any Employee condition automatically terminates employee theft coverage with respect to any employee who has committed a dishonest act as soon as the act is known to the insured or any partner, officer, or director not in collusion with the employee. Coverage on the employee is terminated regardless of whether the act was committed against the insured or others (before or after the employee was hired by the insured) and regardless of whether the employer learns of it before or after policy inception.

If the insured first learns of an employee's dishonest act after the employee has committed an employee theft, the loss will be covered (assuming no other exclusions apply), but coverage with respect to that employee for any further claims will be terminated.

If, in another situation, a claim investigation of an employee theft loss reveals that the insured knew about a prior dishonest act by the same employee, the current claim will not be covered, because coverage for that employee was automatically terminated when the insured learned of the prior dishonest act.

The second part of the Termination as to Any Employee condition gives the insurer the right to cancel coverage with respect to any employee by providing thirty days' advance notice to the insured.

The Employee Benefit Plans condition explains how employee theft coverage applies when the policy includes one or more employee benefit plans as insureds for the Employee Theft insuring agreement. This condition eliminates the need to attach the Employee Retirement Income Security Act of 1974 (ERISA) compliance endorsement to the policy to satisfy the ERISA fidelity bonding requirement. Employee theft coverage was traditionally called a fidelity bond, and the term "fidelity" is still used to refer to employee theft coverage.

Apply Your Knowledge

On August 5, Millright Foods canceled its crime insurance policy, which it had purchased from Insurer A. Millright then purchased a new crime policy from Insurer A's affiliate, Insurer B, which took effect on the cancellation date of Insurer A's policy. Insurer B's policy uses the ISO Commercial Crime Coverage Form. Four months after Insurer B's policy became effective and during its policy period, Millright discovered that one of its former managers, who left Millright's employment on July 15 of that year, had been embezzling funds over the previous three months. Insurer A denied coverage for the loss because the loss was not discovered until after Insurer A's policy was canceled.

How would the Loss Sustained During Prior Insurance Issued by Us or Any Affiliate condition in Insurer B's policy affect coverage for this loss?

Feedback: This condition specifies that the loss will be covered under Insurer B's policy if these requirements are met: the loss is discovered during the policy period shown in the declarations, the loss occurred while the affiliate's insurance was in effect, the current insurance became effective when the prior insurance was canceled, and the loss would have been covered by the present insurance if the insurance had been in force at the time of loss.

DETERMINING WHETHER THE COMMERCIAL CRIME COVERAGE FORM COVERS A LOSS

Knowing how to apply commercial crime coverage to the facts of a case is an important skill. This case study will help you make the transition from knowing policy language to applying policy language to losses to determine whether coverage applies. As you progress through this case study, you can check your understanding of the coverage provided by answering the Knowledge to Action questions.

Case Facts

Office Myria, Inc. (OM) is an office supply store. Each day, the shift manager on duty at the end of the day prepares the deposit from all of the daily receipts and takes the deposit to the night depository of a nearby bank. Each night, $2,000 in cash is stored in a safe for use in the cash drawers the next day.

Brad, the principal owner and president of OM, purchased a commercial package policy that includes the Insurance Services Office (ISO) Commercial Crime Coverage Form (Loss Sustained Form). The Crime and Fidelity Coverage Part Declarations page shows the coverages, limits, and deductibles that Brad selected. See the exhibit "Excerpt From Office Myria's Crime Coverage Declarations Page."

Excerpt From Office Myria's Crime Coverage Declarations Page

Insuring Agreements	Limit Of Insurance Per Occurrence	Deductible Amount Per Occurrence
1. Employee Theft	$100,000	$1,000
2. Forgery Or Alteration	$100,000	$1,000
3. Inside The Premises – Theft Of Money And Securities	$25,000	$1,000
4. Inside The Premises – Robbery Or Safe Burglary Of Other Property	$25,000	$1,000
5. Outside The Premises	$25,000	$1,000
6. Computer And Funds Transfer Fraud	$100,000	$1,000
7. Money Orders And Counterfeit Money	Not Covered	
If "Not Covered" is inserted above opposite any specified Insuring Agreement, such Insuring Agreement and any other reference thereto in this policy are deleted.		

In 20X1, OM sustained several losses. On July 3, 20X1, a thief entered OM through an unlocked window while the store was closed and broke into the safe, causing $1,200 damage to the safe. The thief found only $2,000 in cash in the safe, so he also stole $1,500 worth of electronic devices from the selling floor on his way out. OM repaired the safe and replaced the stolen property promptly after the loss.

Two employees, Daryl (OM's bookkeeper) and Jared (a shipping clerk), in collusion, stole money and merchandise from OM during 20X1. The thefts occurred as shown in the exhibit, "Office Myria Employee Thefts From 20X1." When Daryl and Jared were hired, neither Brad nor anyone else at OM was aware of any criminal history of either of these men.

Because Brad had a high degree of trust in Daryl and did not check the store's accounting records frequently, he did not discover any of the thefts until late December, 20X1, after all the thefts had been committed. During a police investigation, Daryl and Jared blamed one another for the thefts, but later they both confessed to all the thefts. Brad immediately fired both Daryl and Jared. See the exhibit "Office Myria Employee Thefts From 20X1."

Office Myria Employee Thefts From 20X1

Date of Theft	Item(s) Stolen	Value of Stolen Item(s)
April 30, 20X1	Money	$10,000
September 12, 20X1	Merchandise	$15,000
August 20, 20X1	Merchandise	$30,000
November 24, 20X1	Merchandise	$20,000
December 18, 20X1	Money	$35,000
TOTAL		**$110,000**

[DA07924]

Given the facts presented in the case and assuming that no endorsements to OM's policy affect the coverage in these losses, determine whether the commercial crime form will cover the losses, and if so, what amount the insurer will pay for each loss. When answering the questions in this case-based activity, assume that the insured reported each loss to its crime insurer promptly after discovering it, cooperated with the insurer, and maintained records of all property covered under the policy. Otherwise, consider only the information provided as part of this case.

Necessary Reference Materials

To determine whether OM's crime form provides coverage for any losses of money, securities, or other property incurred as a result of criminal acts such as robbery, burglary, and other forms of theft, you need a copy of the crime form and the declarations page.

Overview of Steps

When examining the declarations page and crime form to determine whether coverage applies to each loss, you can apply the four steps of the DICE method. Doing this involves analyzing the policy declarations, insuring agreement, conditions, and exclusions and determining whether any information found at each step precludes coverage at the time of each loss. You should also examine other policy provisions such as the limit of insurance, deductible, endorsements (not applicable in this case), and terms defined in the policy.

Next, you determine the amounts payable for each loss under the applicable policy. Doing this involves analyzing the limit(s) of insurance and any deductibles that apply. Assume OM has no other policy that provides coverage for the same losses.

Determination of Coverage

To determine coverage, you must apply the four DICE steps to the case facts for each of OM's losses.

DICE Analysis Step 1: Declarations

The first DICE step is to review the declarations page to ascertain basic facts about the coverage.

Action Task: Review OM's Common Policy Declarations included with its commercial package policy. See the exhibit "Excerpt From Office Myria's Common Policy Declarations Page."

Excerpt From Office Myria's Common Policy Declarations Page

POLICY NUMBER:

IL DS 00 09 08

COMMON POLICY DECLARATIONS

COMPANY NAME AREA	PRODUCER NAME AREA

NAMED INSURED: **Office Myria, Inc.**
MAILING ADDRESS: **1225 East Nevada Avenue**
Anytown, US 12345
POLICY PERIOD: FROM **03/12/20X1** TO **03/12/20X2** AT 12:01 A.M. STANDARD TIME AT YOUR MAILING ADDRESS SHOWN ABOVE

BUSINESS DESCRIPTION	Office supply store with loading dock

Knowledge to Action

To complete Step 1, answer these questions about the Common Policy Declarations:

- Is OM listed as an insured under the policy?
- Were the losses sustained during the policy period?

Feedback: The declarations page shows OM as the named insured. A review of the insuring agreements is needed to confirm whether coverages apply to each of the losses. The case facts indicate that each of the losses was sustained (and discovered) during the policy period.

DICE Analysis Step 2: Insuring Agreement

The second DICE step is to review the insuring agreements to determine whether those for which coverage is provided apply to the described losses.

Action Task: Refer to the insuring agreements in the excerpt from the crime coverage declarations page, and then examine the applicable insuring agreements from the Commercial Crime Coverage Form.

The $2,000 theft of money from the safe and $1,200 damage to the safe are covered under the Inside the Premises—Theft of Money and Securities insuring agreement.

> We will pay for:
>
> a. Loss of "money" and "securities" inside the "premises" or "financial institution premises":
>
> (1) Resulting directly from "theft" committed by a person present inside such "premises" or "financial institution premises"; or
>
> (2) Resulting directly from disappearance or destruction.
>
> b. Loss from damage to the "premises" or its exterior resulting directily from an actual or attempted "theft" of "money" and "securities", if you are the owner of the "premises" or are liable for damage to it.
>
> c. Loss of or damage to a locked safe, vault, cash register, cash box or cash drawer located inside the "premises" resulting directly from an actual or attempted "theft" of, or unlawful entry into, those containers.[6]

The $1,500 theft of electronic devices is not covered under the Inside the Premises—Theft of Money and Securities insuring agreement, because the stolen property does not qualify as money or securities. This theft is also not covered under the Inside the Premises—Robbery and Safe Burglary of Other Property, because the cause of the loss does not meet the policy definition of "robbery" or "safe burglary."

> 20. "Robbery" means the unlawful taking of property from the care and custody of a person by one who has:
>
> a. Caused or threatened to cause that person bodily harm; or
>
> b. Committed an obviously unlawful act witnessed by that person.[7]

In this case, the cause of loss was not robbery, because the thief did not harm or threaten a person having custody of the property, nor was there any custodian present to witness the thief's obviously unlawful act. Moreover, the cause of loss was not safe burglary because the devices were stolen from the selling floor, not from a locked safe or vault, as is required by the policy definition of safe burglary.

The Employee Theft insuring agreement applies to the employee theft losses committed by Daryl and Jared. Daryl and Jared both meet the policy definition of employee, they committed theft as defined, and their acts of theft resulted in the loss of money and other property as defined.

> We will pay for loss of or damage to "money", "securities" and "other property" resulting directly from "theft" committed by an "employee", whether identified or not, acting alone or in collusion with other persons.[8]

DICE Analysis Step 3: Conditions

The third DICE step is to review the policy conditions to determine whether they preclude coverage at the time of the loss.

Action Task: Refer to the applicable Commercial Crime Coverage Form policy conditions.

OM has complied with the standard policy conditions contained in the Commercial Crime Coverage Form, such as Cooperation, Duties in the Event of Loss, and Records. The only other condition that would apply is the Valuation—Settlement condition. This condition, which explains how money and property are valued, will be helpful to you when you determine the amounts payable for the insured's claims.

If OM had not immediately fired Daryl and Jared, then the Termination As to Any Employee condition (provision E.2.a.) that applies to the Employee Theft insuring agreement would have automatically terminated OM's employee theft coverage with regard to any further acts committed by Daryl or Jared.

DICE Analysis Step 4: Exclusions

The fourth DICE step is to review the policy exclusions to determine whether they exclude or limit coverage of the loss.

Action Task: Refer to the exclusions in the Commercial Crime Coverage Form, (section D).

Based on these loss scenarios, no exclusions apply. However, under different circumstances, two exclusions might have been applicable to the employee theft loss.

If Brad had been aware of any past criminal acts of either Daryl or Jared prior to the policy period, the Acts of Employees Learned of by You Prior to the Policy Period exclusion (D.1.b.) would apply.

If the only evidence of the employee theft loss was the inventory shortage that Brad noticed in January, then the Inventory Shortages exclusion that applies to the Employee Theft insuring agreement (A.1) would apply. However, in this case, Daryl and Jared confessed their crime to the police.

> Insuring Agreement A.1. does not cover:
>
> a. Inventory Shortages
>
> Loss, or that part of any loss, the proof of which as to its existence or amount is dependent upon:
>
> (1) An inventory computation; or
>
> (2) A profit and loss computation.
>
> However, where you establish wholly apart from such computations that you have sustained a loss, then you may offer your inventory records and actual physical count of inventory in support of the amount of loss claimed.[9]

Knowledge to Action

Based on the Inventory Shortages exclusion in the commercial crime form, would OM's inventory records from January of 20X2 serve any useful purpose in OM's claim for merchandise losses from employee theft? Explain your answer.

Feedback: Yes, OM could use the inventory records from January 20X2 to support the amount of loss it claims from the employee theft because Brad was able to "establish wholly apart from such computations" that OM sustained a loss.

Determination of Amounts Payable

Now that you have completed the DICE analysis, you can determine the amounts payable. Doing this involves applying the limits of insurance available to pay each of the losses and any deductibles that apply. Typically, it also involves determining whether more than one policy provides coverage for the same loss; however, in this case no other policy applies. See the exhibit "Office Myria's Claims and Applicable Limits."

The Limit of Insurance provision (B) in the Commercial Crime Coverage Form restricts the amount that the insurer will pay for losses.

> The most we will pay for all loss resulting directly from an "occurrence" is the applicable Limit Of Insurance shown in the Declarations.
>
> If any loss is covered under more than one Insuring Agreement or coverage, the most we will pay for such loss shall not exceed the largest Limit of Insurance available under any one of those Insuring Agreements or coverages.[10]

The Commercial Crime Coverage Form's definition of "occurrence" is crucial in applying the Limit of Insurance provision correctly. Part a. of the definition (F.17.a.) applies specifically to the Employee Theft insuring agreement.

"Occurrence" means:

a. Under Insuring Agreement A.1.:

(1) An individual act;

(2) The combined total of all separate acts whether or not related; or

(3) A series of acts whether or not related; committed by an "employee" acting alone or in collusion with other persons, during the Policy Period shown in the Declarations, except as provided under Condition E.1.k. or E.1.l.[11]

Office Myria's Claims and Applicable Limits

Claim	Applicable Insuring Agreement(s)	Coverage Limit(s)	Claim Amount(s)
July 3, 20X1 Theft:			
• Theft of money from safe ($2,000) • Damage to safe ($1,200) • Theft of small electronics (not covered)	Inside the Premises—Theft of Money and Securities	$25,000	$3,200
20X1 Employee Theft:			
• Theft of money ($45,000) • Theft of merchandise ($65,000)	Employee Theft	$100,000	$110,000

[DA07926]

Consequently, all the separate acts of employee theft that Daryl and Jared committed (for both money and merchandise) qualify as only one occurrence when applying the limit of insurance applicable to employee theft loss. Therefore, the most the crime insurer will pay for OM's employee theft losses is $100,000.

The July 3, 20X1 theft of money from the safe and safe damage claim is within the policy limit for the applicable coverage and will be paid fully, minus the deductible.

The Deductible provision of the crime form explains how the deductible should be applied to a loss.

> We will not pay for loss resulting directly from an "occurrence" unless the amount of loss exceeds the Deductible Amount shown in the Declarations. We will then pay the amount of loss in excess of the Deductible Amount, up to the Limit of Insurance.[12]

The July 3 money theft amounts to $3,200, which is less than the applicable limit of insurance. The insurer will pay OM the amount of loss in excess of the $1,000 deductible: $2,200.

The employee theft losses (one occurrence) amount to $110,000, which exceeds the $100,000 limit of insurance for employee theft. The insurer will pay the amount of the loss in excess of the deductible ($110,000 – $1,000 = $109,000), up to the limit of insurance. Therefore the insurer's loss payment is $100,000. (The deductible comes off the amount of the loss, not the limit.)

EQUIPMENT BREAKDOWN INSURANCE

Because commercial property policies exclude loss caused by mechanical or electrical breakdowns and steam boiler explosions, most businesses need equipment breakdown insurance, which covers those perils.

The Insurance Services Office (ISO) Equipment Breakdown Protection Coverage Form is a typical example of the various equipment breakdown policies offered by insurers. This form contains ten insuring agreements that cover property damage, expediting expenses, business income and/or extra expense, and other loss consequences of equipment breakdown. Some of the leading insurers in this line use independently developed forms but keep them similar to the ISO form in most ways. All equipment breakdown policies, whether standard or independent, contain conditions that distinguish them from other types of policies.

Need for Equipment Breakdown Insurance

Traditionally called boiler and machinery insurance, equipment breakdown insurance covers loss caused by the accidental breakdown of almost any type of equipment that operates under pressure or that controls, transmits, or uses mechanical or electrical power.

Common examples of such equipment include steam boilers (used for heating buildings and other purposes); electrical generating and transmitting equipment; pumps, compressors, turbines, and engines; air conditioning and refrigeration systems; production machinery used in manufacturing operations; and all types of electrically powered office equipment such as copiers, computers, and telephone systems. Nearly all businesses rely on one or more of these types of equipment.

The types of equipment covered by equipment breakdown insurance are covered under the Building and Personal Property Coverage Form, also referred to as the BPP, but only with regard to the perils insured against by the causes of loss forms used with the BPP. The commercial property causes of loss forms exclude electrical breakdown, mechanical breakdown, and steam boiler explosion, all of which can damage such equipment and the property around it.

Equipment breakdown insurance can fill this coverage gap, covering physical damage to both the covered equipment and other property of the insured that results from the accidental breakdown of covered equipment. Equipment breakdown insurance can also cover business income, extra expense, and other losses resulting from such physical damage.

A relatively small line of insurance, equipment breakdown insurance is important for businesses of all sizes. Few insurers have the expertise to underwrite and provide risk control services for equipment breakdown coverage, but many provide it in their commercial package policies through reinsurance arrangements with insurers that specialize in equipment breakdown coverage.

Because of the potentially catastrophic effects of equipment breakdown, loss prevention is a key goal for both the equipment breakdown insurer and the insured. Therefore, the inspection and risk control services provided by equipment breakdown insurers are important adjuncts to the insurance they provide. An insurer's inspection expenses for equipment breakdown coverage often equal or exceed its loss payments.

Insuring Agreements

The ISO Equipment Breakdown Protection Coverage Form contains ten insuring agreements. The coverages that apply in a particular policy are indicated on the policy's Declarations page by either a limit of insurance or the word "included." If neither is noted for a particular coverage, then that coverage does not apply. Several of the insuring agreements function more as coverage extensions than as basic coverages. See the exhibit "Insuring Agreements of the ISO Equipment Breakdown Form."

Insuring Agreements of the ISO Equipment Breakdown Form

- Property Damage
- Expediting Expenses
- Business Income and Extra Expense
- Spoilage Damage
- Utility Interruption
- Newly Acquired Premises
- Ordinance or Law
- Errors and Omissions
- Brands and Labels
- Contingent Business Income and Extra Expense

[DA07890]

The covered cause of loss in the Equipment Breakdown Protection Coverage Form is a "breakdown" to "covered equipment." The form defines breakdown as direct physical loss that causes damage to covered equipment and necessitates the equipment's repair or replacement as a result of any of these malfunctions:

- Failure of pressure or vacuum equipment
- Mechanical failure, including rupturing or bursting caused by centrifugal force
- Electrical failure, including arcing

Various exclusions apply to the definition of "breakdown," such as leakage, defects, or viruses in computer equipment and programs; damage to vacuum or gas tubes; and damage to foundations or structures supporting the equipment.

The policy definition of covered equipment is extremely broad and includes these equipment groupings:

- Equipment built to operate under internal pressure or vacuum
- Electrical or mechanical equipment used in the generation, transmission, or utilization of energy
- Communication and computer equipment

This definition is broad enough to encompass all of the previously discussed types of property, as well as some additional types that insurers are generally not willing to insure under equipment breakdown policies. Accordingly, the definition excludes various types of property that are outside the intended scope of coverage. The list of excluded property includes, but is not limited to, computer media; vehicles, aircraft, and watercraft (including any attached equipment); excavation or construction equipment; parts and tools subject to periodic replacement (such as brake pads); medical diagnostic equipment; and equipment manufactured by the named insured for sale.

Property Damage

Under the Property Damage insuring agreement, the insurer agrees to pay for direct damage to "covered property." The policy definition of covered property differs from, and is much broader than, the policy definition of covered equipment. Covered property means property that the named insured owns or that is in the named insured's care, custody, or control and for which the named insured is legally liable. In either case, the property must be situated at a location described in the Declarations.

Thus, the Property Damage insuring agreement covers loss to a much broader classification of property than covered equipment. The purpose of equipment breakdown coverage is not merely to cover damage to the covered equipment but also to cover damage to other property that results from damage to the covered equipment.

For example, a steam boiler explosion may not only destroy the steam boiler but also damage the building in which the steam boiler is contained as well as the contents of the building. The commercial property causes of loss forms would cover none of this damage because they all exclude damage resulting from steam boiler explosion.

The ISO equipment breakdown form does not include any coinsurance provision applicable to property damage coverage; a coinsurance provision applies only to the business income and extra expense coverage. Debris removal is covered as part of the property damage limit.

Expediting Expenses

The Expediting Expenses insuring agreement covers the reasonable extra cost to make temporary repairs in order to speed up (expedite) permanent repairs or replacement of covered property. An example of expediting expenses is overtime wages paid to speed up repairs.

Reality Check

Coverage for an Explosion From a Steam Boiler

This hypothetical case shows how equipment breakdown coverage applies to the various losses that can result from an accident to covered equipment.

A steam boiler in Galbi Manufacturing's factory exploded, causing destruction of the boiler; bodily injury to some of Galbi's employees; and damage to Galbi's building, Galbi's business personal property, a customer's patterns in Galbi's possession, and a neighboring firm's building.

Because the explosion was an accident to covered equipment, Galbi's equipment breakdown insurance would cover the damage to Galbi's building and business personal property and to its customer's patterns in its possession (its care, custody, or control). Galbi's equipment breakdown insurance would not cover damage to the neighboring firm's building, because equipment breakdown coverage does not cover property of others unless it is personal property in the insured's care, custody, or control at a described location. The equipment breakdown coverage would not apply to bodily injury to Galbi's employees (or to anyone else). Galbi's responsibility for injury to its own employees would be covered under its workers compensation insurance.

[DA07891]

Expediting expenses coverage can overlap with the extra expense coverage available through another insuring agreement of the form. However, expediting expenses coverage is not as broad as extra expense coverage. For example, the cost of renting substitute facilities to continue operations could be covered as extra expense but not as expediting expenses. When expenses fall within both coverages, the insured can collect under either one, but not both.

Business Income and Extra Expense

Equipment breakdown (and resulting damage to covered property in addition to the covered equipment) can interrupt operations and cause the insured to lose business income, incur extra expenses, or both. Accordingly, equipment breakdown policies normally offer business income and extra expense coverage. The ISO form allows the insured to select coverage for both business income and extra expense, or coverage for extra expense only.

The form also offers a Contingent Business Income and Extra Expense insuring agreement that covers the insured's loss of business income and extra expenses resulting from equipment breakdown occurring at a location, shown in the Declarations, that the insured does not own or operate. For example, an insured that manufactures computers might buy this coverage and show the location of the single company that supplies microprocessors to the insured.

Other Insuring Agreements

Several additional insuring agreements are included in the form. The insured can choose the ones that meet their particular business needs. These insuring agreements are available:

- Spoilage Damage—Covers loss caused by the spoilage of perishable goods as a result of a breakdown to covered equipment.
- Utility Interruption—Extends the business income and extra expense coverage to include loss sustained by the insured because of breakdown of equipment owned by a utility or other supplier that has contracted to provide the insured with any of these services: electricity, communications, air conditioning, heating, gas, sewer, water, or steam.
- Newly Acquired Premises—Extends all of the equipment breakdown coverages to property situated at newly acquired locations that the insured has purchased or leased after policy inception.
- Ordinance or Law—When equipment breakdown damages a building, this insuring agreement covers losses (such as increased construction costs) that result from the enforcement of ordinances or laws that regulate the repair or construction of buildings.
- Errors and Omissions—Covers loss or damage that would otherwise not be covered because of certain unintentional errors or omissions made in arranging the insurance, such as incorrectly describing an insured building's location.
- Brands and Labels—Covers the reasonable costs to label damaged merchandise as salvage or to remove the brands or labels from the merchandise before the insurer takes the property for disposition.

Conditions

Most of the general conditions contained in equipment breakdown policies are comparable to those contained in other property insurance policies. The noteworthy conditions that distinguish equipment breakdown policies from other policies include these: Suspension, Joint or Disputed Loss Agreement, and Jurisdictional Inspections.

Suspension

The Suspension condition allows the insurer to immediately suspend equipment breakdown insurance on an item of equipment that the insurer determines to be in a dangerous condition. The insurer can suspend coverage by delivering or mailing a written notice of coverage suspension to the named insured. Once coverage for an item of equipment has been suspended, coverage can be reinstated only by endorsing the policy.

The Suspension condition is reasonable considering the enormous loss potential some equipment breakdown exposures entail. The condition allows a boiler inspector or risk control representative of the insurer to act immediately when imminent danger of an accident exists. Most insureds want a loss-free operation and willingly cooperate when a dangerous situation is discovered. Therefore, the Suspension condition is seldom invoked. However, it serves as a last resort that the insurer can use when the insured cannot or will not cooperate in remedying a dangerous situation.

Joint or Disputed Loss Agreement

When separate insurers provide an organization's equipment breakdown insurance and its commercial property insurance, coverage disputes may occur when the cause of loss is uncertain. For example, disputes may occur when fire breaks out following the breakdown of covered equipment. The insurers may disagree on how much of the damage was caused by breakdown and how much by the fire.

When both policies contain the Joint or Disputed Loss Agreement condition or its equivalent, each insurer will (after receiving a written request from the insured) pay the entire amount of loss that each agrees is covered under its own policy plus one-half of the amount in dispute. In this way, the insured is fully paid without having to wait for the insurers to reach agreement on their respective liabilities.

Jurisdictional Inspections

Many states and municipalities require boilers and other pressure vessels to be inspected by a qualified inspector. The inspectors working for equipment breakdown insurers are usually licensed to perform these inspections, which are often referred to as "jurisdictional inspections." Some insurers' equipment breakdown policies state that the insurer will make jurisdictional inspections for their insureds. The ISO form does not contain such a statement, but most insurers arrange for the required inspections for their equipment breakdown insureds regardless of whether the form includes a jurisdictional inspection provision.

SUMMARY

The ISO commercial crime program includes crime coverage forms that can be added to a commercial package policy and crime policy forms that can be written as monoline crime policies. ISO offers two versions of crime forms, the discovery form and the loss sustained form. Financial institution bonds provide employee dishonesty insurance and other crime coverages designed for banks, insurance companies, and other types of financial institutions.

Insureds can select from among the seven insuring agreements of the ISO Commercial Crime Coverage Form to tailor coverage for their businesses. These insuring agreements cover money, securities, and other property against a variety of covered perils, such as employee theft, forgery or alteration, robbery, safe burglary, theft, disappearance, destruction, computer and funds transfer fraud, and good-faith acceptance of counterfeit money.

The ISO Commercial Crime Coverage Form contains provisions that specify the policy's limits and the manner in which a deductible should be applied.

In the commercial crime form, the exclusions are divided into different groups, depending on whether they apply to all or only some insuring agreements.

The ISO Commercial Crime Coverage Form includes numerous policy conditions that extend or eliminate coverage under various circumstances. While some conditions apply only to particular insuring agreements, such as two that apply to Employee Theft, other conditions apply to all insuring agreements.

You should now be able to apply policy language to commercial crime losses to determine whether the losses are covered and the amount for which they are covered.

Most businesses need equipment breakdown insurance because commercial property policies exclude loss caused by mechanical or electrical breakdown and steam boiler explosion. The ISO Equipment Breakdown Protection Coverage Form contains insuring agreements covering property damage, expediting expenses, business income and extra expense, and several other loss consequences. Equipment breakdown policies contain conditions related to suspension, joint or disputed loss agreement, and jurisdictional inspections, distinguishing them from other types of policies.

ASSIGNMENT NOTES

1. Includes copyrighted material of Insurance Services Office, Inc. Copyright, Insurance Services Office, Inc., 2012.
2. Includes copyrighted material of Insurance Services Office, Inc. Copyright, Insurance Services Office, Inc., 2012.
3. Includes copyrighted material of Insurance Services Office, Inc. Copyright, Insurance Services Office, Inc., 2012.
4. Includes copyrighted material of Insurance Services Office, Inc., with its permission. Copyright, Insurance Services Office, Inc., 2012.
5. Includes copyrighted material of Insurance Services Office, Inc., with its permission. Copyright, Insurance Services Office, Inc., 2012.
6. Copyright, Insurance Services Office, Inc., 2012.
7. Copyright, Insurance Services Office, Inc., 2012.
8. Copyright, Insurance Services Office, Inc., 2012.
9. Copyright, Insurance Services Office, Inc., 2012.
10. Copyright, Insurance Services Office, Inc., 2012.
11. Copyright, Insurance Services Office, Inc., 2012.
12. Copyright, Insurance Services Office, Inc., 2012.

Direct Your Learning

7

Inland and Ocean Marine Insurance

Educational Objectives

After learning the content of this assignment, you should be able to:

- Describe inland marine insurance in terms of these elements:
  - The role of the Nationwide Marine Definition
  - The distinction between filed and nonfiled classes of inland marine business
  - The role of judgment rating
- Summarize the key provisions of each of these traditionally nonfiled classes of inland marine insurance:
  - Contractors equipment
  - Builders risk
  - Transit
  - Motor truck cargo liability
  - Difference in conditions
  - Electronic data processing (EDP) equipment
  - Bailees
  - Instrumentalities of transportation and communication
- Describe what is covered by each of the filed classes of inland marine insurance.
- Describe ocean marine insurance in terms of the following elements:
  - The types of loss exposures that can be covered
  - The role of judgment rating
- Summarize the key provisions of these three main types of ocean marine insurance:
  - Cargo insurance
  - Hull insurance
  - Protection and indemnity insurance

Outline

Inland and Ocean Marine Insurance

7

OVERVIEW OF INLAND MARINE INSURANCE

A century ago, inland marine insurance developed as a way to cover emerging loss exposures linked to transportation. Today, inland marine insurance continues to be a source of flexible coverage solutions.

These concepts provide a foundation for understanding the types of inland marine insurance and why inland marine policy forms and rates are more flexible than those for most other types of insurance:

- Nationwide Marine Definition
- Distinction between filed and nonfiled classes of inland marine business
- Role of judgment rating

Nationwide Marine Definition

The term inland marine insurance was coined in the early 1900s, when United States insurers were restricted to writing one of three general kinds of insurance: fire insurance, casualty insurance, and **marine insurance**. Although fire insurers could insure buildings and their contents against fire and allied perils, they were not permitted to insure against most crime perils. In addition, they were generally not interested in providing fire and allied coverage on property in transit or on valuable property such as jewelry.

Marine insurance
Insurance that, in the U.S., includes both ocean and inland marine coverage and, in the rest of the world, is limited to insurance for vessels and cargo.

Marine insurers, however, were accustomed to covering ocean cargos of all types against many different causes of loss, including theft, while the property was either at sea or ashore. Consequently, they were willing to provide broad perils or "all-risks" coverage on the types of property that fire insurers avoided covering. The inventories of jewelry stores, property in the course of inland transit, and bridges were typical properties covered by marine insurers in the early 1900s. The insurance became known as inland marine insurance.

By the 1930s, inland marine insurance had grown to cover so many types of property that fire insurers believed that marine insurers were encroaching on their territory. To resolve the conflict, in 1933 the National Association of Insurance Commissioners (NAIC) adopted a **Nationwide Marine Definition**, a statement used mainly to determine whether a particular coverage is marine insurance (inland or ocean). The definition restricted the underwriting powers of marine insurers to specified types of property.

Nationwide Marine Definition
Statement of the types of property that may be insured on inland marine and ocean marine insurance forms.

The enactment of legislation in the 1950s permitted a single insurer to offer fire, casualty, and marine coverages. Hence, the Nationwide Marine Definition was no longer needed for restrictive purposes. However, many states continue to use a similar, updated definition to determine whether a particular coverage is marine insurance (either inland or ocean) under their form and rate filing laws. Typically, commercial inland and ocean marine insurance is subject to less rate and form regulation than other lines of insurance. See the exhibit "Summary of Nationwide Marine Definition."

Summary of Nationwide Marine Definition

This summary lists many, but not all, types of coverage that can be classified as marine.

A. Imports

B. Exports

C. Domestic shipments

D. Bridges, tunnels, and other instrumentalities of transportation and communication, such as piers, wharves, docks, pipelines, power and telephone lines, radio and television towers and communication equipment, and outdoor cranes and loading equipment

E. Various types of property owned or used by individuals, such as jewelry, furs, musical instruments, silverware, coin collections, and stamp collections

F. Various types of property pertaining to a business, a profession, or an occupation, such as mobile equipment, builders risks, property in the custody of bailees, live animals, property at exhibitions, and electronic data processing equipment

[DA02503]

Filed and Nonfiled Classes of Business

A variety of inland marine policies cover many classes of business (such as contractors equipment, builders risk, motor truck cargo, and so forth). Insurance regulatory authorities have recognized this diversity by dividing inland marine classes of business into two categories: filed and nonfiled.

The filed classes are the classes of inland marine business for which the policy forms and/or rates must be filed with the state insurance department. Filed classes are characterized by a large number of potential insureds and reasonably homogeneous loss exposures. Examples of filed classes are policies that cover musical instruments and photographic equipment.

Insurance Services Office, Inc. (ISO) and the American Association of Insurance Services (AAIS) file forms and rates for these classes on behalf of their member companies. Many states, however, specify additional classes for which forms and rates must be filed.

Nonfiled classes are the classes of inland marine business for which neither policy forms nor rates must be filed with the state insurance department. The classes of inland marine insurance that are nonfiled vary by state. To avoid violating state laws that require the filing of insurance forms and/or rates, insurers must determine which classes of inland marine insurance can be written on a nonfiled basis in every state in which the insurer wishes to write those classes of business. The term "traditionally nonfiled classes" is sometimes used to denote those classes that are nonfiled in some states but not others.

Nonfiled classes are characterized by a relatively small number of potential insureds, diverse loss exposures, or both. The contractors equipment floater is an example of a class of inland marine insurance that has traditionally been nonfiled because of the diverse loss exposures that can be covered by this type of policy. (The term "floater" is often used to denote an inland marine policy that covers property moved between different locations, or, in other words, "floating" property.)

Many types of property may be covered, ranging from simple hand tools and small power equipment to very large cranes and earthmovers. The property may be used in a variety of locations and climates such as in a desert, in a rain forest, or on the Arctic tundra. It may be used for many purposes, such as to build roads, buildings, pipelines, or other structures, or to remove snow or mow grass in public areas. Policies must be drafted, rates calculated, and underwriting keyed to all of these variables. In states where these policies do not need to be filed with state regulators, insurers can customize appropriate policy provisions and rates for individual insureds.

Role of Judgment Rating

Rating methods for the filed commercial inland marine forms are based on procedures contained in the ISO *Commercial Lines Manual* (*CLM*). The *CLM* does not contain rating methods for the traditionally nonfiled classes of inland marine insurance. However, many nonfiled inland marine policies are so widely written that both their coverage provisions and rates have become standardized to an extent. Motor truck cargo liability insurance, for example, is a common form of inland marine coverage with rates based on many years of loss experience. Insurers active in insuring truck shipments have developed their own manuals and rate schedules for this coverage.

In other cases, the property being insured under a nonfiled policy may be so unusual or the coverage terms so specialized that there is not enough previous loss information to give the insurer a statistically accurate idea of what the coverage should cost. What is a fair price for transporting a priceless painting from one museum to another for a special exhibit? How much should be charged for coverage on a one-of-a-kind piece of machinery that could be damaged as it is custom-fitted and installed in a new factory? How could an insurer rate coverage on a drawbridge?

When faced with such questions, inland marine underwriters must rely on their best judgment to set rates. Judgment rating is a rating method used by underwriters to rate one-of-a-kind risks. As opposed to manual rating (the method used to determine the premium for filed lines of insurance), judgment rating requires a thorough knowledge of the class of business for which coverage is being written. An underwriter might have to draw on expertise in any of several specialized fields—fine arts, heavy equipment, construction, or communications—to determine an adequate rate for the unique risks that are eligible for inland marine coverage. Realistically, rates are also influenced by market conditions.

NONFILED CLASSES OF INLAND MARINE INSURANCE

The largest classes of inland marine business (as measured by premiums written) are the traditionally nonfiled classes. Historically, each insurer has developed its own forms for these coverages, though both the American Association of Insurance Services (AAIS) and Insurance Services Office, Inc. (ISO) offer advisory nonfiled forms for their affiliated insurers. Nonfiled forms can range from preprinted documents and endorsements used by most insureds to one-of-a-kind manuscript policies drafted for unusual risks.

Though there are many other classes of nonfiled inland marine insurance, these are significant examples:

- Contractors equipment
- Builders risk
- Transit
- Motor truck cargo liability
- Difference in conditions
- Electronic data processing equipment
- Bailees
- Instrumentalities of transportation and communication

Contractors Equipment

Contractors equipment floater

A policy that covers mobile equipment or tools while located anywhere in the coverage territory.

Contractors equipment typically represents the largest class of commercial inland marine business. The equipment used by contractors may include cranes, earthmovers, tractors, stone crushers, bulldozers, mobile asphalt plants, portable offices, and scaffolding. All such equipment can be covered under a **contractors equipment floater**.

This policy normally contains a schedule that lists each piece of equipment and its corresponding limit of insurance. A policy may also provide blanket coverage on unscheduled hand tools and miscellaneous equipment.

It is difficult, if not impossible, to maintain a current insurance schedule of all items when several hundred pieces of equipment are used by an insured. A large contractor may therefore obtain blanket coverage applying to all equipment, whether owned, rented, or borrowed by the contractor. A policy providing such blanket coverage is subject to an annual accounting of value of the insured equipment.

Coverage may be provided for named perils only or on an open perils basis, an approach that covers causes of loss that are not specifically excluded. When coverage is on a named perils basis, the perils commonly included are fire, lightning, explosion, windstorm, hail, vandalism, theft, earthquake, flood, collision, overturn, and collapse of bridges and culverts.

Contractors equipment floaters frequently include rental reimbursement coverage, which pays the cost of renting substitute equipment when covered property has been put out of service by a covered cause of loss.

Builders Risk

Although an ISO Builders Risk Coverage Form can be issued as a component of a commercial property coverage part, buildings or other structures in the course of construction can also be insured under a nonfiled inland marine **builders risk policy**. The nonfiled approach is often preferred by both insureds and insurers because it allows more coverage and rating flexibility.

Builders risk policy
Policy that covers a building in the course of construction, including building materials and supplies while on or away from the building site.

Inland marine builders risk policies typically cover the structure under construction, temporary structures at the building site, and building materials that have not yet become part of the building. Building materials are covered while on the insured location, in transit, or in storage at another location. Business income coverage may be provided as part of the policy.

Inland marine builders risk policies usually cover losses on an open perils basis, and many insurers provide coverage for losses usually excluded under standard commercial property forms, such as these:

- Flood
- Earthquake
- Theft of building materials that have not been installed

Many insurers that write inland marine builders risk policies offer an endorsement providing soft costs coverage. Soft costs coverage covers various incidental expenses that might result from a physical loss to a building project, such as additional interest, advertising expenses, or real estate taxes. Incidental expenses may also include additional costs and commissions incurred during lease renegotiation.

Closely related to the builders risk policy is the installation floater, which covers a contractor's interest in building supplies or fixtures that the contractor has been hired to install. It does not cover the entire building, as in the case of a builders risk policy.

Transit

Transit insurance, also called transportation insurance, covers owners of property against damage to their property while in the course of transit by land, air, or water carriers. Shippers use this coverage because their property may be damaged in circumstances under which a carrier has no legal obligation to pay the shipper's loss.

Two basic types of transit insurance are available. The trip transit policy covers a particular shipment of goods specified in the policy. This kind of policy is purchased by occasional shippers. Designed for frequent shippers, the annual transit policy covers all shipments made or received by the insured throughout a one-year policy period.

Examples of property excluded in an annual transit policy include these:

- Contraband is not insurable as a matter of law and is therefore explicitly excluded by most insurance policies.
- Other types of property are commercially insurable but are especially attractive to thieves and therefore expensive to insure (for example, precious metals, furs, jewelry, and money and securities). Most annual transit policies exclude these items.
- Some insurers also exclude certain high-risk commodities such as electronics, tobacco products, alcoholic beverages, or fresh and frozen food.

If coverage for these items is wanted, and the insured is willing to pay an additional premium, the exclusions can be deleted or modified to provide coverage. Coverage may also be obtained under another policy, such as a jewelers or furriers block policy or a crime policy covering money and securities.

Most annual transit policies cover on an open perils basis. For example, flood and earthquake are not excluded.

Many annual transit policies cover only within the continental United States, Alaska, and Canada, including airborne shipments between those places. The continental U.S. does not include Hawaii, Puerto Rico, or any overseas possessions. Such wording precludes the insurer from having to cover air or water shipments to or from overseas locations. Overseas shipments by plane or ship (even between places within the coverage territory) are usually insured under ocean marine cargo policies.

Property covered under an annual transit policy is usually valued at the amount of invoice, including shipping charges, if the property is being transported between buyer and seller. If no invoice applies—such as when a company is shipping its own property between its own locations—the property may be valued at actual cash value.

Motor Truck Cargo Liability

A motor carrier (a trucking company) can be held liable for damage to the property it is transporting in certain circumstances. To cover this exposure, a motor carrier can purchase a **motor truck cargo liability policy**. This form of insurance applies only to cargo damage for which the motor carrier is legally liable. It is not direct property insurance for the benefit of the cargo owner.

Motor truck cargo liability policy
Policy that covers a trucker's liability for damage to cargo of others being transported by the trucker.

In addition to limiting coverage to losses for which the insured is legally liable, some policies also limit coverage to losses caused by specified perils. Other forms cover any loss for which the insured is liable as long as the loss is not subject to any of the exclusions expressed in the form.

The description of covered property usually encompasses most property accepted by the insured for transportation. However, as in transit policies, certain types of valuable property likely to be targeted by thieves are commonly excluded, such as precious metals, jewelry, and fine arts. Some policies exclude liquor and cigarettes, two other commodities that attract hijackers. A motor carrier that transports such commodities can usually have the exclusions deleted in return for an additional premium.

The property is covered only while in or on a land vehicle operated by the insured (including connecting carriers) or while located at the insured's terminal. Terminal coverage, however, is usually limited to a certain time period, such as seventy-two hours. The insurer will usually extend the duration of terminal coverage for an additional premium.

Difference in Conditions

A difference in conditions (DIC) policy can serve a variety of needs. Its basic purpose is to fill in gaps left by the insured's commercial property insurance. Originally, a DIC policy was intended to provide open perils coverage to insureds whose basic policy provided only named perils coverage. DIC policies are still used for that purpose, but with the widespread availability of the Causes of Loss—Special Form, which provides open perils coverage in commercial property policies, organizations now buy DIC policies for these reasons:

- To provide coverage for flood and earthquake exposures not covered by basic policies
- To provide excess limits over flood and earthquake coverages included in basic policies
- To cover loss exposures not covered in basic policies, such as property in transit or loss of business income resulting from theft or transit losses
- To cover property at overseas locations

DIC policies are a nonfiled class of inland marine insurance in most states. Thus, insurers have great flexibility in arranging the insurance to address the specific needs or exposures of their insureds.

Electronic Data Processing Equipment

An electronic data processing (EDP) equipment floater covers computer equipment, software, and electronic data owned by the insured, as well as similar property of others in the insured's care, custody, or control. "Electronic data processing equipment" basically means "computer equipment." Some insurers expand the term to include medical equipment, robotics, and even computerized gaming equipment such as slot machines. Although such equipment is covered as business personal property in commercial property forms, an inland marine EDP equipment floater can provide added benefits. Many EDP equipment floaters cover perils that are not usually covered in commercial property policies, such as mechanical or electrical breakdown. They may also insure covered property while it is in transit or at unlisted locations. Moreover, because EDP equipment is a nonfiled class of inland marine in many states, an EDP equipment floater can be tailored to meet the insured's individual needs.

The policy definition of "equipment" usually includes, but is not limited to, mainframe computers, servers, server racks or server "farms," display terminals, monitors, printers, imaging devices (optical scanners), disk drives and other storage devices, network components, and laptops and other portable devices. The term "data" includes both computer programs—which direct the processing of data—and data files—which store processed data, such as customer mailing lists. "Media," such as disks and tapes, are the materials used to store data.

An EDP policy usually includes coverage for extra expenses incurred as the result of covered loss. Business income coverage can often be added when the insured requests it. Coverage is usually on an open perils basis but without all the exclusions found in the Causes of Loss—Special Form. In addition, breakdown coverage can usually be added to an EDP policy. Subject to a separate deductible, breakdown coverage insures loss to equipment resulting from such perils as mechanical failure, electrical disturbance, and changes in temperature resulting from breakdown of air conditioning equipment.

Equipment and data are usually subject to separate valuation methods. Equipment may be valued at its actual cash value, replacement cost, or upgraded value. Upgraded value is the cost to replace the property with the latest, comparable, state-of-the-art equipment available. For data and media, property can be valued at the actual cost of reproduction or for an agreed dollar amount.

Bailees

Insurers use two basic approaches to insuring bailees for the property in their custody.

The first approach covers loss to customers' goods only if the insured bailee is legally liable for the loss. A common example of this type of coverage is a warehouse operator's legal liability policy, which covers warehouse operators against liability for damage to the property of others being stored in operators' warehouses.

The second approach covers damage to customers' goods, regardless of whether the insured bailee is legally liable for the loss. An inland marine policy that takes this approach is called a bailees' customers policy; this policy covers damage to customers' goods while in the possession of the insured, regardless of whether the insured is legally liable for the damage. Because this type of policy allows the bailee to pay customers' losses even when the bailee is not legally obligated to do so, it can preserve customer goodwill under circumstances in which a legal liability policy would not cover the loss. Bailees' customer policies are written for dry cleaners, laundries, furriers, tailors, upholsterers, and appliance repair shops, among others.

Instrumentalities of Transportation and Communication

Property essential to transportation or communication can be insured under an inland marine policy. The major types of properties in this class are bridges, tunnels, pipelines, and radio and television broadcasting equipment.

FILED CLASSES OF INLAND MARINE INSURANCE

Though an insurer may file its own inland marine rates, rules, and forms, Insurance Services Office, Inc. (ISO) and the American Association of Insurance Services (AAIS) file inland marine coverage forms, endorsements, manual rules, and loss costs for several classes of commercial inland marine business.Insurers affiliated with ISO or AAIS can use these forms and endorsements to compose a commercial inland marine coverage part. The coverage part can be included in a commercial package policy or issued as a monoline policy that provides inland marine insurance only.

The ISO commercial inland marine coverage forms are briefly described in this section. These forms provide coverage on an open perils basis, meaning that they cover direct physical loss by any cause other than those that are specifically excluded. Valuation is typically on an actual cash value basis. However, ISO *Commercial Lines Manual* (CLM) rules permit the valuation clause to be modified to provide for any other basis of valuation to which the insurer and the insured might agree.

Commercial Articles

The Commercial Articles Coverage Form covers photographic equipment and musical instruments used commercially by photographers, motion picture producers, professional musicians, and others. It is not intended for dealers of these types of property. Coverage can be provided on a scheduled or blanket basis.

Camera and Musical Instrument Dealers

The Camera and Musical Instrument Dealers Coverage Form covers the stock in trade (inventory) of camera dealers or musical instrument dealers and similar property of others in the insured's care, custody, or control. Coverage can be provided by endorsement for other types of equipment while it is on the insured's premises.

Equipment Dealers

The Equipment Dealers Coverage Form covers the stock in trade of dealers that sell agricultural or construction equipment. The form also covers similar property of others in the insured's care, custody, or control. Coverage under a reporting form is available.

Physicians and Surgeons Equipment

The Physicians and Surgeons Equipment Coverage Form covers the professional equipment, materials, supplies, and books of physicians, surgeons, and dentists. It also covers the insured's office equipment and (if the insured is a tenant) improvements and betterments that the insured has made to a leased building.

These coverages can be added by endorsement:

- Office equipment while off premises for no more than thirty consecutive days
- Extra expenses following a covered loss
- Money and stamps on premises
- Personal effects of the insured or others while on premises
- Valuable records

Signs

The Signs Coverage Form covers neon, fluorescent, automatic, or mechanical signs. The covered signs must be scheduled with a limit of insurance shown for each item. This form (or a comparable commercial property endorsement) is used by many businesses because commercial property coverage forms severely limit coverage for signs.

Theatrical Property

The Theatrical Property Coverage Form covers stage scenery, costumes, and other personal property used in theatrical productions. It covers similar property of others in the insured's care as well as property owned by the insured. The insured must have used or must intend to use the property in a production stated in the declarations.

Film

The Film Coverage Form covers exposed motion picture film and magnetic tapes or videotapes, including related soundtracks or sound records. The amount of insurance reflects—and the form covers—the cost of reshooting the film if it is lost or damaged.

Floor Plan

The Floor Plan Coverage Form covers merchandise that is being held for sale and financed through a floor plan. The Floor Plan Coverage Form may be used to insure the dealer's interest in the merchandise, the lender's interest in it, or both. Coverage is written on a reporting form basis. The Nationwide Marine Definition includes policies covering floor plan merchandise, but only for merchandise other than automobiles. Therefore, floor plan insurance on automobiles is not handled as inland marine.

Jewelers Block

The Jewelers Block Coverage Form covers the merchandise of retail jewelers, including similar property of others in the insured's care, custody, or control. It was designed to meet the needs of small retail jewelers. Depending on the nature of the insured's operations, this can be either a filed or nonfiled coverage. The filed coverage form covers damage to the insured's stock of jewelry, precious and semiprecious stones, watches, precious metals, and similar merchandise, along with other stock used in the insured's business.

Mail

The Mail Coverage Form is written for banks, trust companies, insurance companies, investment brokers, and other financial institutions that fre-

Reality Check

Financing Merchandise Under a Floor Plan

Retailers (dealers) who offer certain types of high-priced merchandise often open a line of credit with a lender (a finance company or manufacturer) to obtain product inventory. This arrangement, called a floor plan, enables the dealer to display a number of models, colors, or options for products on its sales floor or lot, which encourages sales. Floor plan financing is often used for autos, recreational vehicles, manufactured homes, agricultural and construction equipment, and major home appliances.

Under a floor plan, the lender holds title to each item of merchandise (the collateral) until the dealer sells it. As property is sold, the dealer uses the proceeds to pay the lender for the merchandise, restoring that amount to the dealer's credit line, and the lender transfers the title to the buyer. When sales of floor plan merchandise are slower than expected, the lender can demand payment of interest and depreciation from the dealer for the collateral.

[DA07867]

quently ship securities and other valuable items through a government postal service. The form covers the insured against loss of securities (such as bonds, stock certificates, and certificates of deposit) and other negotiable instruments (such as bills of lading and warehouse receipts) while in transit by first-class mail, certified mail, express mail, or registered mail. Valuable items such as bullion, currency, and jewelry are covered property only if sent by registered mail.

Accounts Receivable

Many businesses would be unable to collect their accounts receivable (monies owed to them) if the records of those accounts were destroyed. This exposure can be significant, but it is easily overlooked.

The Accounts Receivable Coverage Form covers losses (including uncollectible accounts) resulting from destruction of the insured's records of accounts receivable. The insurer pays the amount of accounts receivable the insured is unable to collect because of the destruction of records. The form also covers the cost to reconstruct accounts receivable records, interest on loans made necessary by an inability to collect accounts receivable, and increased collection costs resulting from loss of records. Coverage may be written on either a reporting or nonreporting form.

Because many businesses keep backup (duplicate) copies of all their computer records, including records of accounts receivable, at a secure off-premises location, they do not buy accounts receivable insurance. However, insurers frequently include a certain amount of accounts receivable coverage in their package policies. An insured may use the inland marine form to obtain a higher coverage limit than the insurer is willing to include in a package policy.

Valuable Papers and Records

The Valuable Papers and Records Coverage Form covers printed or otherwise recorded items such as an architect's blueprints and plans, as well as the cost of necessary research to reconstruct the records. Irreplaceable records, such as original manuscripts or rare books, are scheduled with an agreed value shown for each item.

OVERVIEW OF OCEAN MARINE INSURANCE

Parties involved in the transportation of property in vessels are exposed to common and unique hazards. Various types of ocean marine insurance are available to cover those exposures.

The transportation of property in vessels (watercraft) over oceans or other bodies of water creates several types of loss exposures that can be covered by ocean marine insurance. The three most common types of ocean marine insurance policies are cargo, hull, and protection and indemnity. Ocean marine insurers typically develop their own rates for these types of insurance based on their underwriters' judgment.

Ocean Marine Loss Exposures

Ocean marine loss exposures exist for these parties:

- Cargo owners (shippers)
- Vessel owners
- Carriers

Cargo owners, often called shippers, include manufacturers, importers, and exporters. Owners of cargo face the possibility that their cargo could be damaged or destroyed while in transit, either on board the vessel or on land between the vessel and the cargo's point of origin or destination. This loss exposure can be covered by ocean marine **cargo insurance**.

Cargo insurance

Insurance that covers loss of or damage to property shipped primarily by water or, if in foreign trade, by air.

Vessel owners face the possibility that their vessels could be damaged or destroyed by largely the same perils that can damage or destroy the cargo they carry. These perils include the action of wind and waves, striking of rocks or other vessels, shifting of cargo, fire, war, and breakage of machinery. This loss exposure can be covered by hull insurance.

A carrier that is prevented by an accident from delivering the cargo aboard its ship may face an additional exposure, called loss of freight. Freight is the compensation the carrier receives for transporting cargo. If the cargo cannot be delivered as promised, the carrier may lose the freight that the shipper would otherwise have paid. More frequently, however, the shipper guarantees that freight charges will be paid regardless of whether the cargo is delivered, provided that the failure to deliver the cargo results from causes beyond the carrier's control. When freight is guaranteed, the shipper, and not the carrier, is primarily exposed to loss of freight.

A vessel owner's freight exposure can be covered under a freight insurance policy, but such policies are not frequently requested. A shipper's freight loss exposure can be covered under an ocean marine cargo policy by including freight in the valuation clause.

Finally, a vessel owner faces exposure to legal liability for damage to cargo and other property and bodily injury to crew members, passengers, and other persons. If, for example, an oil tanker operator's negligence results in a collision with another vessel, the operator could become liable to the cargo owner for loss of oil, to the owner of the other vessel for damage to that vessel and its cargo, to persons on either vessel injured in the accident, and for the costs of cleaning up a resulting oil spill.

These vessel-related liability exposures can be covered by protection and indemnity (P&I) insurance. Many hull policies also include a collision liability clause, which covers the vessel owner's liability for damage to another vessel and its cargo resulting from collision with the insured vessel.

The Role of Judgment Rating in Ocean Marine Insurance

No advisory organization computes ocean marine loss costs. Moreover, ocean marine insurance is generally not subject to rate-filing laws in the various states. Thus, each insurer writing ocean marine insurance develops its own ocean marine rates, guided by the judgment of its underwriters. A marine underwriter's judgment in rating may be influenced by many factors.

A cargo insurance underwriter usually considers past loss experience, the product being shipped, the type of packing, the trade route over which the product is to be shipped, the time of year, the volume of shipments, port conditions, the ocean and inland carriers, and, significantly, the shipper's reputation and quality of management.

Hull and P&I insurance underwriters consider past loss experience; the size, type, and age of the insured vessel; the area of navigation; the trade in which the vessel is employed; the nation in which the vessel is registered (the loss experience of ships registered under one flag may differ dramatically from ships under another flag); and the vessel owner's reputation and quality of management.

Reality Check

Oil Tanker Collision Loss Exposures

Details of a January 24, 2010, collision between an oil tanker and a barge in Port Arthur, Texas, demonstrate some of the exposures that cargo shippers and owners and operators of vessels face.

According to the U.S. Coast Guard, a vessel towing two barges struck and ruptured the side of the oil tanker *Eagle Otome*. It was estimated that 450,000 gallons of crude oil were spilled into the Sabine Neches Waterway, which was then closed to all marine traffic.[1]

The damage to the tanker represents a property loss exposure of the tanker's owner and a liability loss exposure of the barge operator, who could be held legally liable for the damage to the tanker.

The loss of oil is a property loss exposure of the shipper who owns the oil and pollution liability exposure for the barge owner and possibly the tanker owner, if the tanker owner is held to be partially at fault in the collision.

One or both of the vessel owners or operators could also incur liability because of the waterway's closure to other vessel traffic while the spill is being cleaned up. According to news reports, one officer reported that 150 barges and 15 tankers typically use the waterway daily—so the closure could create a significant economic loss.

Any bodily injuries would have created an additional liability for the responsible vessel owner. Fortunately, no injuries were reported in this case.

Finally, the tanker owner may have suffered loss of freight for the portion of oil that was lost, unless the shipper had guaranteed that the freight charges would be paid.

[DA07901]

OCEAN MARINE INSURANCE POLICIES

While ocean marine insurance may sound exotic, any company whose business involves importing or exporting has ocean cargo loss exposures. Similarly, any enterprise that uses watercraft in its operations has vessel property and liability loss exposures. Ocean marine insurance is used to insure these loss exposures.

Ocean marine insurance is written using a variety of forms. Because ocean marine policies can vary widely, this discussion focuses on the general characteristics of these three most common types of ocean marine policies:

- Cargo
- Hull
- Protection and indemnity

Cargo Insurance

There are two basic types of ocean marine cargo policies. A voyage policy is a policy that covers cargo for a single trip specified in the policy. In contrast, an open cargo policy is a policy that covers all goods shipped or received by the insured during the policy's term and is comparable to an inland marine annual trip transit policy, but without a set policy expiration date. The insured periodically pays premiums to the insurer based on reports from the insured of covered shipments.

The open cargo policy is well suited to the needs of an insured who frequently ships or receives goods overseas. Open cargo policies are often extended to cover air shipments as well as ocean shipments. An open cargo policy does not have an end date; the policy remains in force until either the insured or the insurer cancels it.

Warehouse to Warehouse Clause

Many importers and exporters are not located in a seaport. Consequently, their overseas shipments may be exposed to loss while in transit to the port facility by truck or railcar or by barge on an inland waterway, while aboard the cargo vessel, and while being transported again by land or inland waterway to the final destination.

To accommodate shippers' needs for continuous coverage during the entire course of transit, including inland transportation, ocean cargo policies contain a warehouse to warehouse clause. This clause covers the insured cargo during the ordinary course of transit (including land transit) from the time the cargo leaves the point of shipment until it is delivered to its final destination. If the cargo is discharged at the final port and not delivered to an inland destination, coverage ceases after a stipulated number of days.

The warehouse to warehouse clause is often supplemented by the marine extension clauses, which expand the coverage to include unavoidable deviations from the ordinary course of transit or delays caused by natural disasters, orders of civil authorities, or strikes of port workers. For example, a vessel may become damaged and have to dock for repairs at an unintended port. If the cargo owner arranges for transshipment of the cargo by another carrier to the final destination, the policy will cover the remainder of the trip. The insured must pay the additional premium required by the insurer.

Covered Causes of Loss

In the past, ocean cargo policies insured against specified causes of loss. Today, most ocean cargo policies use the "all-risks" approach. When cargo insurance is written on an "all-risks" basis, the insurer covers any unexpected or fortuitous loss not specifically excluded. Typically, an "all-risks" open cargo policy excludes loss caused by delay, inherent vice, war, strikes, riots, or civil commotion. Coverage for loss caused by strikes, riots, or civil commotion is reinstated in virtually every open cargo policy by endorsement. Loss caused by war can usually be insured under a separate cargo war risk policy.

Virtually every ocean cargo policy contains a sue and labor clause, which is a clause that covers the cost of reasonable measures that the insured is required to take to protect property from damage at the time of loss. In return, the insurer agrees to pay expenses the insured incurs in carrying out this duty.

General average situations arise when some of the vessel's cargo is jettisoned (thrown overboard) or otherwise sacrificed in order to save the entire venture. Under maritime law, all parties to the venture, including the vessel owner and all cargo owners, are required to share the losses of the owner(s) whose property was sacrificed. Similarly, if the vessel owner incurs certain expenses (such as the cost of being towed to a port of refuge) to ensure the safety of a voyage following a collision or other casualty, the vessel owner and all owners of cargo aboard the vessel will be required to share the expenses.

General average

Partial loss that must, according to maritime law, be shared by all parties to a voyage (cargo owners and vessel owner).

Ocean cargo policies specifically cover the insured's liability for general average and salvage charges. "Salvage" refers to situations in which owners of cargo aboard a vessel that falls in distress become liable to pay awards to other parties, such as salvage contractors, that put themselves at risk to rescue the vessel.

Valuation of Property

If a policy covers only one particular voyage, the property can be insured for a specific agreed value. It would be impractical, however, for an open cargo policy to list an individual valuation for every shipment made under the policy, especially if the insured makes many shipments each year. Consequently, the usual practice is to value a shipment of cargo by a formula, which typically includes the amount of invoice, all freight charges included in the invoice, and a stated percentage to cover additional expenses. The stated percentage varies depending on the circumstances, but 10 percent is often used. Thus, a typical valuation of an ocean shipment is calculated as shown:

Amount of invoice + Freight + 10%

Open cargo policies are ordinarily subject to a maximum limit of insurance for cargo shipped on any one vessel. Open cargo loss payments are usually subject to a dollar deductible.

Hull Insurance

A hull is the body of a vessel. Hull insurance covers physical damage to vessels, including their machinery and fuel but not their cargo. Hull insurance also covers provisions and stores for the operation of the vessel. Hull policies ordinarily exclude any cargo on board the vessel, as well as personal effects of passengers and crew.

Hull insurance policies usually cover on a specified perils basis but can also apply on an "all-risks" basis. These are the typically covered causes of loss:

- Perils of the seas—Perils of the seas are accidental causes of loss that are peculiar to the sea and other bodies of water. Examples include abnormally high winds and rough seas, strandings, groundings, and collisions with other vessels or objects.
- Fire, lightning, and earthquake—The inclusion of earthquake provides coverage for the possibility that a vessel might be damaged by earthquake while docked.
- Barratry—Barratry is serious misconduct by the vessel's master or crew that is contrary to the owner's interest, such as a fraudulent or criminal act that causes damage to the vessel.
- All other like perils—"All other like perils" refers to perils similar to the perils specifically listed in the policy. The phrase does not provide "all-risks" coverage.

In addition to these basic perils, many hull policies include an additional perils clause covering losses caused by several other perils, such as electrical breakdown, bursting of boilers, breakage of shafts, latent defects, and negligence of the crew.

Hull policies exclude loss caused by war, piracy, strikes, riots, and virtually any situation in which the vessel is taken by another party. Coverage for many of the excluded perils can be added to the policy by endorsement.

A vessel is normally insured for a value agreed upon by the insurer and the insured. If the vessel sustains a total loss caused by a covered cause of loss, the insurer pays the agreed value stated in the policy. In the event of a partial loss, the insurer pays the cost of repairs.

Most hull policies contain a collision liability clause (also known as a running down clause), which covers the insured's liability for collision damage to other vessels and their cargoes. Collision liability coverage is a separate amount of insurance ordinarily equal to the amount of insurance on the hull. The costs of defending a suit alleging covered damages are also covered, and such costs do not reduce the amount of insurance available for paying damages.

The collision liability clause does not cover liability for bodily injury, nor does it cover property damage resulting from some cause other than collision. Usually, it does not apply to liability for collision damage to any property besides other vessels and their cargoes.

Protection and Indemnity Insurance

Protection and indemnity (P&I) insurance covers vessel owners against various liability claims resulting from the operation of the insured vessel.

P&I insurance is usually provided in a separate policy. These are some of the important sources of liability claims that may be covered by P&I insurance:

- Damage to bridges, piers, wharves, and other structures along waterways
- Injury to passengers, crew, and other persons on the insured vessel
- Injury to persons on other vessels
- Damage to cargo of others aboard the insured vessel

P&I policies cover several miscellaneous exposures as well, such as expenses incurred to remove the wreck of an insured vessel, the costs of entering an unscheduled port to obtain medical assistance for a passenger or crew member, and fines resulting from the violation of laws.

Some P&I policies do not cover the insured's liability for discharging pollutants. Separate pollution liability insurance for vessel owners is available from underwriting syndicates or industry pools.

Reality Check

Application of Ocean Marine Coverages

This hypothetical loss and claim scenario shows how the hull and P&I policies of two vessels typically apply to a collision at sea between the two vessels.

The owners of cargo vessel A and cargo vessel B both have hull insurance and P&I insurance. Vessel A negligently runs into vessel B. Both vessels and their cargoes are damaged. In addition, crew members of vessels A and B are injured. Vessel A is held legally liable for damage to vessel B, to vessel B's cargo, to vessel A's cargo (owned by others), and for injury to crew members on each vessel. Coverage will apply as follows:

- Vessel A's hull policy will cover the damage to vessel A.
- Vessel A's hull policy (under the collision liability clause) will cover vessel A's liability for damage to vessel B and vessel B's cargo.
- Vessel A's P&I policy will cover vessel A's liability for damage to vessel A's cargo and injury to the crew members of both vessels A and B.

[DA07922]

SUMMARY

Inland marine insurance provides a variety of flexible coverage solutions. Many states continue to use an updated NAIC Nationwide Marine Definition to differentiate marine insurance from other types of insurance for form and rate regulation. Inland marine business can be filed or nonfiled with state insurance departments, and underwriters use judgment rating for less common types of nonfiled, inland marine insurance.

ISO and AAIS file various forms on behalf of their members. However, the largest classes of inland marine insurance are, in many states, nonfiled and include contractors equipment, builders risk, transit, motor truck cargo liability, difference in conditions, and electronic data processing equipment.

Filed classes of inland marine insurance include coverage forms for commercial articles, camera and musical instrument dealers, equipment dealers, physicians and surgeons equipment, signs, theatrical property, film, floor plan merchandise, jewelers block, mail, accounts receivable, and valuable papers and records.

The transportation of property in vessels creates several types of loss exposures that can be covered by ocean marine insurance. Insurers typically develop rates for ocean marine insurance based on their underwriters' judgment, which may be influenced by a number of factors.

Ocean marine loss exposures can be insured by three basic types of marine insurance: cargo insurance, hull insurance, and P&I insurance. The open cargo policy covers all goods shipped or received by the insured during the term of the policy. Hull insurance covers the vessel, its machinery, fuel, and supplies. P&I insurance covers vessel owners against various liability claims resulting from the operation of the insured vessel.

ASSIGNMENT NOTE

1. Angel Gonzalez and Naureen Malik, "Collision Causes Crude Oil Spill in Texas," The Wall Street Journal, Digital Network, January 24, 2010, www.online.wsj.com/article/SB10001424052748704562504575021540843701582.html (accessed July 21, 2011).

Direct Your Learning

8

Business Owners, Farm Insurance and Other Specialty Coverages

Educational Objectives

After learning the content of this assignment, you should be able to:

- Describe the typical businessowners policy (BOP) in terms of these elements:
  - The categories of loss exposures that can be covered by a BOP
  - The advantages of the BOP to insurers, producers, and insureds
  - Why BOP eligibility rules are necessary
  - How the BOP is rated
- Contrast the property coverages of a typical businessowners policy with the commercial property coverages available in a commercial package policy.
- Summarize coverages provided by the ISO farm program and how specialty farm coverages help farmers address additional loss exposures.

Outline

Business Owners, Farm Insurance and Other Specialty Coverages

8

OVERVIEW OF THE BUSINESSOWNERS POLICY

The businessowners policy (BOP) is widely used to insure eligible small to mid-size businesses against most of their property and liability loss exposures.

Both Insurance Services Office, Inc. (ISO) and the American Association of Insurance Services (AAIS) have developed businessowners programs for use by their member insurers. In addition, many insurers use their own independently developed BOP forms. This discussion examines these characteristics shared by most BOPs:

- Loss exposures covered by the BOP
- Advantages of the BOP
- The need for BOP eligibility rules
- Rating the BOP

Loss Exposures Covered by the BOP

BOPs usually cover most of the property and liability loss exposures that can be insured under the various ISO commercial package policy coverage parts. Most BOPs cover these common exposures:

- Buildings
- Business personal property
- Personal property of others
- Business income and extra expense
- Premises and operations liability
- Products and completed operations liability
- Contractual liability
- Personal and advertising injury liability
- Employee dishonesty
- Theft of money and securities
- Forgery and alteration
- Equipment breakdown

The BOP does not provide commercial auto coverage for owned autos. However, hired and nonowned auto coverage, as well as a variety of other coverages, can be added to the BOP by endorsement.

Advantages of the BOP

The manner in which the BOP packages basic coverages and uses simplified rating procedures is similar to that of a homeowners policy and offers advantages to the insurer, the producer, and the insured. Packaging several coverages reduces **adverse selection** and, combined with simplified rating, lowers handling costs for insurers.

Adverse selection

In general, the tendency for people with the greatest probability of loss to be the ones most likely to purchase insurance.

Underwriting and processing policies through an automated system rather than through individual underwriting also reduces costs for insurers. The resulting lower premiums and broader coverage enable an insurer and its producers to compete effectively with other insurers and producers. Producers also benefit from the simplified rating procedures when quoting coverage. Insureds gain the convenience and economy of having one policy that meets most of their property and liability insurance needs.

The Need for BOP Eligibility Rules

Every insurer that writes BOPs has eligibility rules limiting its program to applicants for which the BOP approach is designed. These rules are needed because the rating structure of all BOPs contemplates a relatively homogeneous group of small to mid-size insureds. Writing BOP coverage for insureds that do not fall within this group can create a mismatch of premium and exposure.

BOP eligibility rules are based on criteria that relate to business size and complexity of loss exposures. Examples of these criteria are total floor area, building height in stories, annual gross sales, occupancy or business type, and characteristics of the applicant's operations.

Since the first BOP was written in the 1960s, insurers have continually expanded their eligibility rules to remain competitive and to increase or maintain market share. For example, BOP eligibility rules once excluded restaurants and contractors. Most insurers now write BOPs for both, subject to certain size and hazard restrictions required to maintain rating integrity.

Under ISO *Commercial Lines Manual* rules for the BOP, eligible risks, generally, may not exceed 35,000 square feet in total floor area or $6 million in annual gross sales at each location. Furthermore, certain types of businesses are not eligible for the ISO Businessowners Program. Examples of ineligible businesses are automobile-related businesses, bars, financial institutions, general contractors, and buildings occupied in whole or in part for manufacturing.

Insurers that have developed their own businessowners programs may have eligibility rules that are either broader or stricter than ISO's. Because of the variation in businessowners eligibility rules and their ongoing expansion, such rules are not discussed in further detail here.

Rating the BOP

Rating a BOP is much less complicated than rating comparable coverages in a commercial package policy. BOP property coverage is rated based on the amounts of coverage provided for building and personal property. BOP property rates include loadings (built-in charges) for business income and any additional coverages that are automatically included. As a result, the rates do not have to be computed separately for each of those coverages.

The ISO BOP requires separate liability rating for all classes of business. However, in calculating the BOP liability premiums for most classifications, the liability rate is applied to the property insurance amount rather than to a rating basis such as that used to rate commercial general liability (CGL) coverage. For example, under the ISO BOP, the liability premium for an apartment building is based on the amount of building insurance; under the CGL coverage form, the number of apartment units determines the rate. The AAIS BOP program and most independent insurers use separate liability rating only for certain classes of business.

Most insurers that write BOPs for eligible contractors rate the liability coverage apart from the property coverages by applying a separate liability rate to the insured's payroll, receipts, or number of full- and part-time employees.

Typically, the BOP rater or processor enters some basic data into a computer application, which automatically calculates the premium. BOP rating incorporates these variables:

- Territory. (For example, tornadoes are more frequent in the Midwestern United States; theft losses are higher in metropolitan areas; and so forth.)
- Type of construction. (For example, frame, joisted masonry, or fire resistive.)
- Public fire protection.
- Occupancy of the building.
- Presence of sprinklers.
- Deductible. (The standard deductible for most insurers is $250 or $500 per loss. The deductible can be increased or decreased, with a corresponding premium adjustment.)

If the insured wants increased limits for liability insurance, the rates are increased by appropriate factors. If the insured has purchased optional coverages, the policy premium is increased either by adding a premium charge for each optional coverage requested or by applying an increased rate factor to the insured values.

BUSINESSOWNERS PROPERTY COVERAGE

In most ways, the property coverage in a typical businessowners policy (BOP) is comparable to the commercial property coverages that can be included in a commercial package policy. For insurance professionals who are already familiar with the commercial property forms, an effective way to learn about BOP property coverage is to contrast these two types of property coverage.

A typical businessowners policy (BOP) offers most of the options available under commercial package policies, but some differences exist. Major property coverage differences between most BOPs and Insurance Services Office, Inc. (ISO) commercial property coverage forms can be highlighted under these topics:

- Covered causes of loss and valuation provisions
- No coinsurance
- Shorter list of property not covered
- Automatic seasonal increase provision
- Business income and extra expense coverage included
- Other property coverages

Covered Causes of Loss and Valuation Provisions

The ISO commercial property program offers three causes of loss forms—basic, broad, and special. Most insurers offer only two versions of the BOP property coverage—a named perils form, similar to the commercial property broad form, and a special form. The special form predominates; in fact, some independent forms offer only the special form, with an endorsement available to change coverage to named perils.

The standard valuation provision in BOPs is replacement cost, whereas the standard valuation provision in commercial property policies is actual cash value. Most insurers offer actual cash value as an option for BOPs, just as replacement cost is an option in commercial property policies.

No Coinsurance

BOPs were originally written without a coinsurance or another insurance-to-value requirement in the policy. Insurers relied on producers and underwriters to be certain that the insured carried insurance equal to full insurable values. Although coinsurance requirements can be suspended in commercial property policies by the agreed value option, underwriters are careful in granting that option. As a result, most commercial property forms (other than BOPs) written for smaller insureds are subject to coinsurance.

Because many insurers felt that BOP insureds were not carrying adequate amounts of insurance, ISO introduced an insurance-to-value provision in its BOP forms similar to the insurance-to-value provision in homeowners policies. To collect full replacement cost, the insured must carry insurance equal to at least 80 percent of the insurable value of the covered property. Otherwise, recovery is limited to actual cash value or a proportion of the loss equal to the amount of insurance carried divided by 80 percent of the insurable value, whichever is greater.

Subsequently, ISO introduced an option to remove the insurance-to-value requirement by endorsement. Although many insurers currently do not include an insurance-to-value provision in their BOPs, its use is becoming more widespread. The American Association of Insurance Services (AAIS) has included an insurance-to-value requirement similar to the ISO provision in its most recent BOP form.

Shorter List of Property Not Covered

In most BOPs, the list of property not covered is considerably shorter than the comparable list of property not covered in the Building and Personal Property Coverage Form (BPP). There are two principal reasons for this difference:

- Some of the "property not covered" exclusions in the BPP are not needed in a BOP because they apply to types of businesses that are not eligible for BOP coverage. For example, wharves or docks are often not excluded in BOPs because the types of insureds eligible for BOP coverage rarely have them.
- Insurers are willing to offer broader coverage because the insureds eligible for a BOP are generally lower-risk, more homogeneous types of businesses. For example, cost of excavations, underground pipes, foundations below the lowest floor, and retaining walls, all of which the BPP excludes, are often not excluded in BOPs.

Automatic Seasonal Increase Provision

Some BOPs provide a novel solution to the problem of fluctuating values. A seasonal increase provision is a provision commonly included in BOPs that addresses fluctuating personal property values by automatically increasing the amount of insurance for certain time periods. A seasonal increase provision functions somewhat like the peak season endorsement, which also provides differing amounts of insurance for certain time periods. However, the seasonal increase provision applies automatically. Provided the insured carries an amount of insurance equal to at least 100 percent of its average monthly personal property value for the twelve months preceding the loss, the business personal property limit will automatically increase by 25 percent.

The seasonal increase provision can be advantageous for an insured whose inventory has increased beyond the personal property limit at the time of a loss. For example, if Bill's Gift Shop carried a $100,000 limit for personal property and had an average monthly personal property value of $100,000 for the twelve months immediately before a loss, it could collect up to $125,000 for the loss. If Bill's Gift Shop carried $95,000 of insurance, or even $99,000, the amount would not be increased. And, of course, if the loss were $150,000, Bill would still be underinsured. Some BOP insurers offer a peak season endorsement in addition to the seasonal increase provision to enable the insured to meet an expected seasonal surge in values that will exceed 25 percent.

Business Income and Extra Expense Coverage Included

One of the distinguishing features of most BOPs is the automatic inclusion of business income and extra expense coverage. In commercial package policies, business income and extra expense coverage is provided by a separate form and is subject to its own underwriting requirements, such as a completed business income worksheet. Insurers seldom require any special underwriting for business income or extra expense coverage in a BOP.

Moreover, business income and extra expense coverage under the BOP is usually not subject to coinsurance, a monthly limitation, or even a total dollar limit. However, most BOPs apply a time limit that is not present in the commercial property business income forms. Under a typical BOP, business income loss and extra expenses are payable for up to twelve consecutive months following the occurrence of the direct physical damage. Some BOPs limit ordinary payroll coverage to ninety days.

Some insurers apply a dollar limit in addition to the twelve-month limitation. For example, some BOPs limit business income and extra expense coverage to an amount equal to 20 percent of the building insurance limit plus 100 percent of the personal property insurance limit. This can be a significant difference from the twelve-month limitation. In one case, an office tenant with a $25,000 personal property insurance limit (and no building coverage) sustained a business income loss in excess of $1 million. Because the loss was incurred in less than twelve months and the tenant's BOP business income coverage did not have a dollar limit, its insurer paid over $1 million. Under the alternative approach just described, payment would have been limited to $25,000. However, insurers that use this approach may offer the option to remove the dollar limitation for an increase in premium.

At one time, most BOP insurers did not offer business income coverage for dependent property exposures. However, dependent property coverage can be important, for example, to a small business located in a shopping mall if the business depends on one or more large "anchor stores" to draw customers to the insured's store. ISO, AAIS, and many independent insurers now offer this coverage either as an option or as part of their standard form. Under this coverage, the insurer will pay for a business income loss sustained because of physical loss or damage by a covered cause of loss at the premises of a dependent property. Some insurers offer all business income and extra expense coverage only as an option, not as part of their standard BOP form.

Other Property Coverages

To reduce complexity and to minimize the number of policies required, many coverages that would require separate policies or separate coverage parts in the commercial package program are either included as part of the BOP or available as options. The trend has been for an ever-increasing number of coverages and endorsements to be included in BOP programs. Although this trend conflicts with the goal of simplification, it makes the BOP policy suitable for a growing number of insureds. However, not all insurers offer all options, and certain insureds cannot find the exact coverage combination that they would like in any insurer's BOP. See the exhibit "Property Coverages Available in BOPs."

Property Coverages Available in BOPs

- Employee dishonesty
- Money and securities, when special-form property coverage applies; or burglary and robbery, when named-perils property coverage applies
- Forgery
- Interior and exterior glass (if not included as part of the building and personal property coverage)
- Outdoor signs
- Mechanical breakdown
- Money orders and counterfeit money
- Computer coverage
- Accounts receivable
- Valuable papers and records

[DA02603]

The limits for these coverages are often quite low, with minimal or no options for higher limits. The coverages also may not be as broad as those available in the commercial package program or in separate policies. However, they generally satisfy the needs of most small businesses.

Some coverage options are almost never offered under BOPs because they are not needed by the small businesses for which BOPs are designed or because they require individualized underwriting attention.

FARM INSURANCE

Some farms or ranches are operated by families and include both a residence and farm-related structures such as barns or silos. Other farms are operated by agribusiness corporations and are worked by employees who may or may not live on the farm property.

To accommodate both family farms and commercial farm operations, the Insurance Services Office, Inc. (ISO) farm program uses a modular approach in providing farm insurance coverage. When the insured is a family operation, a form covering residential property loss exposures is included with forms to cover the farm property loss exposures. For agribusiness operations, the Farm Dwelling form can be omitted if no residential buildings are insured.

Specialty farm coverage can be used to meet the needs of customers that are not included within the ISO farm program.

ISO Farm Program

The ISO farm program includes various forms and endorsements that can be combined in either a separate farm policy or a commercial package policy.

The Farm Dwellings, Appurtenant Structures and Household Personal Property Coverage Form contains four coverages, which are comparable in most respects to Coverages A through D of homeowners policies. See the exhibit "Farm Property—Farm Dwellings, Appurtenant Structure and Household Personal Property Coverage Form."

Farm Property—Farm Dwellings, Appurtenant Structure and Household Personal Property Coverage Form

Coverage A—Dwellings

Coverage B—Other Private Structures Appurtenant to Dwellings

Coverage C—Household Personal Property

Coverage D—Loss of Use

Coverage B excludes structures, other than private garages, that the named insured uses principally for farming purposes. Similarly, Coverage C insures only household personal property and excludes farm personal property other than office fixtures, furniture, and office equipment. Loss or damage to trees, plants, or other types of crops grown for farming purposes are excluded.

The Farm Property—Farm Personal Property Coverage Form contains two coverages:

- Coverage E—Scheduled Farm Personal Property
- Coverage F—Unscheduled Farm Personal Property

The insured can choose either or both of these coverages. Coverage E applies to only those classes of farm personal property for which a specific limit of insurance is shown in the Declarations page. The types of property that can be insured under Coverage E include farm products, materials, and supplies; farm equipment; various types of livestock; and several other classes of farm personal property. In addition to insuring specified classes of farm personal property, Coverage E can also be used to cover individually scheduled items of farm personal property, such as a particular tractor or combine owned by the insured. Coverage restrictions and sublimits apply to some of the eligible classes of property.

Coverage F insures unscheduled farm personal property under a single limit. To discourage underinsurance, Coverage F is subject to an 80 percent coinsurance requirement. Coverage F excludes an extensive list of property, such as household personal property, animals other than livestock, racehorses or show horses, certain crops and poultry, and vehicles primarily designed and licensed for road use.

The Farm Property—Barns, Outbuildings, and Other Farm Structures Coverage Form, Coverage G is used to insure all types of farm buildings and structures other than the dwelling and private garages.

Three levels of covered causes of loss can be purchased under the ISO farm program: Basic, Broad, and Special. All the policy provisions for these three levels of coverage are contained in the Causes of Loss Form—Farm Property. The insurer marks the declarations page accordingly to indicate which level of coverage applies.

The basic causes of loss in the farm policy are the same as those found in the commercial property Causes of Loss—Basic Form, plus four additional perils: theft, collision, earthquake (covering livestock only), and flood (livestock only). The collision peril has three aspects: collision damage to covered farm machinery; death of covered livestock resulting from contact with vehicles; and collision damage to other farm personal property. The earthquake and flood perils apply only to loss (by death) of covered livestock.

The broad causes of loss in the ISO farm program include all the basic causes of loss, plus all other named perils included in the commercial property causes-of-loss broad form and the homeowners Broad Form. Death of livestock resulting from some additional perils is also covered. These additional perils are electrocution, drowning, accidental shooting, attacks by dogs or wild animals, and accidents in loading or unloading.

The special causes of loss coverage corresponds to the coverage provided by the homeowners Special Form and the commercial property Causes of Loss—Special Form. Most of the exclusions of the farm coverage form are identical to, or closely resemble, the exclusions and limitations found in the commercial property Special Form. However, some are modified either to address the particular loss exposures of farms or to emulate homeowners Special Form coverage. Livestock, poultry, and many other types of farm products are not eligible for farm Special Form coverage under ISO manual rules.

Apply Your Knowledge

Which one of the following Farm Property Coverage Parts would be appropriate for covering specified classes of farm personal property?

a. Coverage A
b. Coverage G
c. Coverage E
d. Coverage C

Feedback: c. Coverage E provides coverage for a specified class of farm personal property such as farm products, materials, and supplies; farm equipment; various types of livestock; and several other classes of farm personal property.

Specialty Farm Coverages

Standard farm policies do not cover some loss exposures for which farmers frequently need coverage. Examples of the specialty coverages that can meet farmers' needs are crop-hail insurance, federal crop insurance, and animal mortality insurance.

Private insurers offer a traditional form of crop insurance called crop-hail insurance. Crop-hail policies cover crop loss resulting from hail and are frequently extended to cover additional perils such as fire, windstorm accompanying hail, damage caused by livestock, and vehicles. Such policies may also cover harvested crops against named perils while being transported to the first place of storage.

Various crop insurance programs are also available from the Federal Crop Insurance Corporation (FCIC), a governmental insurer subject to the Risk Management Agency (RMA), a division of the United States Department of Agriculture. One of FCIC's crop insurance plans is Multiple Peril Crop Insurance (MPCI) which insures farmers against unexpected production losses from natural causes, including drought, excessive moisture, hail, wind, flood, hurricanes, tornadoes, and lightning. MPCI policies do not cover losses resulting from neglect, poor farming practices, or theft. These programs are marketed and serviced by participating private insurers but are reinsured by the federal government.

The livestock coverage provided by most farm policies is not adequate for some farmers and ranchers. In addition, nonfarmers often own valuable animals that they would like to insure for their full value. Farm policies normally cover loss of livestock only by specified causes, such as electrocution, accidental shooting, or drowning. Owners of high-valued animals often want to insure against loss of their animals by any fortuitous cause, including illness or disease.

One example of livestock coverage designed to meet special needs is animal mortality insurance. Animal mortality insurance is essentially term life insurance on animals. This type of insurance may be purchased to cover farm animals such as valuable horses, registered cattle, or calves being grown and exhibited under sponsorship of a club (such as 4-H). Animal mortality insurance is also purchased by owners of racehorses, show dogs, circus animals, and laboratory animals. Animal mortality insurance generally covers against loss of the insured animal by death resulting from accident, injury, sickness, or disease, or by theft, subject to exclusions.

SUMMARY

The businessowners policy (BOP) is designed to insure eligible small to mid-size businesses. Common exposures generally included in the BOP are buildings, business personal property, personal property of others, business income and extra expense, premises and operations liability, and several others. With its package approach and simplified rating procedures, the BOP can meet the needs of insurers, producers, and policyholders.

These are the main differences between BOP property coverage and the ISO commercial property coverage forms:

- Covered causes of loss in the BOP are usually offered on either a broad form or special form basis.
- Replacement cost is the standard BOP valuation provision.
- Some BOPs have no coinsurance, and others have insurance-to-value requirements other than coinsurance.
- BOP property not covered provisions list fewer items.
- BOPs contain automatic seasonal increase provisions.
- BOP business income and extra expense coverage is automatically included, often with no dollar limit.

Insurance coverage for farm operations can be provided under the ISO farm program, which uses a combination of forms to provide coverage that meets the need of different types of farm operations. Specialty farm coverages can be used for loss exposures that are not fully covered or are excluded in the ISO farm program.

Index

Page numbers in boldface refer to pages where the word or phrase is defined.

SYMBOLS

A

B

C

D

E

F

G

H

I

J

L

M

N

V

W

Y